Illicit Sex within the Justice System

Illicit Sex within the Justice System:

Using Weak Power to Legislate, Regulate and Enforce Morality

By

Carmen M. Cusack

Cambridge
Scholars
Publishing

Illicit Sex within the Justice System:
Using Weak Power to Legislate, Regulate and Enforce Morality

By Carmen M. Cusack

This book first published 2017

Cambridge Scholars Publishing

Lady Stephenson Library, Newcastle upon Tyne, NE6 2PA, UK

British Library Cataloguing in Publication Data
A catalogue record for this book is available from the British Library

Cover Art: Bhoja and Adee, Charaka and mother, the White Tigers, Audubon Zoo!

ISBN (10): 1-4438-9146-0
ISBN (13): 978-1-4438-9146-2

TABLE OF CONTENTS

LIST OF FIGURES

INTRODUCTION

Illicit Sex within the Justice System: Using Weak Power to Legislate, Regulate, and Enforce Morality argues that the state's power to regulate morality by using the law and law enforcement appears to have been diluted, in part, by immoral behavior occurring within the justice system (Durkheim, 2008). This dilution results from two entropies. First, immorality skews decision-making causing members of the justice system selectively to enforce laws that protect their secrets, excuse their indiscretions, promote their agendas, and deregulate or decriminalize conduct and activities that satisfy their desires. Second, exposure (e.g. media coverage) of immoral conduct within the justice system may suggest to the public that the state's reasons for regulating morality are not genuine or important; and that enforcement of morality laws against the people may be hypocritical of justice members (e.g. government officials) or perhaps unconstitutional. "Traditional *sexual* mores are in deep decline," which may explain why the government has relinquished some power—in order to accommodate immorality indulged in by its own members and leaders; for example, by decriminalizing adultery and failing to implement heart balm statutes (Grossman & Friedman, 2011, p. 104). "Chastity is no longer the issue. But fairness is....This might well be the lesson" (Grossman & Friedman, 2011, p. 104). With relenting public interests in morality, the government appears increasingly to have responded to progressive notions of sexuality and equality. However, the two phenomena may seldom directly correlate. Yet, some members of the justice system and society may blame certain groups, such as women and homosexuals, for deregulation of morality (e.g. secondary victimization) (Reddington & Kreisel, 2009). These groups may benefit from or be harmed by decaying tradition and "moral" structure in some regards as much as hegemonic beneficiaries in other regards. In some cases, immorality breaches tradition or social expectations, but not the law; and some political groups advocate for stricture or tolerance (Durkheim, 2008, p. 314).

Thomas Hobbes (2013) was a political philosopher from the 16th century upon whose work American founders relied for political and philosophical guidance while framing the Constitution (Merrymen, 2007). In his Introduction of *Leviathan,* Hobbes (2013) grounded governmental power in nature, and explored the concept of natural law as a basis for outlawing crimes against nature, such as unnatural sex acts (e.g. bestiality and incest) (RS 14:89, 2016). Most illicit (i.e. deviant) types of sexual intercourse (e.g. adultery) are not crimes against nature.

Hobbes (2013) claimed that human law aspires to manifest God's will when it models the State after living organisms.

> Nature (the art whereby God hath made and [governs] the world) is by the art of man, as in many other things, so in this also imitated, that it can make an Artificial Animal. For seeing life is but a motion of Limbs, the [beginning] whereof is in some [principal] part within; why may we not say, that all Automata (Engines that move themselves by springs and [wheels] as doth a watch) have an [artificial] life? For what is the Heart, but a Spring; and the Nerves, but so many Strings; and the [Joints], but so many [Wheels], giving motion to the whole Body, such as was intended by the Artificer? Art goes yet further, imitating that [Rational] and most excellent [work] of Nature, Man. For by Art is created that great LEVIATHAN called a COMMON-WEALTH, or STATE, (in [Latin] CIVITAS) which is but an [Artificial] Man; though of greater stature and strength than the [Natural], for whose protection and [defense] it was intended; and in which, the [Sovereignty] is an [Artificial] Soul, as giving life and motion to the whole body; The Magistrates, and other Officers of Judicature and Execution, [artificial Joints]; Reward and Punishment (by which [fastened] to the seat of the [Sovereignty], every [joint] and member is moved to [perform] his duty) are the Nerves, that do the same in the Body [Natural]; The Wealth and Riches of all the particular members, are the Strength; Salus Populi (the Peoples Safety) its [Business]; Counsellors, by whom all things [needful] for it to know, are suggested unto it, are the Memory; Equity and [Laws], an [artificial] Reason and Will; Concord, Health; Sedition, [Sickness]; and [Civil] War, Death. Lastly, the Pacts and Covenants, by which the parts of this Body [Politic] were at first made, set together, and united, resemble that Fiat, or the Let Us Make Man, pronounced by God in the Creation (Hobbes, 2013, p. 32).

By embodying humanity, state and federal governments seize authority to reinforce and perpetuate their power over their constituents. They can empower people to instill in society a duty to the government that serves to define, promote, and enforce morality.

> They also that have authority to teach, or to enable others to teach the people their duty to the [Sovereign] Power, and instruct them in the knowledge of what is just, and unjust, thereby to render them more apt to live in [godliness], and in peace among themselves, and resist the [public] enemy, are [Public] Ministers: Ministers, in that they [do] it not by their own Authority, but by [another]; and [Public], because they [do] it (or

> should [do] it) by no Authority, but that of the [Sovereign]. The Monarch, or the [Sovereign] Assembly only hath immediate Authority from God, to teach and instruct the people; and no man but the [Sovereign, receive] his power Dei Gratia simply; that is to say, from the [favor] of none but God: All other[s], receive theirs from the [favor] and providence of God, and their [Sovereigns]; as in a Monarchy Dei Gratia & Regis; or Dei Providentia & Voluntate Regis (Hobbes, 2013, p. 199).

Total control over the people may be accomplished by a government that regulates and criminalizes private moments, expressions of love, and bodily pleasure (e.g. sadomasochism, incest, and prostitution) (Cusack, 2015; Cusack, 2016; Cusack, 2016).

United States Supreme Court Justice Antonin Scalia acknowledged this in his dissent in Obergefell v. Hodges (2015), which gave homosexuals the right to marry same-sex partners thereby further allowing private homosexual conduct to be regulated by the government (e.g. bigamy) (Cusack, 2013).

> If, even as the price to be paid for a fifth vote, I ever joined an opinion for the Court that began: 'The Constitution promises liberty to all within its reach, a liberty that includes certain specific rights that allow persons, within a lawful realm, to define and express their identity,' I would hide my head in a bag. The Supreme Court of the United States has descended from the disciplined legal reasoning of John Marshall and Joseph Story to the mystical aphorisms of the fortune cookie (Obergefell v. Hodges, 2015, p. 2630).

His stunning retort to the majority elucidated the standard used to justify the government's control over intimate expression.

Justice Scalia complained that the judiciary usurped the people's power to "self-rule" by ruling that morality-based bans on gay marriage were unconstitutional (Obergefell v. Hodges, 2015, p. 2627).

> The Constitution places some constraints on self-rule—constraints adopted *by the People themselves* when they ratified the Constitution and its Amendments. Forbidden are laws 'impairing the Obligation of Contracts,' denying 'Full Faith and Credit' to the 'public Acts' of other States, prohibiting the free exercise of religion, abridging the freedom of speech, infringing the right to keep and bear arms, authorizing unreasonable searches and seizures, and so forth. Aside from these limitations, those powers 'reserved to the States respectively, or to the people' can be exercised as the States or the People desire. These cases ask us to decide whether the Fourteenth Amendment contains a limitation that requires the States to license and recognize marriages between two people of the same

> sex. Does it remove *that* issue from the political process (Obergefell v. Hodges, 2015, p. 2627)?

He answered his rhetorical question with disapproval for the majority in this case.

> Of course not. It would be surprising to find a prescription regarding marriage in the Federal Constitution since, as the author of today's opinion reminded us only two years ago (in an opinion joined by the same Justices who join him today):
> '[R]egulation of domestic relations is an area that has long been regarded as a virtually exclusive province of the States.'
> '[T]he Federal Government, through our history, has deferred to state-law policy decisions with respect to domestic relations.'
>
> But we need not speculate. When the Fourteenth Amendment was ratified in 1868, every State limited marriage to one man and one woman, and no one doubted the constitutionality of doing so. That resolves these cases. When it comes to determining the meaning of a vague constitutional provision—such as 'due process of law' or 'equal protection of the laws'—it is unquestionable that the People who ratified that provision did not understand it to prohibit a practice that remained both universal and uncontroversial in the years after ratification. We have no basis for striking down a practice that is not expressly prohibited by the Fourteenth Amendment's text, and that bears the endorsement of a long tradition of open, widespread, and unchallenged use dating back to the Amendment's ratification. Since there is no doubt whatever that the People never decided to prohibit the limitation of marriage to opposite-sex couples, the public debate over same-sex marriage must be allowed to continue (Obergefell v. Hodges, 2015, p. 2627).

He challenged judicial activism that famously observed "penumbras" and "emanations" of privacy in the Bill of Rights and has expanded protections for one hundred years (Griswold v. Connecticut, 1965, p. 484; Pierce v. Society of the Sisters, 1925; Whitman, 1855). He chastised social movements that seek to tear down the establishment by destroying traditional marriage. He compared the gay rights movement to the 1960s hippies, who also contended for freedom and recognition outside traditional, monogamous, lifelong, and patriarchal marriage.

> 'The nature of marriage is that, through its enduring bond, two persons together can find other freedoms, such as expression, intimacy, and spirituality.' (Really? Who ever thought that intimacy and spirituality [whatever that means] were freedoms? And if intimacy is, one would think Freedom of Intimacy is abridged rather than expanded by marriage. Ask the nearest hippie. Expression, sure enough, *is* a freedom, but anyone in a

> long-lasting marriage will attest that that happy state constricts, rather than expands, what one can prudently say.) Rights, we are told, can 'rise…from a better informed understanding of how constitutional imperatives define a liberty that remains urgent in our own era.' (Huh? How can a better informed understanding of how constitutional imperatives [whatever that means] define [whatever that means] an urgent liberty [never mind], give birth to a right?) And we are told that, '[i]n any particular case,' either the Equal Protection or Due Process Clause 'may be thought to capture the essence of [a] right in a more accurate and comprehensive way,' than the other, 'even as the two Clauses may converge in the identification and definition of the right.' (What say? What possible 'essence' does substantive due process 'capture' in an 'accurate and comprehensive way'? It stands for nothing whatever, except those freedoms and entitlements that this Court *really* likes. And the Equal Protection Clause, as employed today, identifies nothing except a difference in treatment that this Court *really* dislikes. Hardly a distillation of essence. If the opinion is correct that the two clauses 'converge in the identification and definition of [a] right,' that is only because the majority's likes and dislikes are predictably compatible.) I could go on. The world does not expect logic and precision in poetry or inspirational pop-philosophy; it demands them in the law (Obergefell v. Hodges, 2015, p. 2630).

Justice Scalia then directed his dissent toward his colleagues. "It is one thing for separate concurring or dissenting opinions to contain extravagances, even silly extravagances, of thought and expression; it is something else for the official opinion of the Court to do so. Of course the opinion's showy profundities are often profoundly incoherent" (Obergefell v. Hodges, 2015, p. 2630). He summarized his point that the Court had committed a *coup d'état* because it ended a democratic "debate" "in an opinion lacking even a thin veneer of law" (Cusack, 2014; Obergefell v. Hodges, 2015, p. 2628).

The government has often claimed that it does not have an interest in regulating healthy, "normal," and traditional sexual conduct (Cusack, 2013; Cusack, 2013; Cusack, 2013; Cusack, 2017). Unhealthy and harmful conduct consistently has been regulated by the government. Definitions of "unhealthy" and "harmful" have changed as women, homosexuals, and others have emerged into powerful political arenas. For example, laws criminalizing HIV transmission have had greater penalties than laws criminalizing sexual transmission of other diseases; and some gay rights activists have described these laws as being bigoted and unfair (Cohen, 2015; Cusack, 2013). Another example is that seduction was previously a crime because a woman was seduced with a false promise of marriage. However, in many jurisdictions (e.g. Texas) a defendant could in good faith promise to marry a prosecutrix; and remain wed for two years. Then, his indictment would be dismissed. "Debauchery and carnal intercourse without seduction" was "no offense" (Cusack, 2012; Neal, 2009, p. 44). "The offenses" at which these laws were "aimed" were "the seduction and debauchery accomplished by the promises and blandishments the man" offers "in effecting the ruin and disgrace of the female; and where the seduction and debauchery is accomplished by promises of marriage, upon which the female relies, and thus surrenders her person, and gives to the man the brightest jewel in the crown of her womanhood" (Neal, 2009, p. 44). "It is the broken promise which the law will regard as the [essence] of the offense" (Neal, 2009, p. 44). Female chastity is no longer emphasized as the crux of a woman's person or the essence of her virtue. Women's rights activists consider those laws to have been sexist and patriarchal. Yet, as in both examples, when progressive strides against inequality are made against the *status quo* and law, each minority population may suffer when laws designed to provide greater safety and security become unenforced. As these types of political, cultural, social, and legal debates unfurl, members of the justice system may seek to institute public morality while privately participating in immoral, deviant, and nontraditional conduct.

If members of the justice system (i.e. rulers) can hide the harm they cause, as defined by the law and to some extent culture, then they can control the people without being controlled by their own systems or the people, thereby intentionally implementing a broken system that results in a zero-sum game against the people, who unknowingly, naively, or regretfully forfeit trust and freedom to members of a sexual oligarchy rather than a representative democracy (Cusack, 2012). For example, under the premise that every male has experienced lifetime rape or sexual abuse, victimization correlated in many cases with systemic acceptance, secrecy, and tolerance that fostered obedience to patriarchy. "This monopolization may be effected either legally or conventionally" (Gerth & Mills, 1946, p. 193). Patriarchy that represses free speech, threatens safety, and unnecessarily restricts liberty is an affront to the purpose of government, the Leviathan, and society (Cusack, 2014).

If the people believe that the government is comprised of individuals, who benefit from patriarchy in professional, social, or personal capacities, then they will be unwilling to attempt to enforce their rights or advocate for change. "Individuality is in this way organized as a basis of knowledge that can be deployed as an instrument of regulation" (Brown, 2006, p. 41). "Organic social ethics, where religiously sub-structured, stands on the soil of 'brotherliness,' but, in contrast to mystic and acosmic love, is dominated by a cosmic, rational demand for brotherliness. Its point of departure is the experience of the inequality of [moral or] religious charisma" (Gerth & Mills, 1946, p. 338). For the absolute charisma of virtuoso" morality, "this relativization is indeed objectionable and estranged" (Gerth & Mills, 1946, p. 339). Males, who complain about rape and sexual abuse, may be dubbed "emasculated," "homosexual," or "turned-out" (Cusack, 2015). This classification places the onus of sexual power on the victim to reinstall patriarchal control, demonstrate male might, and distinguish male victims from complainant female victims of sexual assault and rape, who have been portrayed by law and society as losing power, being ruined by men, and being "sluts" (McAfee, 2015; Slut Leanne, 2011).

> Understanding contemporary political life pertains to tracing of the formation and regulation of the modern subject through a discursive equation of certain beliefs and practices…[B]ehaviors or beliefs…are in turn regulated…as a means of ordering, classifying, and regulating individuals in the…mass society….[T]his kind of…construction of the homosexual in modernity through the convergence of various scientific, administrative, and religious discourses…., medicine, psychiatry, pedagogy, religion, and sexology…[is] increasingly constitutive of identity such that homosexual *acts* come to be seen as expressions of the homosexual *subject.* Homosexual acts become signs of the core truth of this subject, which is now also reduced to its desires; its sexual desires are the truth of this subject. No longer is one defined by being of this village or that family, this language group or that vocation, but rather by a particular and fundamental sexual or other persona—an identity rooted in desire and behavior (Brown, 2006, p. 41).

These domineering, oligarchical, objectifying, and oppressive mental and sociosexual constructs are imbedded into governance, law, politics, and the justice system (Aiken, 1962). They may harm members of minority and hegemonic groups and protect a sexual oligarchy.

Sexual oligarchy defies the American notion of governance.

> There be other names of Government, in the Histories, and books of Policy; as Tyranny, and Oligarchy: But they are not the names of other [Forms] of Government, but of the same [Forms] misliked. For they that are discontented under…Tyranny; and they that are displeased with Aristocracy, called it Oligarchy: so also, they which find themselves grieved under a Democracy, call it Anarchy, (which signifies want of Government;) and yet I think no man believes, that want of Government, is any new kind of Government: nor by the same reason ought they to believe, that the Government is of one kind, when they like it, and another,

> when they mislike it, or are oppressed by the [Governors] (Hobbes, 2013, p. 159).

A sexual oligarchy is formed by numerous anarchistic members of the justice system, who participate in public enforcement of morality, but break the law by committing sexual deviance in their private lives and in the course of their public duties.

When the oligarchy persecutes sex crimes, they may opportunistically distill obscenities through investigations, interviews, depositions, courtroom testimony, and the press. Salacious speech and tawdry details are unveiled at the government's command, perhaps giving rise to public perception that the government may be a gateway for moral corrosion and perversion. For example, during the 1900s, locals congregated in courtrooms to indulge in sexual details described by witnesses, attorneys, and judges. In the 1900s and presently, despite strict regulations on sexual speech, the government's power to force sexually explicit speech at trial has caused the government to seem intentionally or unintentionally to have monopolized and made available obscenity. To victims, this may feel like racketeering or prostitution because sexual details describing their bodies are conscripted by the government in exchange for protection, sold by the press, and consumed by sex-crazed members of the public, some of whom are thrilled and others, who are repulsed by sexual immorality and interested in prosecution.

> Women who allowed themselves to be stripped naked before windows or who agreed to intimacy on the mere pretext of an errand-run were hardly ordinary specimens of the fairer sex. In the world outside the courtroom, these articulated cultural markers of difference afforded narrator and listeners a bit of amusement and pleasure as well as alerting the listeners to potential leads for their own future sexual pursuits. Inside the courtroom, these tales of sexual intrigue also provided entertainment to all participants, save the prosecuting witness herself. But more importantly, when expressed in the principal forum for social and political decision making, intimate narratives and the practice of sexual storytelling took on qualities of necessity, even legitimacy (Hayes, 2014, p. 193).

Repeatedly, throughout history and in the present, the government's parameters for acceptable speech, depictions, and conduct have been contextualized and legitimized by the government's desire to have command and control over sexual behavior, identity, intimacy, and refrain. The government's purposes and methods may appear to be self-serving, rather than protective of the people, and marginalizing of people's sexual autonomy. This phenomenon has occurred simultaneously with the sexual liberation movement and establishment of rights for children, animals, women, and gay people, with the latter two frequently questioned in light of moral decomposition (Cusack, 2012).

Fig. 0.1, Site where Larry Flynt was shot when he was tried for obscenity, Lawrenceville, Georgia.

Fig. 0.2, Site where Larry Flynt was shot when he was tried for obscenity, Lawrenceville, Georgia.

The effect of sexual liberation on culture and law has been evident in how society has responded to pornographic materials (Attorney General v. "Tropic of Cancer," 1962; Miller, 1994; Roth v. U. S., 1957; U.S. v. One Package of Japanese Pessaries, 1936). In 1965, *Memoirs of a Woman of Pleasure* was considered to be obscene in a civil equity suit made by the Attorney General of Massachusetts (*Memoirs of a Woman of Pleasure* v. Attorney General, 1966). The U.S. Supreme Court carefully distinguished obscenity from material that possesses redeeming value, yet is exploited for sexual use (Cusack, 2016; *Memoirs of a Woman of Pleasure* v. Attorney General, 1966; U.S. v. Dost, 1986). Today, Playboy fundraises for the Democratic Party and Larry Flynt is considered by some people to be a hero of free speech because he was shot by a racist serial killer after he published interracial pornography. However, others believe that he is a pervert. For example, Bob Guccione, editor of the pornographic magazine *Penthouse*, said of Flynt, "He is a sick, demented character. He is no hero" (*New York Times Magazine,* 1997).

Negative effects of pornography's influence on society are evident to legislators, who have successfully implemented zoning bans against adult establishments (Barnes v. Glen Theatre, 1991; Hudson, 2002; Los Angeles v. Alameda Books, 2002; McCullen v. Coakley, 2014; Paris Adult Theatre v. Slaton, 1973; Renton v. Playtime Theatres, 1986; Ward v. Rock Against Racism, 1989; Young v. American Mini Theatres, 1976). Municipalities may form parameters to keep specific kinds of businesses certain distances from schools, churches, residential neighborhoods, and other places that may be sensitive to consequences of sexual arousal, drunkenness, and randy behavior (i.e. secondary effects). For example, zoning laws may regulate pornography theaters and massage parlors.

Municipalities have overcome First Amendment challenges by stipulating that prohibitions are not against the content of speech exhibited, sold, or promoted by establishments. The laws protect property value, family-life, and other interests from secondary effects. A series of cases challenged the secondary effects doctrine by distinguishing particular effects, such as prostitution, sexual assault, and public intoxication, and claiming that laws were irrational and unconstitutional. The U.S. Supreme Court uses an intermediate-level scrutiny to analyze a law that is content neutral on its face. If too a great a burden is placed on speech by time, place, and manner regulations that are not sufficiently tailored, then laws are unconstitutional prior restraints on speech. An undue burden is one that limits the exact kind of speech proscribed by the time, place, or manner regulations. Anti-skid row zoning regulations pass intermediate scrutiny.

Pornography and immorality negatively impact the private lives of justice system members, some of whom have sought sex addiction treatment (Cusack, 2014). Sex addiction is "everywhere" "and it's" affecting people of "all ages" (LeBlanc, 2017). Many seek therapeutic and communal intervention through moral organizations, such as the Catholic Church (U.S. Conference of Catholic Bishops, 2006). Attendees may escape institutional culture by attending a men's group where they overcome addiction using a 12-step program. For example, My House Men's Group discusses addiction to internet pornography. Almost all members have histories of abuse that are "connected to addiction;" however, the group does not discuss abuse as a cause of addiction (LeBlanc, 2017). They view pornography addiction as being a neurological problem akin to heroin addiction; yet, a priest attends the meetings each month to have confession. A group leader described their problem as an addiction to lust that is capable of destroying families, jobs, and lives. Although, they discuss related philosophies, such as their beliefs that sex should be "unitive" and "fruitful"; and they "feel bad" for "sex slaves," "who are in captivity," the group focuses on recovery (LeBlanc,

2017). They believe that lawmakers would need to ban all pornography to end lust addiction, but they do not view anti-pornography laws as being morality-based. They believe that pornography is a threat to public safety and general well-being.

Prisons, discussed in Chapter Four, are an archetypal example of how government institutions may disintegrate morality. A serious danger for inmates is prison staff's sexual immorality. American prisons' brutality and immorality has raised concerns throughout the world. Although concerns may be justified under a retributive theory of justice, prisons' corrosive effects on society are inexcusable (Dressler & Garvey, 2012).

Prison staff may rape, coerce, pimp, or unfairly barter with inmates; others may participate in voluntary sexual contact (Cusack, 2014). All sexual contact with inmates is prohibited, thus voluntary acts are nonconsensual. Society may want inmates and staff to be coercive to worsen prisons' reputations to deter crime. However, institutions tend to claim that sexual violations mostly affect homosexuals and juveniles (Schmitz, 2017). Although this is untrue, abuse of homosexuals, juveniles, and transgender inmates is a serious problem (Taylor & Fritsch, 2011). Members of the justice system seem unable or unwilling to regulate morality within prisons sufficiently to prevent deviance and protect victims. Recent studies of institutional deviance suggest that researchers may have problematically adopted sexist attitudes that potentially perpetuate sexual deviance. Rather than blaming institutional settings, culture, and paradigmatic shifts in consciousness, some research has blamed women for working as prison guards.

Deleterious moral vortices in other justice environments are similar to sociosexual degeneration experienced in prisons. However, not every example of an individual employee serves this argument; and the majority of justice system members may functionally serve the people and competently perform duties assigned to them by the Leviathan. Nevertheless, an overwhelming pattern emerges from numerous examples of uncovered sexual deviance within the justice system suggesting to the public that moral corrosion is sponsored by or tolerated within the government. The people may conclude that laws regulating morality are unfairly imposed on them, but not the oligarchy. As the press reports sexual misconduct within the justice system, the public, comprised of deviants, moralists, liberationists, and other groups, is confronted, enticed, threatened, offended, perplexed, and put in a position to doubt and challenge the government's authority.

For many individuals, political views spring from or may be the basis for their moral compasses. Partisanship evident in institutional culture and speech may influence structure, morals, and deviance. It may be particularly difficult to train justice members to alter or suspend their political views while at work (Cusack, 2015; DiFranco, 1993; DiFranco, 2012; Madonna, 2015).

Democrats and Republicans have differing views about crime and punishment (Lerman & Page, 2016). These views affect their political power, which reciprocally alters how the public interprets and implements justice. For example, imprisonment rates directly increase with the strength of the Republican Party. Candidates claim to be tough on crime. In office, Republicans fund prison expansion; support increased capital sentences; and legalize various methods for capital punishment. Crime control is a top priority for Republican voters, who believe in punishment and enforcement, not prevention or rehabilitation, like Democrats. Republican voters are likelier than Democrats to want increased sentences. Democrats believe more often than Republicans that poor people, African Americans, and Hispanics are likelier to receive disproportionately higher sentences (Cusack, 2014; Lerman & Page, 2016). One reason may be that they are targeted by lawmakers, who engage in deviance. For example, a Republican state representative sponsored a bill to increase proscriptions against public sex, but was arrested after he offered oral sodomy to a male undercover police officer in exchange for $20 (Cusack, 2014; Fox News, 2007).

Partisan politics differently affect regions throughout the country (Lerman & Page, 2016). For example, incarceration and sentencing debates have been cores of California politics for decades; but, similar issues have been irrelevant in Minnesota's penal development. California Democrats would like to limit incarceration to allocate prison beds to serious offenders, not drug users, non-violent offenders, or other similar types of criminals (Okorocha, 2013). They advocate for reform and rehabilitation. Republicans in California have wanted to incarcerate drug-users, who may receive education and access to specialized programs (e.g. labor) (Harvin, 2016; Lerman & Page, 2016). In Minnesota, the Republican Party tends to follow typical Party platforms, but penology is essentially a non-issue. The Democratic-Farm-Labor Party appears to be disinterested in political issues relating to corrections. They advocate for prevention, law enforcement, reform, education, and treatment. They believe that prisons should be designed to punish violent criminals, not provide them with recreation.

Politicization shapes members' attitudes, identities, professional orientation, and relationships (Lerman & Page, 2016). This effect is particularly salient in prison guards' attitudes toward rehabilitation as a predominant purpose of incarceration in California and Minnesota. Politicization may be less likely to affect which rehabilitative programs officers believe to be valuable in California and Minnesota. Guards' beliefs about the general purpose of incarceration may be guided by politicized attitudes; yet, result in similar deviant conduct. For example, a Republican may believe that inmates (e.g. sex offenders) should suffer. A Democrat may become sexually involved with an inmate, who appears to deserve forgiveness and a second chance. Worldviews influence institutional definitions and willingness to enforce rules using morality as a guide. Institutional integrity, which may be corrupted by sex and monetary gain, is a touchstone.

Chapter One

Power, Sex, and the Justice System

Morality is the basis for laws criminalizing allegedly deviant sexual depictions and activities, such as child pornography, bestiality, and public indecency (Slifkin, 2006). States' use of police power to enforce moral legislation has been challenged, and by some accounts, diminished by superseding doctrines and constitutional requirements for laws (Haberfeld & Cerrah, 2008; Lawrence v. Texas, 2003). Equal protection, substantive due process, free speech, and the establishment clause are a few constitutional requirements that have stamped out states' ambitions to regulate private and public sexual behavior. The state's power to regulate public sexual behavior may be invoked under their authority to maintain safety and order, and in many cases, this power has been used to implement widespread regulation of private activities. One example was states' longstanding regulation of public and private acts of sodomy on the grounds that total bans deterred male prostitution, cottaging (i.e. closeted use of public spaces), public indecency, voyeurism, and exploitation of minors. Although female-female cunnilingus was prosecuted, sodomy laws were typically enforced to punish female fellators and homosexual males. Labeling victimless sex crimes, such as cottaging, with sexual abuse demonstrated animus against homosexual adult males. Crimes against nature laws, which presumably correlated humans' physical actions with spiritual consequences in nature or in the wild, communicated that the most debased components of each crime were somehow congruent (Durkheim, 2008, p. 259). For example, they have "convey[ed]" that "all the worst elements of homosexuality and bestiality" "could possibly" be related; and "[i]t is not enough…to represent homosexuality fused with bestiality, but indeed" to "convey *all the very worst* elements of both" (Morrissey, 2013, p. 244). Yet, many male homosexuals sought companionship and sex in bathhouses and other public places as oases because homosexual men have been oppressed by domestic life that suppresses their genuine interests, pressures them to restrict their sex drives, and forces them to work within a construct that does not satisfy their urges (i.e. heterosexual married life) (Skiba, Hoppus, & Barker, 1999; Skiba, Hoppus, & Barker, 2001).

According to legislators, their goals to maintain public safety and decorum were legitimate, yet their means were not because they unreasonably criminalized a substantial amount of private conduct. Decades later, society began to view some prohibitions against sodomy as violating equal protection and due process. Because the government could not demonstrate that these laws were reasonably, substantially, or necessarily related to rational, important, or compelling state interests, the laws were stricken and the government was forced to narrowly tailor laws that directly prevented behavior that could be outlawed (Cusack, 2012; Kahneman, 2011).

Tradition is a guiding principle in law; for example, it is the basis for substantive due process rights and case law precedence. "The most obvious and generally accepted element of tradition is what T.S. Eliot has called its 'pastness'….The problem is finding an alternative" that continues to be suitable today (Glenn, 2004, p. 5). In addition to tradition, members of the justice system may rely on personal discretion, cronyism, and cultural influences to interpret and formulate laws that regulate which sexual conduct (e.g. pornographic depictions) ought to be illegal. Political commitments, religion, philosophies, and political dialectics (e.g. patriarchy) may motivate the government to label acts and speech as "bad" or "good" (Schaeffler, 1999).

Thomas Hobbes (2013) idealized relationships between legislative labels and implicit forfeiture of power by the people in exchange for protection from anarchy and tyranny.

> But whatsoever is the object of any [man's] Appetite or Desire; that is it, which he for his part [called] Good: And the object of his Hate, and Aversion, [evil]; And of his contempt, Vile, and Inconsiderable. For these words of Good, [evil], and Contemptible, are ever used with relation to the person that [used] them: There being nothing simply and absolutely so; nor any common Rule of Good and [evil], to be taken from the nature of the objects themselves; but from the Person of the man (where there is no Common-wealth;) or, (in a Common-wealth,) From the Person that [represented] it; or from an Arbitrator or Judge, whom men disagreeing shall by consent set up, and make his sentence the Rule thereof (Hobbes, 2013, pp. 58-59).

To maintain tradition, leaders appointed by the people ought to be the individuals with the greatest amount of experience, foresight, or reason.

> [B]ecause in Deliberation the Appetites and Aversions are raised by foresight of the good and [evil] consequences, and sequels of the action whereof we Deliberate; the good or [evil] effect thereof [depends] on the

> foresight of a long chain of consequences, of which very [seldom] any man is able to see to the end. But for so far as a man [sees], if the Good in those consequences be greater than the [evil], the whole chain is that which Writers call Apparent or Seeming Good. And contrarily, when the [evil exceeds] the good, the whole is Apparent or Seeming [Evil]: so that he who hath by Experience, or Reason, the greatest and surest prospect of Consequences, Deliberates best himself; and is able, when he will, to give the best counsel unto others (Hobbes, 2013, p. 65).

Hobbes' explanation of entitlement to rule suggests that virtue, foresight, and authority may be developed through trial and error possibly involving immoral experiences (Hobbes, 2013). Members of the justice system may use their positions to achieve notoriety or increase their own pleasure and aggrandize their own egos.

> The POWER of a Man, (to take it Universally,) is his present means, to obtain some future apparent Good. And is either [Original], or [Instrumental]. [Natural] Power, is the eminence of the Faculties of Body, or Mind: as extraordinary Strength, [Form], Prudence, Arts, Eloquence, Liberality, Nobility. [Instrumental] are those Powers, which acquired by these, or by fortune, are means and Instruments to acquire more: as Riches, Reputation, Friends, and the Secret working of God, which men call Good Luck. For the nature of Power, is in this point, like to Fame, increasing as it proceeds; or like the motion of heavy bodies, which the further they go, make still the more hast (Hobbes, 2013, p. 81).

People in power, who use public power for personal gain (i.e. anarchists) may consolidate their personal power (i.e. oligarchy) by surrounding themselves with likeminded people, fanatics, and morally complicit people (e.g. packing the court).

> The Greatest of humane Powers, is that which is compounded of the Powers of most men, united by consent, in one person, [Natural], or [civil], that has the use of all their Powers depending on his will; such as is the Power of a Common-wealth: or depending on the wills of each particular; such as is the Power of a Faction, or of divers factions leagued. Therefore to have servants, is Power; To have Friends, is Power: for they are strengths united.
>
> Also Riches [joined] with liberality, is Power; because it [procures] friends, and servants (Hobbes, 2013, p. 81).

When members' deviance is discovered, their reputations may be tarnished and cause the government to appear to be blemished, unreliable, weak, or useless.

Members of the government are endorsed and elected because of their reputations for being able to provide, defend, and protect; and people rely on the government's reputation for punishing lawbreakers in order to deter criminals.

> Reputation of power, is Power; because it [draws] with it the [adherence] of those that need protection.
>
> So is Reputation of love of a [man's] Country, (called Popularity,) for the same Reason. Also, what quality [whatsoever makes] a man beloved, or feared of many; or the reputation of such quality, is Power; because it is a means to have the assistance, and service of many. Good [success] is Power; because it [makes] reputation of [Wisdom], or good fortune; which makes men either [fear] him, or rely on him.
>
> Affability of men already in power, is [increase] of Power; because it [gains] love.
>
> Reputation of Prudence in the conduct of Peace or War, is Power; because to prudent men, we commit the government of our selves, more willingly than to others.
>
> Nobility is Power, not in all places, but [only] in those Commonwealths, where it has [Privileges]: for in such [privileges consists] their Power (Hobbes, 2013, pp. 81-82).

Thus, coalitions of personal power may usurp the government's power.

Many members of the justice system participate in sexual oligarchy. For example, politicians, courts, and members of law enforcement consistently have surrounded themselves with people, who support, benefit from, and are entertained by their misuse of power. Sometimes, they directly abuse power to control and indulge in sex and obscenity. For example, law enforcement officers have abused victims by inappropriately ordering victims to exhibit their bodies to document evidence of rape (Cusack, 2014). Some of these officers have been disciplined and occasionally prosecuted. Others have pruriently utilized for gratification evidence (e.g. photos) of dead and living adult, child, and animal victims.

Testimony may be used to titillate; however, this effect is not necessarily prosecutable or actionable under civil remedies. A tragic example occurred in Cox Broadcasting v. Cohn (1975). Seventeen year-old Cynthia Cohn was raped and killed on April 10, 1972 by six juvenile males. The press passionately discussed details of the crime and the prosecution of one defendant, who did not plead guilty to attempted rape or rape, like the other five defendants. A reporter used documents made available in open court to publish through Cox Broadcasting the details of the victim's identity. Under Georgia law it was a misdemeanor for any person to broadcast or publish the name of a rape victim (Ga. Code Ann. §

26-9901, 1972). The victim's father sued under the criminal statute for damages resulting from a violation of his right to privacy. Cox made a novel claim that the information was privileged under Georgia law and under the federal Constitution's First Amendment protection of the press and the Fourteenth Amendment right to privacy. The trial court found that Cox was liable under the criminal statute and could not defend under the federal Constitution.

Fig. 1.1, Cox Broadcasting Building, Fulton County, Georgia.

Georgia's Supreme Court held that the criminal statute did not provide a civil remedy for invasion of privacy (Cox Broadcasting v. Cohn, 1975). The court also held that the defendant could find no relief in tort law. To receive damages for the tort of public disclosure, the father's zone of privacy had to have been wilfully or negligently violated without regard for the extreme offense that would have been experienced by a reasonable person. Intrusions under the First Amendment may be balanced against abrogation of the right to privacy. The Georgia court reheard the argument that the victim's identity was a matter of public interest that superseded the criminal statute, which applied when the victim's name was not a matter of public interest.

The U.S. Supreme Court reversed. The Court held that freedom of the press is protected under the First and Fourteenth Amendments (Cox Broadcasting v. Cohn, 1975). "In other words, the First Amendment has a penumbra where privacy is protected from governmental intrusion" (Griswold v. Connecticut, 1965, p. 483). However, public records contained the victim's name (Cox Broadcasting v. Cohn, 1975). The victim's father did not have a privacy interest in her name. The state government of Georgia "stoutly defend[ed]" it's position, which the Court upheld because "[i]ts claims are not without force" (Cox Broadcasting v. Cohn, 1975, p. 487). It may be ultimately defined" that "there *is*" no "zone of privacy surrounding" public records (Cox Broadcasting v. Cohn, 1975, p. 487). However, it surrounds "every individual, a zone within which the State may protect him from intrusion by the press, with all its attendant publicity" (Cox Broadcasting v. Cohn, 1975, p. 487). The dead victim could not assert a privacy interest.

The U.S. Supreme Court quoted verbiage stating that "[t]o satisfy a prurient taste the details of sexual relations are spread broadcast in the columns of the daily papers. To occupy the indolent, column upon column is filled with idle gossip, which can only be procured by intrusion upon the domestic circle. The intensity and complexity of life" "have rendered necessary,...under the refining influence of culture," "solitude and" "essential...enterprise and invention" (Cox Broadcasting v. Cohn, 1975, p. 487). "[T]hrough invasions upon...privacy,...mental pain and distress, far greater...harm" has been created (Cox Broadcasting v. Cohn, 1975, p. 487). However, "such invasions" are "confined to the suffering of those... subjects of journalistic" interest (Cox Broadcasting v. Cohn, 1975, p. 487).

> [A]s in other branches of commerce, the supply creates the demand. Each crop of unseemly gossip, thus harvested, becomes the seed of more, and, in direct proportion to its circulation, results in a lowering of social standards and of morality. Even gossip apparently harmless, when widely and persistently circulated, is potent for evil. It both belittles and perverts. It belittles by inverting the relative importance of things (Cox Broadcasting v. Cohn, 1975, p. 487).

"[T]hus" minimizing "the thoughts and aspirations of" the state and its "people" "[w]hen personal gossip attains the dignity of print, and crowds the space available for matters of real interest to the community, what wonder" "the ignorant and thoughtless mistake" of "its relative importance. Easy of comprehension" "that weak side of human nature...is never wholly cast down by the misfortunes and frailties" (Cox Broadcasting v. Cohn, 1975, p. 487). "More compellingly, the century has experienced a strong tide running in favor of the so-called right of privacy. In 1967, [the Court] noted that…at common law in 30 States plus the District of Columbia," "the right of privacy [was] by this time recognized and accepted in all but a very few jurisdictions" (Cox Broadcasting v. Cohn, 1975, p. 488). "Nor is it irrelevant here that the right of privacy is no recent arrival in the jurisprudence of Georgia, which has embraced the right in some form since 1905" (Cox Broadcasting v. Cohn, 1975, pp. 488-489). "These are impressive credentials for a right of privacy, but" no "tangible intrusion" was at issue (Cox Broadcasting v. Cohn, 1975, p. 489). Therefore, the state's credentials were worthless. It was its forcible argumentation, mentioned by the Court, which originally prevailed in this matter. The argument "in which the plaintiff claim[ed] the right to be free from unwanted publicity about his private affairs, which, although wholly true, would be offensive to a person of ordinary sensibilities" failed because the Supreme Court of Georgia dismissed the state's interest in and power to protect the victim's father's privacy right. This all but sealed the case for Cox, which was able to exploit the rape and death of a teenager because Georgia's highest court found sufficient proof that because public records contained her name, the press could publish it in contravention of precedence and law. Georgia's law could not prevent Cox from capitalizing on her name despite her father's privacy interest.

> Because the gravamen of the claimed injury is the publication of information, whether true or not, the dissemination of which is embarrassing or otherwise painful to an individual, it is here that claims of privacy most directly confront the constitutional freedoms of speech and press. The face-off is apparent (Cox Broadcasting v. Cohn, 1975, p. 489).

The Court went further and held that "the press may not be made criminally or civilly liable for publishing information that is neither false nor misleading but absolutely accurate, however damaging it may be to reputation or individual sensibilities" (Cox Broadcasting v. Cohn, 1975, 489). This holding diminished traditional respect (i.e. privacy) granted by society to living or murdered rape victims, and fortified the press' ability to sexually humiliate women and arouse audiences with vivid specifics.

Courts have openly aired garish details of sex crimes, such as statutory rape or sodomy, to the delight of the press and attendees, including jurors. Sexual exploitation of victims has often been sexist and served to control participants with gender roles.

> In this way, courtroom narrations of sex—those given by individuals directly involved in the act *and* those supplied by peeping Toms—offered

> actual sexual incidents a vicarious life beyond the experience itself, and in the decorous public setting of the courthouse, no less. The young men's salacious testimony proved a source of titillation to court spectators. [For example, in] the days after their appearance on the witness stand, several local residents filed into the defendant's barn to judge the placement of the bed and the location of the window, all in hopes of ascertaining the kinds of sinful activity the youth might have engaged in during that moonlit night. There is some evidence to suggest that sexual storytelling was not an entirely masculine pastime. This proof yet again originates from the courtroom disclosures of character witnesses (Hayes, 2014, p. 189).

"Battles" have been waged over which lurid descriptions could be uttered in the "public sphere" (Hayes, 2014, p. 151). "[C]ontests that pitted moralists against both sex reformers and obscene print publishers… represent a narrow accounting of a public sexual culture full of eroticization" (Hayes, 2014, p. 151). In the 19th century, those seeking "titillation" turned to "venues," such as courthouses in Illinois for "regularly authorized candid sexual storytelling" (Hayes, 2014, p. 151). Quixotic attraction to "eroticized fanfare" was satisfied by tales of illegal "seduction, breach of promise of marriage," and "disputes in domestic law" (Hayes, 2014, p. 152). Courthouses were hospitable to "erotic sensationalism, voyeurism, sexual boasting, and bawdy humor," which "flourish[ed]" and "command[ed] authority" (Hayes, 2014, p. 153). Dirty descriptions "shucked the archaic clothing of" a legitimate legal "action," and attracted deviants to the legal realm (Grossman & Friedman, 2011, p. 95). Reactions from "prurient spectators" fueled "salacious headlines" (Hayes, 2014, p. 153).

> Instead of seeing the era of Comstock [laws] as a time in which public discourse about sexuality went underground….amative spectacles of rural and small-town courthouses….infused all levels of the juridical process—from the examination of litigants and witnesses to the closing arguments directed at the jury to the briefs that provided appellate judges with the facts and arguments of the trial. Nineteenth-century courts were not simply spaces to regulate print obscenity or to police sexuality, rather the courts themselves, in their examinations of 'illicit sex,' produced 'obscenity' (Hayes, 2014, pp. 153-154).

Acknowledging the "erotic underbelly" of "legal order fundamentally reshapes" interpretations of American power and the regulation of sex (Hayes, 2014, p. 154).

Media outlets, witnesses, litigants, attorneys, law enforcement officers, and judges have publicly disclosed intimate details that shamelessly promoted obscenity and braggadociously explored and controlled sex.

> [A]s a whole [it] had the effect of inciting—rather than quelling—a raucous culture of sexuality. The discourse...contributed to this legal climate of unabashed eroticism in different, but nonetheless complementary, ways. Newspapers' coverage of sexual trials generated erotic sensationalism, whereas young women's courtroom testimony fuelled community voyeurism. Sexual suits offered male witnesses and litigants public platforms for sexual aggrandizement, and they presented lawyers with respectable venues for telling dirty jokes (Hayes, 2014, p. 154).

During this era, tawdry talk and scrawling's were outlawed and condemned, but became central to trials that purported to stamp out immorality. These acts were improper, dismissive, and possibly, subversive toward law.

During the 19th century, progressive sexual attitudes were developing, but the oligarchy's exploitation of its power stifled liberation. In effect, naughty distillations were an immoral *coup d'état* perpetrated by members of the government and media against the government's purported moral purpose.

> As state and federal obscenity laws clamped down on the public sexual conversation at large—particularly on the individuals who insisted on portraying female sexual agency—a climate of unadulterated eroticism emerged front and center in the one public venue where discussions of this aspect of female sexuality endured without threat of prosecution (Hayes, 2014, p. 156).

In the 19th century, adultery and fornication were immoral acts, which have since all but been condoned by decriminalization and by examples of legislators, law enforcement, judges, and other members of the justice system. Yet, the media, system, and public continue to be riveted and influenced by exploitive court proceedings surrounding new legislation protecting victims, sexual minorities, and women from sexual claims (e.g. harassment). As members of the justice system continue to use the government's power and their discretion to decriminalize or ignore deviant acts considered to be *passé*, they also effectively decriminalize previously *avant garde* sexualities and problematic sex acts (e.g. harmful sadomasochism) by ignoring establishments and subcultures catering and pandering to these interests (Cusack, 2012; Cusack, 2013; Cusack, 2016; Cusack, 2017). They also exploit, sensationalize, eroticize, and glamorize the few prosecutions that are pursued by the government.

> While scopophilic pleasure in any kind of sexual display can be interpreted as a kind of voyeurism, the term has specific appeal in the context of watching illicitly recorded material: Watching unwanted observation material—

> potentially involving people we know—adds a very specific element of erotic and voyeuristic appeal" (Rosewarne, 2016, p. 245).

Sex trials are like a two-sided coin. They sensationalize and advertise obscene sexual details under the guise of regulating and seeking to punish perverted acts, and sometimes mere words (e.g. propositions, solicitation, and sexual harassment).

Though the 19th century focused on propriety, current political and social influences continue to demonstrate "concern for genteel notions of respectability," such that "female-narrated depictions of sex…[possess] an aura of the forbidden and the illicit" (Hayes, 2014, p. 163). Police reports, trials, and media interviews have become acceptable outlets for creating and absorbing sexuality possessed in this discourse. For example, the entertainer Madonna based her decision not to report rape on this. During the late 1970s, Madonna was raped by a man in New York, New York. She said that she never sought legal recourse because of the public record and humiliation required by the system to prosecute.

> I was raped. I guess people know that now….The rest is not worth talking about….I was told that if I wanted to press charges…[then, I would need] a physical examination[.] I would have to go before the court….[T]hey're going to ask you all these personal questions; and, you've already been violated—so, then do you want to talk about it? Do you want to make it public? No, it's just not worth it. It's too humiliating (Madonna, 2015).

"Reporters [have] anticipated that if reading about sexual testimony offered pleasure, this would be all the more so when those intimate narratives were recounted by pretty prosecuting witnesses" (Hayes, 2014, p. 167). The press may intentionally describe a rape victim in detail to entice the audience. For example, a reporter may describe Madonna's experience of being raped in one paragraph, but then describe her immodest fashion.

The press may also correlate a victim's age with the degree of sympathy owed to her by society, such that young victims are portrayed as being more sympathetic than older victims. An example of this occurred in the case of Daniel Holtzclaw, the serial rapist, who worked as a police officer (Brandes, 2016). The press repeatedly mentioned that one of the victims was a child (i.e. 17 years old) to garner interest from the public by suggesting that he had sexually abused children. Holtzclaw is discussed further in Chapter Six.

The law often analyzes sexual assault in terms of penetration. Therefore, men are accused far more of sexual assault than women; and in some jurisdictions women cannot be convicted of rape (Cusack, 2014).

Investigations, trials, and press reports about sexual assault inevitably depict males as sexual aggressors, which further perpetuates stereotypes about unquenchable male libidos. This may have the effect of fulling this rhetoric so that some men aspire to be archetypical, hypermasculine rapists. Their day in court and subsequent legal records become bragging rights and memorializations of their prowess and status as unrestrainable Lotharios. They are able to discuss their sexual maneuvers, positions, preferences, and pleasures to investigators, lawyers, judges, jurors, relatives, spectators, community members, and the press, which sometimes makes details available online for the entire world to view. Sexual trials that air dirty details may treat criminals like world class Olympians demonstrating their exceptionally sexually deviant behavior on a world stage. Even though moral members of the justice system may attempt to use law to achieve justice for rape victims, many of whom have suffered a hate crime based on gender, the justice system's failure to control how tawdry details are revealed and dispersed further emphasizes sexism and a sexual double standard. The double standard exists not only between penetrators and non-penetrators, but also between those, who have power over sex and those, who do not. Furthermore, while public records and humiliation may deter sex crimes to some extent, public spectacles also normalize sex crimes by demonstrating how routine, if not mundane, sex crimes are (Pollock, 2013). Only the most sensational sex crimes are highlighted by the press, but thousands of sex crimes are mentioned annually by the press and hundreds of thousands of cases are recorded by police and courts.

CHAPTER TWO

MORALITY, TRADITION, LAW, AND POWER

Laws in the United States preserve Americans' way of life, which is rooted in Christian traditions and values (Cusack, 2015; Cusack & Waranius, 2015; Lanoue, 2011; Smith, 2009). Christian values traditionally condemned non-marital sex, premarital sex, and crimes against nature (Eisenstadt v. Baird, 1972). Generally, scriptures, secular knowledge, customary beliefs, and moral discernment were used as the bases for construction of moral rules; however, these values have been interpreted according to social and political trends (e.g. industrialization and alienation), as well as in response to civic needs (Baum, 2006; Greeley, 2004; Grossman & Friedman, 2011; Lanoue, 2011). For example, homosexuality may be tolerated when key or important groups or individuals are homosexual (Limbaugh, 2010). "The native, the fanatic, the fundamentalist, and the bigot are what must be overcome by the society committed to tolerance" (Brown, 2006, p. 184). "'Learning tolerance' thus involves divesting oneself of relentless partiality, absolutist identity, and parochial attachments, a process understood as the effect of a larger, more cosmopolitan world-view and not as the privilege of hegemony" (Brown, 2006, p. 184). Liberation and morality in the United States have been defined according to androcentric and patriarchal values that allegedly benefited males individually (e.g. adulterer Reverend Dr. Martin Luther King, Jr.) and as a group, and focused on depicting men as rational creatures capable of managing impropriety by using free will and higher thought (Cusack, 2016; Mikkelson, 2017). Laws also severed to protect female dignity by exalting purity, virginity, and maternity (Cusack, 2012; Cusack, 2015). Privately, moral behavior attested to spiritual and cultural purity, and publicly it demonstrated that society was under God's control and ordained by God. Interpretations of "morality" may change, but the Christian God is unchanging. Morality relates not only to the establishment of tradition, it causes laws and government to seem permanent and God-like (Cusack, 2015).

Fig. 2.1, Coker v. Georgia, Ware State Prison, Waycross, Georgia

One problem with overturning or diluting the government's morality power is that society loses some conventions, which have benefited many groups; for example, children have been protected from sexual exploitation. An example of reduced criminalization of immoral conduct is that rape is no longer a capital offense for civilians (Coker v. Georgia, 1977; UCMJ art. 120, 2017). During the 1970s, the defendant in Coker v. Georgia (1977) was serving time in the original Ware Correctional Institution for murder, rape, kidnapping, and aggravated assault convictions. He then escaped. Ware State Prison can currently mobilize bloodhounds to apprehend escaped inmates; however, throughout the time that he evaded apprehension, Coker committed armed robbery and raped a woman (Coker v. Georgia, 1977; Gramiak, 2016). He was sentenced to death, but the U.S. Supreme Court held "that death is indeed a disproportionate penalty for the crime of raping an adult woman" (Coker v. Georgia, 1977, p. 597). The Court did "not discount the seriousness of rape as a crime," which they found to be "highly reprehensible, both in a moral sense and in its almost total contempt for the personal integrity and autonomy of the female victim and for the latter's privilege of choosing those with whom intimate relationships are to be established" (Coker v.

Georgia, 1977, p. 597). The Court stipulated that although rape is an "ultimate violation of self," it is less serious than murder (Coker v. Georgia, 1977, p. 597). Rape is “a violent crime because it normally involves force, or the threat of force or intimidation, to overcome the will and the capacity of the victim to resist. Rape is very often accompanied by physical injury to the female and can also inflict mental and psychological damage” (Coker v. Georgia, 1977, pp. 597-598). The Court described the “public injury” caused by rape, which “undermines the community's sense of security” (Coker v. Georgia, 1977, p. 598). This Court did not entirely discard the traditional notion that “[r]ape is without doubt deserving of serious punishment; but in terms of moral depravity and of the injury to the person and to the public,” the Court held “it does not compare with murder, which does involve the unjustified taking of human life” (Coker v. Georgia, 1977, p. 598). Justice Byron White, writing for the majority, deemphasized the degree of suffering experienced by rape victims. “Life is over for the victim of the murderer; for the rape victim, life may not be nearly so happy as it was, but it is not over and normally is not beyond repair” (Coker v. Georgia, 1977, p. 598). His comments identified that political attitudes toward rape were fluctuating. Previously, society believed that robbing a woman’s virtue was akin to “social death” for the victim even though the law allowed one exception, marital rape (Megale, 2011, p. 92). As attitudes shifted and the Coker Court held that rape is not “irrevocab[le]," marital rape exceptions began to evaporate (Coker v. Georgia, 1977, p. 598).

The severe stigma of rape also dissipated as non-procreative sex was decriminalized (i.e. sodomy and prophylactics) (Griswold v. Connecticut, 1965; Lawrence v. Texas, 2003). This legal progression seems to be unrelated to the establishment of fundamental rights for homosexuals. Yet, political gains for lesbians and male homosexuals are tangentially related to how the Court reshaped sexuality for women and rape victims.

In Bowers v. Hardwick (1986), the Court analyzed whether homosexuality was comparable with marriage. “No connection between family, marriage, or procreation on the one hand and homosexual activity on the other has been demonstrated, either by the [Georgia] Court of Appeals or by respondent. Moreover, any claim that these cases nevertheless stand for the proposition that any kind of private sexual conduct between consenting adults is constitutionally insulated from state proscription is unsupportable” (Bowers v. Hardwick, 1986, p. 191). The Court specifically stated that morality undergirded the case; but, the legal question of whether homosexuality was a fundamental right precluded the Court from further analyzing morality because homosexuality was not a fundamental right.

"This case does not require a judgment on whether laws against sodomy between consenting adults in general, or between homosexuals in particular, are wise or desirable. It raises no question about the right or propriety of

Fig. 2.2, Georgia Supreme Court, Atlanta, Georgia.

state legislative decisions to repeal their laws that criminalize homosexual sodomy, or of state-court decisions invalidating those laws on state constitutional grounds" (Bowers v. Hardwick, 1986, p. 190). Although this Court's *dicta* was later controverted and its holding overturned in Lawrence v. Texas (2003) and Obergefell v. Hodges (2015), the *Bowers* Court held that homosexual conduct inside one's home was not protected under the Fifth and Fourteenth Amendments. "Plainly enough, otherwise illegal conduct is not always immunized whenever it occurs in the home. Victimless crimes, such as the" "possession in the home of drugs, firearms, or stolen goods" are not excused in private (Bowers v. Hardwick, 1986, p. 195). The Court explained that moral fibers are tethered, and disentangling them causes a slippery slope (Cusack, 2017). "[I]f respondent's submission is limited to the voluntary sexual conduct between consenting adults, it would be difficult, except by fiat, to limit the claimed right to homosexual conduct while leaving exposed to prosecution adultery, incest, and other sexual crimes even though they are committed in the home. We are unwilling to start down that road" (Bowers v. Hardwick, 1986, pp. 195-196). Justice Byron White said that the "Court is most vulnerable and comes nearest to illegitimacy when it deals with judge-made constitutional law having little or no cognizable roots in the language or design of the Constitution" (Bowers v. Hardwick, 1986, p. 194).

The Court described how the government's internal tension is a battleground for interpretations of morality and sexuality.

> [T]his is so was painfully demonstrated by the face-off between the Executive and the Court in the 1930's, which resulted in the repudiation of much of the substantive gloss that the Court had placed on the Due Process Clauses of the Fifth and Fourteenth Amendments. There should be, therefore, great resistance to expand the substantive reach of those Clauses, particularly if it requires redefining the category of rights deemed to be fundamental. Otherwise, the Judiciary necessarily takes to itself further authority to govern the country without express constitutional authority. The claimed right pressed on us today falls far short of overcoming this resistance (Bowers v. Hardwick, 1986, pp. 194-195).

> Even if the conduct at issue here is not a fundamental right, respondent asserts that there must be a rational basis for the law and that there is none in this case other than the presumed belief of a majority of the electorate in Georgia that homosexual sodomy is immoral and unacceptable. This is said to be an inadequate rationale to support the law (Bowers v. Hardwick, 1986, p. 196).

However, a law need to be only rational and reasonably related to its asserted purpose, unless it impinges on a fundamental right.

> The law, however, is constantly based on notions of morality, and if all laws representing essentially moral choices are to be invalidated under the Due Process Clause, the courts will be very busy indeed. Even respondent makes no such claim, but insists that majority sentiments about the morality of homosexuality should be declared inadequate. We do not agree, and are unpersuaded that the sodomy laws of some 25 States should be invalidated on this basis (Bowers v. Hardwick, 1986, p. 196).

The Court used rational review in Lawrence v. Texas (2003) to establish a right to privacy, which protected consensual, non-harmful sexual conduct between homosexuals. In Obergefell v. Hodges (2015), same-sex marriage was legalized for homosexual and heterosexual couples; for example, those seeking to establish legally protected partnerships; victims of domestic violence (e.g. "man haters"); people whose bodies are monuments to war; and iconoclasts (Crace, 1999; Cusack, 2013; Cusack 2013; Gerth & Mills, 1946; Michael, 1987). Because sodomy laws were irregularly enforced and some only applied to homosexual conduct, extending the right to privacy using rational review to all consensual private conduct between adults avoided discussions about gender-based morality and turned the discussion to sexuality-based morality, where it has remained strong since *Lawrence* (2003; Baehr v. Miike, 1996).

In his dissent in Obergefell v. Hodges (2015), Justice Antonin Scalia scolded judicial activists.

> The substance of today's decree is not of immense personal importance to me. The law can recognize as marriage whatever sexual attachments and living arrangements it wishes, and can accord them favorable civil consequences, from tax treatment to rights of inheritance. Those civil consequences—and the public approval that conferring the name of marriage evidences—can perhaps have adverse social effects, but no more adverse than the effects of many other controversial laws. So it is not of special importance to me what the law says about marriage. It is of overwhelming importance, however, who it is that rules me. Today's decree says that my Ruler, and the Ruler of 320 million Americans coast-to-coast, is a majority of the nine lawyers on the Supreme Court. The opinion in these cases is the furthest extension in fact—and the furthest extension one can even imagine—of the Court's claimed power to create 'liberties' that the Constitution and its Amendments neglect to mention. This practice of constitutional revision by an unelected committee of nine, always accompanied (as it is today) by extravagant praise of liberty, robs the People of the most important liberty they asserted in the Declaration of

> Independence and won in the Revolution of 1776: the freedom to govern themselves (Obergefell v. Hodges, 2015, pp. 2626-2627).

Justice Scalia summarized his admonishment by admitting that "[t]he stuff contained in today's opinion has to diminish this Court's reputation for clear thinking and sober analysis" (Obergefell v. Hodges, 2015, p. 2630).

Justice Scalia explained the damaging effect of judicial advocacy on the democratic process.

> Until the courts put a stop to it, public debate over same-sex marriage displayed American democracy at its best. Individuals on both sides of the issue passionately, but respectfully, attempted to persuade their fellow citizens to accept their views. Americans considered the arguments and put the question to a vote. The electorates of 11 States, either directly or through their representatives, chose to expand the traditional definition of marriage. Many more decided not to. Win or lose, advocates for both sides continued pressing their cases, secure in the knowledge that an electoral loss can be negated by a later electoral win. That is exactly how our system of government is supposed to work (Obergefell v. Hodges, 2015, p. 2627).

> Buried beneath the mummeries and straining-to-be-memorable passages of the opinion is a candid and startling assertion: No matter *what* it was the People ratified, the Fourteenth Amendment protects those rights that the Judiciary, in its 'reasoned judgment,' thinks the Fourteenth Amendment ought to protect. That is so because '[t]he generations that wrote and ratified the Bill of Rights and the Fourteenth Amendment did not presume to know the extent of freedom in all of its dimensions….' One would think that sentence would continue: '…and therefore they provided for a means by which the People could amend the Constitution,' or perhaps '…and therefore they left the creation of additional liberties, such as the freedom to marry someone of the same sex, to the People, through the never-ending process of legislation.' But no. What logically follows, in the majority's judge-empowering estimation, is: 'and so they entrusted to future generations a charter protecting the right of all persons to enjoy liberty as we learn its meaning.' The 'we,' needless to say, is the nine of us. 'History and tradition guide and discipline [our] inquiry but do not set its outer boundaries.' Thus, rather than focusing on *the People's* understanding of 'liberty'—at the time of ratification or even today—the majority focuses on…'principles and traditions' that, *in the majority's view*, prohibit States from defining marriage as an institution consisting of one man and one woman. This is a naked judicial claim to legislative—indeed, *super*-legislative—power; a claim fundamentally at odds with our system of government (Obergefell v. Hodges, 2015, pp. 2628-2629).

Justice Scalia again expressed outrage about the judiciary's decision to strike morality-based legislation. "Except as limited by a constitutional prohibition agreed to by the People, the States are free to adopt whatever laws they like, even those that offend the esteemed Justices' 'reasoned judgment.' A system of government that makes the People subordinate to a committee of nine unelected lawyers does not deserve to be called a democracy" (Obergefell v. Hodges, 2015, p. 2629). He explained that five justices' arrogance was their motive for weakening the government.

> The five Justices who compose today's majority are entirely comfortable concluding that every State violated the Constitution for all of the 135 years between the Fourteenth Amendment's ratification and Massachusetts' permitting of same-sex marriages in 2003. They have discovered in the Fourteenth Amendment a 'fundamental right' overlooked by every person alive at the time of ratification, and almost everyone else in the time since. They see what lesser legal minds—minds like Thomas Cooley, John Marshall Harlan, Oliver Wendell Holmes, Jr., Learned Hand, Louis Brandeis, William Howard Taft, Benjamin Cardozo, Hugo Black, Felix Frankfurter, Robert Jackson, and Henry Friendly—could not. They are certain that the People ratified the Fourteenth Amendment to bestow on them the power to remove questions from the democratic process when that is called for by their 'reasoned judgment.' These Justices *know* that limiting marriage to one man and one woman is contrary to reason; they *know* that an institution as old as government itself, and accepted by every nation in history until 15 years ago, cannot possibly be supported by anything other than ignorance or bigotry. And they are willing to say that any citizen who does not agree with that, who adheres to what was, until 15 years ago, the unanimous judgment of all generations and all societies, stands against the Constitution (Obergefell v. Hodges, 2015, pp. 2629-2630).

After *Bowers* (1986), but before *Lawrence* (2003) and *Obergefell* (2015), the State of Georgia decriminalized consensual sodomy when a male defendant's convictions for cunnilingus performed on a female were overturned (Powell v. State, 1998). Anthony San Juan Powell was charged with rape and aggravated sodomy when he had consensual vaginal and oral sex with his wife's 17 year-old niece (Powell v. State, 1998). The niece denied that she granted consent, but the defendant was acquitted of those charges. Powell was found "guilty of sodomy, thereby establishing that the State did not prove beyond a reasonable doubt that the act was committed 'with force and against the will' of the niece" (Powell v. State, 1998, p. 327). Powell claimed that the anti-sodomy statute violated his right to privacy. The pre-*Lawrence* (2003) court distinguished Powell's case from *Bowers* (1986).

Fig. 2.3, Georgia State Capitol, Atlanta, Georgia.

Privacy rights protected by the U.S. Constitution are not at issue in this case. Thus, not applicable to this discussion are [holdings in] Bowers v. Hardwick…, where the U.S. Supreme Court ruled that the right of privacy protected by the U.S. Constitution did not insulate private sexual conduct

> between consenting homosexual adults from state proscription because the U.S. Constitution did not 'extend a fundamental right to homosexuals to engage in acts of consensual sodomy' (Powell v. State, 1998, p. 329).

Powell reiterated that pre-*Lawrence* (2003), a "proscription against sodomy was a valid exercise of the State's police power in furtherance of the public's moral welfare" (Powell v. State, 1998, p. 334). "'Police power' is the governing authority's ability to legislate for the protection of the citizens' lives, health, and property, and to preserve good order and public morals" (Powell v. State, 1998, p. 329). "To justify the State in thus interposing its authority on behalf of the public, it must appear, first that the interests of the public generally...require such interference; and second, that the means are reasonably necessary for the accomplishment of the purpose, and not unduly oppressive upon individuals" (Lawton v. Steele, 1894, p. 137).

> Thus, the suggestion that O.C.G.A. § 16-6-2 is a valid exercise of the police power requires us to consider whether it benefits the public generally without unduly oppressing the individual. Since, as determined earlier, the only possible purpose for the statute is to regulate the private conduct of consenting adults, the public gains no benefit, and the individual is unduly oppressed by the invasion of the right to privacy (Powell v. State, 1998, p. 334).

The government asserted that police power may be used to prohibit private conduct in "furtherance of 'social morality,'" which gives "due regard to the collective will of the citizens of Georgia," and "is a constitutional basis for legislative control of the non-commercial, unforced, private sexual activity of those legally capable of consenting to such activity" (Powell v. State, 1998, pp. 334-335). The government invoked a majoritarian definition of "morality" to establish its authority (Powell v. State, 1998, p. 335). "It is well within the power of the legislative branch to establish public policy through legislative enactment. It is also without dispute that oftentimes the public policy so established and the laws so enacted reflect the will of the majority of Georgians as well as the majority's notion of morality" (Powell v. State, 1998, p. 335). The court then engaged in judicial activism and openly admitted to changing legal directives established by elected officials. "[I]t does not follow…that simply because the legislature has enacted as law what may be a moral choice of the majority, the courts are, thereafter, bound to simply acquiesce" (Powell v. State, 1998, p. 335). They softened their stance by invoking judicially-created levels of scrutiny capable of overturning laws that excessively impinge on fundamental rights and the Fourteenth Amendment. "'Social morality legislation,' like any legislative enactment, is subject to the scrutiny of the judicial branch under our tripartite system of 'checks and balances'" (Powell v. State, 1998, p. 335). Members of the court documented their bigoted personal opinions while issuing the judicial opinion. "In undertaking the judiciary's constitutional duty, it is not the prerogative of members of the judiciary to base decisions on their personal notions of morality. Indeed, if we were called upon to pass upon the propriety of the conduct herein involved, we would not condone it" (Powell v. State, 1998, p. 335). The judiciary, which interprets the law, broadly characterized itself as heroically being "charged with" "scrutinizing the law, the interests it promotes, and the means by which it seeks to achieve those interests, to ensure that the law meets constitutional standards" (Powell v. State, 1998, p. 335). The court generalized that "many believe that acts of sodomy," whether heterosexual or homosexual, "involving consenting adults" "are morally reprehensible" (Powell v. State, 1998, p. 335). However, "this repugnance alone does not create a compelling justification for state regulation of the activity" (Powell v. State, 1998, p. 335). Georgia's Supreme Court found that the law infringed on Powell's right to privacy; and the court overturned his conviction for sodomy.

Fig. 2.4, Site of the Office of the Attorney General of Georgia, Atlanta, Georgia.

After *Lawrence* first struck a law prohibiting sodomy, laws criminalizing non-harmful, private heterosexual or homosexual sexual conduct between consenting adults have been held to be unconstitutional (Lawrence v. Texas, 2003). A related phenomenon, but not reciprocal effect, is that during that 30 year "wave of abolitions," sexual conduct previously considered to be a violation of self, culture, and society was decriminalized alongside violent and deeming hate crimes against women (Grossman & Friedman, 2011, p. 101). Although gendered crimes, like the rape of Betty Jean Owens by four males, have been considered to be hate crimes because European American males intentionally target African American females, the act of rape is hateful (Dressler & Garvey, 2012). It is the relevant act that victimized Owens and was famously prosecuted. The European American males intended to rape an African American female, and the African American males accompanying Owens were allowed to flee at gunpoint before she was attacked. Generally, legislatures have failed to codify rape as a hate crime even though bills have been proposed several times and rape intrinsically and socially demonstrates hate in the form of gendered animus and supremacy.

Insert Fig. 2.5, Site where Betty Jean Owens was abducted by four males, Tallahassee, Florida.

Positive and negative causes and effects are evident in the dilution of strict, traditional boundaries. Historically, American male victims of rape have remained silent, and violations of males' bodies have not been viewed similarly to violations of female bodies. Although in the past, males' status, power, and dignity may have been considered defiled by any homosexual conduct, and particularly by rape, women's bodies have been viewed in terms of their husbands' rights (Eisenstadt v. Baird, 1972). Violations damaged her emotional, social, and physical value to him and tampered with society's symbolism. As laws changed, ideas progressively distinguished unconventional forms of sex, such as voluntary sodomy, from rape. However, the government relinquished itself from its tradition of treating sex crimes against adult women as an ultimate affront to society. Traditionalists, such as husbands relying on the government to enforce domestic patriarchy, lost some footing as the government liberated female rape victims from castigatory social stigmas associated with being raped.

Without the government's help enforcing tradition, distinctions between *malum prohibitum* and *malum in se* could be lost or excessively blurred. Harmful and harmless sex acts arbitrarily may be pried from or remain under the government's control regardless of the effects and destruction, for example on the human spirit and dignity. Harmless crimes, such as women and men being topless in the same designated public spaces, continue to be regulated; yet, cartoon depictions of *bukkake* (i.e. ejaculation by multiple males on one female) have been tolerated by society (e.g. Wikipedia) and protected by courts (Cusack, 2011; Cusack, 2014). Loss of all enforceable moralism not only would permit adults to begin to participate in immorality and disclose previously clandestine immorality, but would also eliminate systemic foundations for youths' beliefs in moral behavior, likely contributing to immoral and abusive behavior (Cusack 2014; Ginsberg v. New York, 1968).

Youth unobligated by law may not believe in morality or participate in moral restraint. A study of juveniles incarcerated for sexual abuse hypothesized that they would demonstrate lower levels of moral development than youth, who had not committed sex offenses (Beerthuizen & Brugman, 2010). Sexual abusers relied on preconventional reasoning to rationalize sexual behavior, but not necessarily non-sexual behavior. Although these youth violated morality-based laws, their reasoning disregarded convention. If moral conventions ceased (i.e. progressive notions of sexuality eradicated tradition) and all conventional attitudes towards sex were to become unenforceable, then youth may behave as sex offenders. Moral restraint may not develop without deterrence. Restraint is not always developed in relation to deterrence, but often in relation to perception of convention and proscriptions that deter deviance. Even without moral regulation, if convention could be maintained, sexual impropriety could be punished by society at large with shaming and disqualification from civic and professional positions. However, some critics of moral imposition would argue that no rational relationship between sexual behavior and legally actionable crimes or turpitude exists without morality laws (Walsh, Eckhardt, & Russell, 2006). Linking sexual behavior with disparaging or unethical conduct enforces tradition founded in common law, gender, and sexuality norms, but may serve no modern purposes (Greeley, 2004).

Immoral actors may breech tradition and thereby violate others of accepted and customary rights, which may not be enforceable by law, but without which society and individuals within it would experience depravity and be subjected to vileness. For example, previously it was a crime to make a false promise of marriage to induce sexual consent and conduct; however, it is now legal (Hayes, 2015). However, lying about intent to consummate a marriage to induce marriage may be grounds for annulment if the marriage is not consummated. Inducing consent to have sex by omitting facts or making false statements about being free from certain sexually transmitted diseases (STDs) may be noncriminal, but may be grounds for annulment (Conway v. Deane, 2007; Macy v. Dep't of Justice, 2012; Cusack, 2012; Cusack, 2013; Cusack, 2015). Misrepresentations about a non-serious STD (e.g. HPV) may be comparable with lying about sexual history, number of partners, and other traditionally foundational aspects of sexual conduct and consent. Courts may analyze whether lies and omissions are immaterial or material misrepresentations.

Inducees may alleged civil and criminal fraud. Courts may analyze whether fraud is in fact or in the inducement (Cusack, 2016). Lying about being cys-gender when an alleged defrauder is transgender, or omitting biological sex when that information is material to inducement of consent, may be a misrepresentation comparable with lying about sexuality, intent to consummate, or fertility, which may be grounds for annulment (Bilowit v. Dolitsky, 1973; Dodrill v. Dodrill, 2004; In re Marriage of Glatfelter, 2004; Lopez v. Lopez, 1968; Singhal, 2013).

Misrepresentation or omission of transgenderism (e.g. transsexualism) has not been heard by the U.S. Supreme Court. The number of criminal complaints may be low or unspecified. However, the right to choose an intimate partner of a specific sex, gender, and sexuality is guaranteed under the First, Fifth, and Fourteenth Amendments (Griswold v.

Connecticut, 1964; Obergefell v. Hodges, 2015). For example, people have a right exclusively to engage in sexual conduct with transsexuals. People have a right to choose, live-out, and express their own sexualities. Sexuality necessarily and directly, not incidentally or relatedly, may correlate with the biological sex of an intimate partner. People have the right to be free from forcible or unwanted same-sex or opposite-sex conduct resulting when a transgender person misrepresents his or her biological sex. Legal sex and gender may be immaterial in comparison to the significance of biological sex. Though transsexuals may allege that their presented sex (i.e. post-operative) and legal sex induce consent, inducees may rely on the presumption that their presented sex is their biological sex (Gudorf, 2009; In the Matter of the Estate, 2001). Inducees may argue that because a small fraction of Americans are transgender (less than .03%), infrequent incidences of secretive sex reassignment and gender presentation should not dramatically impinge on the majority's First, Fifth, and Fourteenth Amendment rights. To protect inducees from unwelcomed conduct, inducees should not be obligated to inquire about sex partners' biological sex. Rather, the law requires transgender individuals to disclose their biological sex to obtain informed consent (Cusack, 2013).

Misrepresentation of biological sex may be fraud in fact and fraud in the inducement. For example, if a woman consents to be penetrated by a male's penis, but she is penetrated by an object or a digit, then she may be the victim of fraud in fact (Cusack, 2015; Cusack, 2016). If she consents to be digitally penetrated by a man, believing that she is consenting to digital penetration by a biological male, then she may be a victim of fraud in the inducement. Some courts may consider either scenario to be fraud in fact or fraud in the inducement. Sex is more than an "external condition[];" and may be "subversive of the true essence of" union (Abrams, et al., 2015; Chudnow v. Chudnow, 2001, p. 1; Gloucester County School Board v. G. G., 2016; In re Marriage of Meagher, 2005; LeBlanc, 2016; Stepp v. Stepp, 2004, p. 1).

Social conundrums resulting when people lie about sex have been confronted by some legislation seeking to criminalize certain sexual misrepresentations and omissions (Cusack, 2013). For example, some laws criminalize nondisclosure of specific STDs (e.g. hepatitis and HIV); and a few jurisdictions prohibit a significant amount of misrepresentative speech (e.g. bigamy) (Cusack, 2013; Cusack, 2013). Anti-HIV laws have been attacked for allegedly targeting homosexual men (Conway v. Deane, 2007; Cusack, 2013). For some defrauded individuals, such as individuals induced to have sex by transgender people, few remedies may be invoked

(Cusack, 2014; Cusack & Waranius, 2012; Waranius, 2011). Victims may choose to remain silent because they have already been victimized and do not want to memorialize the event or be shamed and exploited by justice members eager to hear sexual details (Hayes, 2015). In this scenario, the government has failed to protect the victim, but has also succeeded according to some apologists discouraging the government from persecuting misrepresentative sexualities.

The law is supposed to protect secretive transgender persons from retaliatory attacks. Crimes of passion ought not to be tolerated (Cusack, 2015; Cusack, 2015). Legal remedies for inducees are progressing and will continue to be forged. Arguments for informed consent may mirror birth control activism because it peacefully established privacy rights (e.g. choice). Birth control is problematic when consent for procreative conduct is not expressly granted (e.g. nonconsensual insemination) (Cusack, 2014). This problem confronts fertile individuals, who unknowingly have sex with transgender people of the opposite biological sex.

Closeted and openly transgender persons often complain that police and prosecutors are unwilling to believe them, support them, and enforce the law (In the Matter of E.P.L., 2009; Pub L 111-84 § 4701 *et seq.*, 2009). Transgender individuals may be labeled as being deviants by members of the system. Justice members may associate transgender people with pejorative ideas about "raging" "homosexuality, fetishism, transvestism, pornography, prostitution, bondage and discipline, sado-masochism violence or other unlawful acts" (Gottschalk v. San Francisco, 2013, pp. 1155-1156; Koons, 2009, p. 287). Some transgender individuals may identify as being "heterosexual" (Gottschalk v. San Francisco, 2013, p. 1155). However, transgender people may fear that if they identify as "heterosexual," then they will not be entitled to heightened protection (Gottschalk v. San Francisco, 2013, p. 1155). Many transgender people disclose their transitions to intimate partners. They may object to lying and omissions. Lying and omissions by closeted transgender people may further stigmatize already vulnerable openly transgender individuals (Kothmann v. Rosario, 2013).

To moderate sex, the government is entrusted with enough power to allow some sexual conduct while punishing sexual abuse, harm, and misconduct (Coelho, 2006). Hobbes (2013) discussed how the government achieves this (Cusack, 2014).

> And he that [carries] this Person, as called [SOVEREIGN], and said to have [Sovereign] Power; and every one besides, his SUBJECT.
> The attaining to this [Sovereign] Power, is by two [ways]. One, by [Natural] force; as when a man [makes] his children, to submit themselves,

> and their children to his government, as being able to destroy them if they refuse, or by [War subdue] his enemies to his will, giving them their lives on that condition. The other, is when men agree amongst themselves, to submit to some Man, or Assembly of men, voluntarily, on confidence to be protected by him against all others. This later, may be called a [Political Commonwealth], or [Commonwealth] by Institution; and the former, a [Commonwealth] by Acquisition (Hobbes, 2013, p. 147).

The state becomes an agreement between all people, including citizens and representatives, to authorize action on behalf of the people that enforces peace and protection for all. Laws are based on the people's and representatives' experience. They extrapolate consequences, and warn their children about those consequences.

> [H]e foresees what [will] become of a Criminal, re-cons what he has seen follow on the like Crime before; having this order of thoughts, The Crime, the Officer, the Prison, the Judge, and the [Gallows]. Which kind of thoughts, is called Foresight, and Prudence, or Providence; and sometimes [Wisdom]; though such conjecture, through the difficulty of observing all circumstances, be very fallacious. But this is certain; by how much one man has more experience of things past, than another; by so much also he is more Prudent, and his expectations…[seldom fail] him. The Present [only] has a being in Nature; things Past have a being in the Memory [only], but things To Come have no being at all....And though it be called Prudence, when the Event [answers] our Expectation; yet in its own nature, it is but Presumption (Hobbes, 2013, pp. 41-42).

Fluidity in government, which responds to generations' needs may be the solution. However, conventions, norms, and notice of the law to youth, may be difficult to maintain unless the law is predicated on experience and is consistently passed down through generations.

Problematically, governance erodes agreements between children, parents, and representatives when enforcement selectively applies to some groups, but not others; or when progressive attitudes are hidden along with immoral conduct by representatives and governmental agents, who impose on the people traditions that they do not share. The government's power cannot be built on "false grounds" (Aero Spark Plug Co. v. B. G. Corporation, 1942; Halderman v. Pennhurst State School & Hospital, 1982, p. 661; Hobbes, 2013).

> That we must seek to construe a statute in a way that renders it constitutionally permissible is another way of saying that we must presume that the legislature has intended to do the right thing. Hobbes noted that 'all laws, written and unwritten, have need of interpretation,' but in the course

> of such interpretation 'the intention of the legislator is always supposed to be equity: for it were a great contumely for a judge to think otherwise of the sovereign'....This same presumption, of the constitutionality of legislative enactments, also reflects that legislatures properly have a voice in interpreting and applying constitutions (AA Mechanical v. Superior Court, 1997, p. 370).

Conscientiousness among legislators ensures that they will properly attend to constructing, authorizing enforcement of, and following the law.

The Constitution may forbid a law designed to reserve sexual promiscuity as a delicacy for those, who are above the law, and enforce morality on the people as a form of corporeal and mental control; and yet, many of the framers openly and quietly participated in liberal, extramarital, and homosexual conduct (Flynt & Eisenbach, 2011; Segrave, 1990). In his book, *One Nation Under Sex, Hustler* Magazine editor and free speech advocate, Larry Flynt, claimed that Benjamin Franklin, Alexander Hamilton, George Washington, James Madison, and other framers had premarital sex and extramarital affairs (Cusack, 2015; Flynt & Eisenbach, 2011).

> Today we tend to imagine the people who built the early Republic to have been dignified and composed as the historic documents they left behind. The founders were indeed noble and gracious, but they were also earthy, lusty and as interested in sex and sex scandal as we are today. Like America's leaders throughout history, the Founders had vigorous sex drives and vibrant sex lives that played a major role in building our nation (Flynt & Eisenbach, 2011, p. 5).

Perhaps they flouted convention because they opposed oppressive control (e.g. monarchies); were "jetting the stuff of far more arrogant republics;" or they only seemed to support traditional morality because that is what the people wanted (Alden v. Maine, 1999; In re Opinions of the Justices, 1936; Whitman, 1855, p. 916). Though it bound them legally to standards that they could not meet, they acted on behalf of the people. The federal Constitution forbids state governments from intruding into protected, private sexual conduct; however, lawmakers could attempt to pass laws entitling them to heightened protection from governmental intrusion, persecution, and regulation under special exemptions. For example, the government could pass a law entitling legislators to the benefits of legal marriage without the requirement of being licensed or divorced.

Lawmakers could attempt to inhibit promiscuity and progressive notions of family-life by passing zoning ordinances that prohibit non-traditional families and cohabitation (Greeley, 2004). A substantial amount of private immorality may be unregulated by the government, but reserved for members of the oligarchy, who operate within traditional gender roles and family structures. For example, Belle Terre is a village on Long Island that generally restricted residential land use to single-family homes (Village of Belle Terre v. Boraas, 1974). The ordinance defined the word "family" using a traditional definition, but also included cohabitation, which was a crime in some states and disfavored by society (Village of Belle Terre v. Boraas, 1974). "[O]ne or more persons related by blood, adoption, or marriage, living and cooking together as a single housekeeping unit, exclusive of household servants. A number of persons but not exceeding two (2) living and cooking together as a single housekeeping unit though not related by blood, adoption, or marriage shall be deemed to constitute a family" (Village of Belle Terre v. Boraas, 1974, p. 2).

Six students sued to share a home. The Court held that the state's use of police power was legitimate. "[T]he line 'which in this field separates the legitimate from the illegitimate assumption of power is not capable of precise delimitation. It varies with circumstances and conditions.'...'If the validity of the legislative classification for zoning purposes be fairly debatable, the legislative judgment must be allowed to control'" (Village of Belle Terre v. Boraas, 1974, p. 4).

The Court cited Louisville Gas Co. v. Coleman (1928).

> When a legal distinction is determined, as no one doubts that it may be, between night and day, childhood and maturity, or any other extremes, a point has to be fixed or a line has to be drawn, or gradually picked out by successive decisions, to mark where the change takes place. Looked at by itself without regard to the necessity behind it the line or point seems arbitrary. It might as well or nearly as well be a little more to one side or the other. But when it is seen that a line or point there must be, and that there is no mathematical or logical way of fixing it precisely, the decision of the legislature must be accepted unless we can say that it is very wide of any reasonable mark (Louisville Gas Co. v. Coleman, 1928, p. 41).

The Court found that a locality could draw a line using the state's police power.

> It is said, however, that if two unmarried people can constitute a 'family,' there is no reason why three or four may not. But every line drawn by a legislature leaves some out that might well have been included. That exercise of discretion, however, is a legislative, not a judicial, function. It is said that the Belle Terre ordinance reeks with an animosity to unmarried couples who live together. There is no evidence to support it; and the provision of the ordinance bringing within the definition of a 'family' two

> unmarried people belies the charge (Village of Belle Terre v. Boraas, 1974, p. 8).

The Court found that the state could prevent groups of non-family members from residing together.

The *Belle Terre* Court (1974) cited Berman v. Parker (1954).

> Miserable and disreputable housing conditions may do more than spread disease and crime and immorality. They may also suffocate the spirit by reducing the people who live there....They may indeed make living an almost insufferable burden. They may also be an ugly sore, a blight on the community which robs it of charm, which makes it a place from which men turn. The misery of housing may despoil a community as an open sewer may ruin a river. We do not sit to determine whether a particular housing project is or is not desirable. The concept of the public welfare is broad and inclusive....The values it represents are spiritual as well as physical, aesthetic as well as monetary. It is within the power of the legislature to determine that the community should be beautiful as well as healthy, spacious as well as clean, well-balanced as well as carefully patrolled (Berman v. Parker, 1954, pp. 32-33).

The plaintiffs argued "that the newcomers' rights of privacy" is violated by public inquiry into their living arrangements; "that it is of no rightful concern to villagers whether the residents are married or unmarried;" and the definition of family that intrudes into private life, "is antithetical to the Nation's experience, ideology, and self-perception as an open, egalitarian, and integrated society" (Village of Belle Terre v. Boraas, 1974, p. 7).

The Court found that "[t]he ordinance places no ban on other forms of association, for a 'family' may, so far as the ordinance is concerned, entertain whomever it likes" (Village of Belle Terre v. Boraas, 1974, p. 9).

> A quiet place where yards are wide, people few, and motor vehicles restricted are legitimate guidelines in a land-use project addressed to family needs. This goal is a permissible one within *Berman* v. *Parker, supra.* The police power is not confined to elimination of filth, stench, and unhealthy places. It is ample to lay out zones where family values, youth values, and the blessings of quiet seclusion and clean air make the area a sanctuary for people (Village of Belle Terre v. Boraas, 1974, p. 9).

The *Belle Terre* Court's decision was consistent with other U.S. Supreme Court decisions that enforced the importance of traditional family-life and asserted the government's interest in controlling private affairs using the state's power to police morality (Village of Belle Terre v. Boraas, 1974).

The U.S. Supreme Court held in Moore v. City of East Cleveland (1977) that the government could not criminalize cohabitation of extended families in single-family occupancies. "[T]he traditional relation of the family" is "a relation as old and as fundamental as our entire civilization" (Griswold v. Connecticut, 1964, p. 496).

> [W]e have not an intrusion into the home so much as on the life which characteristically has its place in the home....The home derives its pre-eminence as the seat of family life[; a]nd the integrity of that life is something so fundamental that it has been found to draw to its protection the principles of more than one explicitly granted Constitutional right (Poe v. Ullman, 1961, pp. 551-552).

The Court held that the government must protect (i.e. control) "the family precisely because the institution of the family is deeply rooted in this Nation's history and tradition. It is through the family that we inculcate and pass down many of our most cherished values, moral and cultural" (Moore v. City of East Cleveland, 1977, p. 504).

> Ours is by no means a tradition limited to respect for the bonds uniting the members of the nuclear family. The tradition of uncles, aunts, cousins, and especially grandparents sharing a household along with parents and children has roots equally venerable and equally deserving of constitutional recognition. Over the years millions of our citizens have grown up in just such an environment, and most, surely, have profited from it. Even if conditions of modern society have brought about a decline in extended family households, they have not erased the accumulated wisdom of civilization, gained over the centuries and honored throughout our history, that supports a larger conception of the family. Out of choice, necessity, or a sense of family responsibility, it has been common for close relatives to draw together and participate in the duties and the satisfactions of a common home. Decisions concerning child rearing, which *Yoder, Meyer, Pierce* and other cases have recognized as entitled to constitutional protection, long have been shared with grandparents or other relatives who occupy the same household—indeed who may take on major responsibility for the rearing of the children. Especially in times of adversity, such as the death of a spouse or economic need, the broader family has tended to come together for mutual sustenance and to maintain or rebuild a secure home life (Moore v. City of East Cleveland, 1977, pp. 504-505).

The Court added that within the right to family-life protected under substantive due process, there was a "choice of relatives" in various "degree[s] of kinship," and "to live together may not lightly be denied by the State" (Moore v. City of East Cleveland, 1977, pp. 505-506). The

Court did not overturn its holding in *Belle Terre* that "social homogeneity is…a legitimate interest of the government" (Village of Belle Terre v. Boraas, 1974, p. 7). The government's enforcement of family-life used the sovereign's police power to enforce "homogeneity" in both cases (Village of Belle Terre v. Boraas, 1974, p. 7).

Local governments may use the state's police power. In Hunter v. Pittsburgh (1907), the Court used Dillon's Rule, which describes the state as an absolute sovereign, to limit power granted to any form of local government to only those expressly granted or implied by the state, or less frequently, those that are essential to the locality (Greenberg, 2010). There is a presumption that state authority and governance is reasonable and granted to municipalities to effectuate certain tasks; however, if there is any reasonable doubt that a state has granted power to a corporation (e.g. Village of Belle Terre), then the doubt itself signifies that it has yet to be granted. The Court held in *Hunter* that no charter for any incorporation or municipality is rightful in any capacity, but for the power vested in it by the state (Hunter v. Pittsburgh, 1907). The U.S. Supreme Court relied on well-settled principles that thc policy, wisdom, justness, or fairness of any local act is subject only and exclusively to the state. Only meritorious federal questions will rise beyond the power of the state. *Hunter* made it clear that regardless of whether a state constitution permits or denies special legislation, the power to enforce any enactment will come only from the power of the state (Hunter v. Pittsburgh, 1907). Therefore, the strength of state sovereignty may deflate the illusion of independent corporate or local power.

Though proponents of local governance have created a debate between local autonomy and uniform laws, there is no getting around the Tenth Amendment without a particularly strong Home Rule that can be proven to overcome the presumption that the state always acts reasonably. It is clear that at the county, municipal, town, or school level, all rules and ordinances are subject to the state's power. Not only are rules and ordinances subject to the state's reasonable whims, they are nascent because of the state's interest in providing for constituents at a local level (City of New York v. State, 1990). There cannot be a doubt that localized forms of governments (e.g. school boards) are not independent forms of government because their existence and standing against the state in any court is contingent on the state's permission.

Localized forms of government have attempted to use race-, sex- and gender-conscious policies to control socialization and thereby impact sex, marriage, and reproduction (Cusack, 2015). For example, race-, sex-, and gender-conscious school policies are permitted to exist at the local level because of their provision at the state level (City of New York v. State, 1995; Regents v. Bakke, 1978). While some states may follow Dillon's rule, and some states may permit special legislation, all legislation regarding schools is permitted at the state level unless a federal issue is concerned. As *Hunter* explains, a benefit of non-federalist, state-guided legislation is that regions of the country follow different policies (Hunter v. Pittsburgh, 1907). Some policies cover an area as large as a state and some policies affect districts; however, in no case does the federal government's position on race-, sex-, and gender-conscious legislation subsume the entire United States unless there is a federal issue. Unfortunately, much of the state legislation in this arena has followed *Hunter's* suit, where minority progress has been forbidden because of the fear that it would come at the expense of the majority (Coalition for Economic Equity v. Wilson, 1997; Hunter v. Pittsburgh, 1907).

Enforcement of patriarchal values used to maintain oligarchical control and the moral majority has also resulted in minority discrimination in housing (Hunter v. Pittsburgh, 1907). Sexual minorities and single mothers lawfully have been discriminated against because they are impoverished; however, they are poorer because they are marginalized by society, abused, dominated, scorned, and excluded (Cusack, 2015). Although economically impoverished people are not a suspect class, often times, economically impoverished minorities have immutable ethnic, sexual, and gender traits (Counting Crows, 1999; Gerth & Mills, 1946). Under the protection of state sovereignty, zoning laws have eliminated the furtherance of integration because of economic reasoning.

When courts analyze whether racism and sexism were motivating factors in the prevention of housing for economically disadvantaged people, they may overlook strong data showing that regionally, economically disadvantaged people are highly likely to be minorities (Village of Arlington Heights v. Metropolitan Housing Development, 1977). Instead, courts will use *Hunter* to look at the ordinance or municipal decision on its face (Hunter v. Pittsburgh, 1907). Perhaps courts may consider discussions leading to the decision (e.g. meeting minutes) or consider groups in similar situations to determine if a minority was truly being discriminated (City of Cleburne v. Cleburne Living Center, 1985). Courts can completely neglect considerations of race, sex, gender, marital status, and other factors, so long as a municipality has overtly complied with state and federal discrimination policies and has not overtly discriminated against a protected class, which may not include, for example, homosexuals (Craig v. Boren, 1976; Romer v. Evans, 1996; Village of Belle Terre v. Boraas, 1974). At the state court level, locals' bigoted and biased attitudes need not be considered. The construction placed on a statute by the state court of last resort is binding on the federal courts (Hunter v. Pittsburgh, 1907). Underlying racism, homophobia, sexism, and marital bias that motivate economically lopsided ordinances at the local level need not be vetted under state authority that calls for nothing more than reasonable explanations for economically discriminatory policies.

By diminishing any real or independent power of local governments, *Hunter* also set the stage for states to be able to use local governments as unofficial enforcers of political agendas (Hunter v. Pittsburgh, 1907). Furthermore, by allowing the will of the people to pass local legislation, the state need not soil itself with controversial legislation. In many instances, where the state wishes to deny special protection (e.g. women), they need only remain silent on the issue. When the issue is raised in localities, which are public corporations, the state's lack of position effectively enforces anti-minority legislation (Equality Foundation v. City of Cincinnati, 1997). When local governments contradict the state's political agenda, the state has three extreme recourses: 1) authorize the local government to transgress against state policy through litigation, which is unlikely; 2) abolish the transgressing public corporation's authority; and 3) invoke Dillon's Rule (City of New York v. State, 1990; New Orleans Campaign for a Living Wage v. City of New Orleans, 2002).

The *Hunter* Court discussed state power (Hunter v. Pittsburgh, 1907).

> Municipal corporations are political subdivisions of the state, created as convenient agencies for exercising such of the governmental powers of the state as may be entrusted to them….The number, nature, and duration of the powers conferred upon these corporations and the territory over which they shall be exercised rests in the absolute discretion of the state. Neither their charters, nor any laws conferring governmental powers, or vesting in them property to be used for governmental purposes, or authorizing them to hold or manage such property…constitutes a contract with the state within the meaning of the Federal Constitution. The state, therefore, at its pleasure, may modify or withdraw all such powers, may take without compensation such property, hold itself, or vest it in other agencies, expand or contract the territorial area, unite the whole or a part of it with another municipality, repeal the charter and destroy the corporation. All this may be done, conditionally or unconditionally, with or without the consent of the citizen, or even against their protest. In all these respects the state is supreme, and its legislative body, conforming its action to the state Constitution, may do as it will, unrestrained by any provision of the Constitution of the United States (Hunter v. Pittsburgh, 1907, pp. 178-179).

In most situations, the political agenda of the state will only be strengthened by the municipality's power; and in very few circumstances actually threatened (Cusack, 2017).

Cities and other municipalities sometimes enjoy broad discretion under the reasonableness standard because of the state charter. Even the minority opinions on Hutchison v. State (1980) allow cities to contract for exactions because of the state power, not independently of it; and state compacts provide for broad discretion by agencies that are empowered by the states (Cusack, 2017). But for *Hunter's* explicit references to the federal government's impotence regarding state issues that do not present federal questions, the federal government could argue against state sovereignty as well as local governance that affects multi-state regions and natural resources management, which has been associated with gender and race implications (Cusack, 2015; Hunter v. Pittsburgh, 1907). There is no reason to believe that *Hunter* impeded local governance, but instead, it promulgated the very force that permits and drives local governance, which is state power (Hunter v. Pittsburgh, 1907).

In some cases, corporate power is so strong that it need not have the power to govern at a public level. Private corporations like Pfizer, using the power of cities, which use the state's power, can now take private land and claim a public use. In Kelo v. City of New London (2005), the people saw an unprecedented decision that allowed a city to exercise eminent domain in taking private land and effectively grant it to a private corporation as long as there was a reasonable explanation that showed a public use. In *Kelo*, this extreme power did not raise the levels of scrutiny as long as a public purpose was alleged (Kelo v. City of New London, 2005).

Kelo is a far cry from *Hunter* (Hunter v. Pittsburgh, 1907; Kelo v. City of New London, 2005). *Hunter* attempted to distinguish between private property and property owned by the state. Where *Kelo* permitted taking private property for a public use, *Hunter* specifically said that the government was not omnipotent to do so (Hunter v. Pittsburgh, 1907; Kelo v. City of New London, 2005). Social temperament during *Hunter* warned of the corruption that could come from a powerful locality (Hunter v. Pittsburgh, 1907). It was this fear that perhaps motivated the *Hunter* Court to restrict local power (Hunter v. Pittsburgh, 1907). Eminent domain raises a federal question that was answered by the U.S. Supreme Court in favor of a powerful, private corporation whose interests extended the power that any city had previously exercised (Kelo v. City of New London, 2005).

In light of recent jurisprudence, *Hunter* is not as important today (Hunter v. Pittsburgh, 1907). Contemporary questions of law are no longer about blurred lines between local and state power. The people know that all local power is derived from state power. The serious question that the people are facing with regard to state power are the federal issues arising at a local level, which affect state sovereignty, and the alarming indistinction between private and public property.

Constituents, whose behavior is restricted by local or state laws, may sue to strike the law as being unfairly enforced against them (Alden v. Maine, 1999). However, because people generally are not grouped by the court with specific protected classes (e.g. legal aliens), then their assertions may fail. Sovereign immunity is an example of how lawmakers may make rules exempting their sexual deviance from certain kinds of legal consequences. Sovereign immunity is the principle that the state, and municipalities are chartered by the state, cannot be sued without consent (i.e. waiving immunity) (Frug, Ford, & Barron, 2006).

Under some circumstances, state agencies and municipalities may be sued for damages arising from employee misconduct during the scope of their official duties. Members of the justice system acting in the scope of their employment may be granted qualified immunity so that they may not be held personally liable for tortious or criminal conduct. An essential caveat is that members will not be immunized if their conduct violated a clearly established right. However, courts are quick to interpret conduct and laws to find that victims' rights were not clearly established (Orovitz, 2012).

Morality laws may not be applicable to members of the justice system under typical circumstances. The public effectively may be on notice that this kind of enforcement is practiced because of the frequency of members behaving immorally without legal consequences. Unless an Amendment to a state constitution is passed requiring politicians and law enforcement officers to be held to the same moral standards as the people, then they cannot be compelled by the public to make laws that require them to be morally constrained similarly to non-members of the public. The judiciary could interpret existing laws unfairly to infringe on protected rights, but due to the separation of powers, the judiciary cannot make laws that morally constrain or regulate members of the government. As long as a law passes strict scrutiny, then it would survive a due process challenge claiming that morality-based laws are unnecessary as demonstrated by their inapplicability to governmental employees. The state could claim sovereign immunity and exempt itself and all government actors from all immoral acts performed during the course of government business, including, for example, prison guards raping inmates.

Though cultural melting pots, like metropolitan areas in United States, may experience differing definitions of "morality," a consensus represented and guided by law must dictate the scope of moral actions among the people, including members of the justice system. However, oppressive or excessively restrictive laws that do not protect the people or are arbitrarily enforced may not be justified. Members of the justice system must follow the law and may be required to make truthful representations about their private lives to the public. When they are identified by the press as being immoral, scandals may erupt, even when sexual immoralities are legal. This pattern may be longstanding, but is corrosive to tradition and maintenance of sociosexual wellbeing—the basis, perhaps, for implementing morality-based laws.

CHAPTER THREE

BEHAVIOR, PUBLIC PERCEPTION, LEADERSHIP, AND SCANDAL IN AMERICA

Organizational behavior studies, social science research, and other authorities demonstrate the effects of institutional immorality, such as mistrust and lawbreaking (Conroy, et al., 2017; Cropanzano, Folger, & Goldman, 2003; De Vries & Sobis, 2016; French, 2005; Helena Stein & Cropanzano, 2011; Shalvi, et al., 2011; van Der Lee, Ellemers, & Scheepers, 2016; Wiltermuth, et al., 2013; Zak, 2011). People must trust the justice system in order for society to function; for example, people must trust child protective services and police to help vulnerable victims. A cost-benefit analysis demonstrates that society's ability to protect people from immorality (e.g. molesters) justifies restrictions on liberty for members of the public and government. When members of the government commit sexual misconduct, it reduces people's desire to buy into the system (Lerner-Wren, 2012).

Thomas Hobbes, an influence on U.S. framers, identified how unvirtuous passion, particularly among leaders, causes instability (Hobbes, 2013).

> As for the Passions, of Hate, Lust, Ambition, and [Covetousness], what Crimes they are apt to produce, is so obvious to every [man's] experience and understanding, as there [needs] nothing to be said of them, saving that they are infirmities, so annexed to the nature, both of man, and all other living creatures, as that their effects cannot be [hindered], but by extraordinary use of Reason, or a constant severity in punishing them. For in those things men hate, they find a [continual], and [unavoidable] molestation; whereby either a [man's] patience must be everlasting, or he must be eased by removing the power of that which [molests] him; The former is difficult; the [latter] is many times impossible, without some violation of the Law. Ambition, and [Covetousness] are Passions also that are perpetually incumbent, and pressing; whereas Reason is not perpetually present, to resist them: and therefore [whenever] the hope of impunity appears, their effects proceed. And for Lust, what it wants in the lasting, it hath in the vehemence, which [suffices] to weigh down the apprehension of all [ease], or uncertain punishments (Hobbes, 2013, p. 240).

The public may remove or demand resignation from leaders, who are exposed as being deviants (Greenberg, 2010). When the public merely suspects or believes that leaders participate in immoral conduct, they may tolerate it because it permits them to rationalize, and possibly justify, their own immoral conduct (Shalvi, et al., 2011). The result is immoral leaders leading the people to break laws and participate in immoral behavior. People may already feel violated by members of government whose behavior or demeanor indicates secrets. A sense of being subjected to the government's power, when it is ignored and utilized by deviant rulers, threatens the people's will to obey laws and weakens positive effects of social order (Singer, 2007).

Social order has evolved in recent decades in an attempt to allot to females the same rights and power given to men. Gender differences tolerated, anticipated, and promoted by tradition and culture may create gender-neutral and gender-specific violations and double standards. For example, some males may feel that they can be sexually deviant as long as civic engagement is not impaired. Women may feel that they can be sexually deviant as long as they are helping to solve social problems. These differences may onset early and begin to manifest in society before members of the justice system assume power and fail their constituents (Malin, Tirri, & Liauw, 2015).

Moral motivation for civic performance among adolescents may explain subsequent differences between men and women in their political participation. A study of 1,578 high school seniors confirmed general beliefs that females are more civic-minded and altruistic (Malin, Tirri, & Liauw, 2015). Morally, they were politically motivated to help others and society. Boys, however, were value-oriented indicating that their desire to behave morally would be subject to cost-benefit analysis. In government workplaces, such as states attorney's offices, police forces, the judiciary, and child protective services, gender is stratified by profession for example; most judges are male, while most social workers are female (Cusack, 2014). Males are likelier to work in high power positions where they create, interpret, and enforce laws. They mainly may be responsible for certain kinds of misconduct (e.g. penetrative rape) and foreseeably prone to commit sexual misconduct (Cusack, 2013). Society may be likelier to shame and castigate females, who violate gender roles and sociosexual norms (Lips, 2006). Because men represent the majority of justice members, the question may become: Do policies establish organizational norms or does disregard for policies establish organizational norms (Martinez, et al., 2013)? The answer may depend on whether groups of men and organizations believe that moral policies are beneficial to them. Furthermore, do cultural (e.g. ethnic or organizational) interpretations of laws establish or legitimize norms or institute policies? Gendered and cultural interpretations of "immorality" and "conduct" (e.g. verbal harassment) are relevant to society's responses to context-specific behavior.

Studies show that perceptions of sexual immoral conduct are relative. For example, 107 young adults ranked from worst to best the severity of 30 stigmatizing labels (Lietz, 1981):

> Murderer, Rapist, Armed Robber, Pimp, Drug Pusher, Pick Pocket, Prostitute, Bigamist, Homosexual Female, Confidence Man, Stripper, Homosexual Male, Emotionally Disturbed, Retarded, Atheist, Epileptic, Unlicensed Driver, Fat Person [over 300 pounds], Learning Disabled, High School Dropout, Welfare Recipient, Cancer Patient, Physically Handicapped, Spanish Person, Black Person, Middle-Aged [40 to 65 years old], Protestant, Catholic, and White Person (Lietz, 1981).

Thus, it was better to be labeled a stripper than a homosexual female, but not a homosexual male; and being labeled a homosexual was better than being labeled a bigamist (Lietz, 1981).

Varying sentences and fines for crimes demonstrate that sexually immoral conduct may be harshly or mildly punished depending on numerous objective and subjective factors; for example, degree of harm imposed on victims (Aiken, 1962). Moral standards and correlating "spiritual" or social principles are not necessarily definitive or explanatory of variations in punishments throughout local, state, and federal statutes (Durkheim, 2008, p. 259). The study of stigmatizing labels found that sex, ethnicity, and educational setting contributed to differences suggesting that culture and indoctrination may correlate with individuals' perceptions of harm, immorality, and necessity of punishment (Lietz, 1981).

One apparent trend in gendered cultural institutionalization of morality has manifested in the United States since at least the 19th century. Men, who are prosecuted for sexually immoral acts, may revel in telling details more than women.

> [Male] defendants implicated in sexual trials [may possess]...a distinct advantage, as they...[may] draw on male traditions of erotic storytelling to win over the men acting as judge and jury. Disclosing one's sexual conquests before these legal officials, however,...[may involve] more than mere commentary on the promiscuity of female partners. First and foremost, erotic storytelling...[affirms] a manhood that...[associates] male sexual experience and bravado with virility. As we have seen, this identification did not necessarily translate into a successful legal strategy.

> However, in authorizing defendants and male witnesses to deploy this socialization tradition, the courts…[may help to] popularize already circulating ideas about aggressive sexual expression as an integral aspect of manhood, inseparable from the masculine identity. In other words, the legal system perhaps…[unconsciously normalizes] the very types of sexual…[deviance] they were supposed to police. In many ways, this counterintuitive outcome of legal sexual regulation is perhaps the least surprising of its many unintentional effects (Hayes, 2015, p. 194).

This cultural characteristic subtly may be one reason that municipalities and states will take responsibility for misconduct committed in the scope of employment (e.g. qualified immunity) by justice members, who are predominantly male. Qualified immunity allows the government to accept some responsibility and demonstrate their power over individuals' sexual actions. Yet, it is a self-validating mechanism for demoralizing the people while establishing sexual oligarchies.

The public may associate government power with exploitive masculinity because a disproportional number of males work in the justice system; and therefore, more male than female members commit sexual deviance. For example, more male police officers commit sexual misconduct than female officers. Outwardly, society may believe that the government's power to police morality is legitimate; and therefore, they obey police and the law.

> We are all taught from an early age that we must obey police orders. Police enforce the laws of our state and are in a position of authority. They protect us, sometimes by placing themselves in danger to ensure the safety of the general public. On occasion, however, some individual officers abuse their authority by committing intentional acts of violence under the color of their authority. Some officers have been physically abusive, some have raped, and some have even killed. Who is responsible for the good cop who has gone bad? The individual officer of course will be tried for his crime, but is the municipality who hired him also responsible (Neumann-Ribner, 1993, p. 457)?

Hobbes (2013) discussed how qualified immunity reflects on the government and society as a whole. He distinguished between private sexual deviance and misconduct committed under color of law. This distinction has become more relevant in recent years as salacious media coverage excitedly broadcasts intimate details about the private lives of justice members (e.g. extramarital affairs).

> In a Body [Politic], if the Representative be one man, whatsoever he does in the Person of the Body, which is not warranted in his Letters, nor by the Lawes, is his own act, and not the act of the Body, nor of any other Member thereof besides [himself]: Because further than his Letters, or the Lawes limit, he [represents] no [man's] person, but his own. But what he does according to these, is the act of every one: For of the Act of the [Sovereign] [everyone] is Author, because he is their Representative unlimited; and the act of him that recedes not from the Letters of the [Sovereign], is the act of the [Sovereign], and therefore every member of the Body is Author of it (Hobbes, 2013, pp. 186-187).

The government's power to excuse itself from responsibility (i.e. sovereign immunity) and excuse justice members (i.e. qualified immunity) may be perceived as being unfair. People's power is traded to the Leviathan, but the Leviathan's power is not traded back when individual officials err. Therefore, immunity may seem like a waste. Yet, to assume any kind of responsibility for individual authority figures' breach of the law demoralizes the people. Assumption of responsibility may insinuate that authority figures not only lack the ability to follow the laws that they are entrusted to make and enforce, but also that the Leviathan lacks the capacity to protect people from the harms for which it exists. The Leviathan facilitates sexual immorality and harm.

Rape by police officers is foreseeable, which may make responsible parties liable; however, it may also have the effect of desensitizing the public to immorality underlying rape by legitimizing it with state approbation when the state settles lawsuits with victims (Applewhite v. City of Baton Rouge, 1979; Baumeister v. Plunkett, 1996; Benoit v. Capitol, 1993; Miller v. Keating, 1977; Orgeron v. McDonald, 1994; Turner v. State, 1986). For example, a member of the Los Angeles Police Department raped a woman in 1981 while he was on duty. The victim was a drunk driver, who was forcibly raped by the officer in her home after he decided that he would not arrest her. He was sentenced to eighteen months incarceration, and the civil Superior Court entered a judgment of $150,000 against the municipality, which was a *respondeat superior* for the officer.

Policy rationales for finding against the municipality include deterrence and adequate victim compensation. However, to assume that these policy rationales will be effective is also to assume that the government allowed or facilitated the rape, *ergo*, failed as a Leviathan to safeguard the people from harm and acted complicity in rape. Rape by an officer is no longer viewable as a lone and rogue violation of the government's trust and authority. It becomes recognized as a systemic problem, foreseeable, and yet, ignored by a powerless government. This perception of the government by courts and the people provides a shaky foundation from which to utilize police power to control people's private and public sexual conduct. It results in a potential for all people, irrespective of moral leanings, to believe that police power is a misuse of governmental authority because police foreseeably participate in sexual misconduct that makes them the kind of people the government wants to punish.

> Obviously, a rape is not within the duties of a police officer. Police officers do possess considerable power and authority such as detaining people at gunpoint, placing them in handcuffs, removing them from their homes, ordering them into police cars, frisking them (which entails nonconsensual touching), and even using deadly force. Therefore, 'it is neither startling nor unexpected that on occasion an officer will misuse that authority by engaging in assaultive conduct.' The actual abusive conduct does not need to be anticipated, as long as it is reasonably foreseeable. The risk of sexual abuse is broadly incidental to the law enforcement profession (Neumann-Ribner, 1993, pp. 460-461).

Sexual misconduct by justice members is so foreseeable to the legislature that some legislation specifically waives sovereign immunity and authorizes the people to sue the state when members, such as police officers, sexually assault citizens during the course of duty (California Government Code § 815 *et seq.,* 2016). The admission of rampant and uncontrollable sexual immorality is further acknowledged by generous civil rights-oriented legislation, such as in California Torts Claims Act, which not only holds officers responsible for sexual assault, it holds all governmental agents responsible for non-physical, social, and emotional forms of sexual misconduct, including harassment. One reason is because the authority, in and of itself, contributes to the perpetrator's ability to complete the misconduct. The Leviathan becomes a conspirator.

Positions within the justice system, for example law enforcement, may attract individuals with low self-esteem and unresolved traumas from childhood, who lack socialization, seek validation, and are prone to behavior issues.

> Law enforcement naturally attracts people who desire positions of control and authority. The people who may be suffering from poor self esteem and feelings of inadequacy are only masking those feelings when given the badge, gun and uniform. When stress occurs or the officer has a fight with his spouse or his boss is demanding too much of him, it is only natural that he needs to release his tension. Not every officer will turn to rape as a release, but for some, the authority he has will help him rape. The power

> thrust is a motivator for sexual offenses. It makes him feel strong, adequate and in control. Thus, it is foreseeable that some officers will take advantage of their authority (Neumann-Ribner, 1993, p. 467).

This is why courts hold that rape by an on-duty police officer is within the scope of his or her employment, which makes the government responsible.

In Osborne v. Lyles, the Ohio Supreme Court said that employers are liable for an employee's tortious conduct when, "the behavior giving rise to the tort must be 'calculated to facilitate or promote the business for which the servant was employed'" (Osborne v. Lyles, 1992, p. 829).

> Police officers occupy a unique position in our society. They are responsible for enforcing the law and protecting society from criminal acts. They are given the authority to detain and to arrest and, when necessary, to use deadly force. As visible symbols of that formidable power, an officer is furnished a distinctively marked car, a uniform, a badge, and a gun. Those who challenge an officer's proper authority or who obstruct the performance of an officer's duties is subject to criminal prosecution. When law enforcement officers abuse their authority by committing crimes against members of the community, they violate the public trust. This may seriously damage the relationship between the community and its sworn protectors, by eroding the community's confidence in the integrity of its police force (Neumann-Ribner, 1993, p. 473).

Even without outward manifestations of power and capacity to enforce one's will, employment by the government suggests authority.

Legislators, courts, and the people rely on the doctrine of *respondeat superior* to claim and award tort damages. However, by this same reasoning, the government, which may demand too much sexual puritanism and cause excessive sexual repression among citizens, while paying for officers' misconduct, may create a boiling point resulting in sexual crimes committed by people. Since this kind of result is foreseeable, and the government cannot pay for every person's crimes, then perhaps the government should eliminate one cause of sexual stress, which is use of police power to enforce morality.

> [Arguably, when] a municipality is held liable for the tortious acts of its officers committed within the scope of employment, that government is acknowledging to the public that it is working with and for the people. It is taking responsibility for breaking the public's trust. The community will more likely gain back its confidence for police integrity if the government assumes responsibility and admits the wrong done. The imposition of liability places the city in a position to be more cautious in its hiring

> practices, training, supervision and policies to prevent future abuse of authority (Neumann-Ribner, 1993, p. 473).

However, it may be more truthful, cost effective, and progressive-minded to acknowledge disintegration within the moral fabric of the government and formulate institutional attitudes, culture, internal policies, and laws that appropriately govern authority figures and equally govern the people, rather than foreseeing liability, excusing conduct, or assuming responsibility for sexual misconduct (Monell v. New York City Dept. of Social Services, 1978). Authority figures are infrequently brought to justice. This corrodes people's faith in government. When the state pays for tortious and criminal sexual conduct, it may have the effect of legitimizing immorality because taxpayers pay for the state's assumption of responsibility; and taxpayers may feel entitled to behave immorally because they pay for that behavior.

A serious cause and effect of sexual misconduct in government workplaces is antisocial behavior, which infects society. Studies show that although culture associates flirtation, socializing, and sexual behavior, antisocial workplaces are likelier to have greater reports of unwanted sexual behavior (Timmerman & Bajema, 2000). One reason may be that unwanted sexual behavior relates to anti-social attitudes. Another reason may be that social environments perceive flirtation as being normal. A third reason may be that friends do not report co-workers' inappropriate conduct. These scenarios contribute to current regulation and imposition of traditional attitudes by force of law, which may be discordant with actual practices correlating with leadership in governmental workplaces. Three variables may contribute to unwanted sexual behavior: 1) negative organizational social climate; 2) perception of unequal treatment of women; and 3) negative attitudes toward work-family-life balance (Timmerman & Bajema, 2000). When the government attempts excessively to impose morality, while failing to control foreseeable immoral sexual conduct in its ranks, society and private workplaces emulate immoral conduct. This may further exacerbate unwanted sexual behavior; and therefore, require increased governance or changes in law. Respect for traditional families and monogamy is eroded; male sexual prowess and female acquiescence is pronounced; and the social climate becomes oppressive.

Society may not yet know how progressively to respond to immoral sexual conduct that is legal, albeit deviant. Government policies, practices, and culture ignoring or condoning consensual sex in the workplace may lead to abuse of discretion or miscommunication; or act as a valve for rape complaints. People may be misled by television, film, romance literature, and other media and entertainment suggesting that sexual contact in the workplace, particularly in government workplaces is a norm, validator, or indication of fulfilment.

Polices for firing or transferring employees whose conduct may have been immoral and inappropriate, but was consensual, may disparately affect women (Anderson & Hunsaker 1985; Ferber & Loeb, 1997; Folgero & Fjeldstad, 1995; Hochschild, 1996; Lobel, et al., 1994; Loe, 1996). This further emphasizes the government's role as the controller of sex and enforcer of traditional gender roles while diminishing its role as a protector of people. Generally, women, especially in government, work in lower-level positions and they are likelier than high-power individuals to be transferred or terminated. Courts have held that this response is legal even if it has a discriminatory effect, which seems to violate equal protection. Government agencies may frame their decisions to appear to include independent causal factors. Private organizations emulating governmental policies that pass muster are not held to the same constitutional standards when their polices do not infringe on civil rights. Some organizations' culture, such as in the military, facilitates and encourages socialization, sexual relationships, and formations of families, including alternative-lifestyle families (Spight, 2005).

Government institutions may be so skewed toward maintaining unspoken rules of patriarchy and sexual privilege that transfer or dismissal, rather than arrest, may result when nonconsensual sex has been alleged. One exception to the traditional male-dominated paradigm occurs in prisons when male inmates have voluntary, but nonconsesual, sex with female guards (Cusack, 2014; Cusack, 2015). However, female guards are routinely subjected to sexual harassment by inmates, which may result in their unlawful dismissal for complaining. The paradigm is maintained through culture and policies (Cusack, 2014).

> Fully understanding how behaviors such as these come to be labeled consensual or coercive raises fundamental questions that call out for systematic study by sociologists: How pervasive is consensual sexual activity in the workplace? How do workers distinguish between wanted and unwanted sexual advances? What are the consequences of consensual sexual behavior for men's and women's careers? How do organizations distinguish between wanted and unwanted sexual activity? And why do some organizations accommodate consensual sexual relationships, and others resist or prohibit them (Williams, Giuffre, & Dellinger, 1999)?

Many justice system employees are not stigmatized by sex scandals, but are immediately rehired elsewhere. Within their organizations, they may be stigmatized by low libido or prowess; indifference toward sexual culture; perceived lack of control or power; poor commitment to participating in organizational culture; perceived antisociality; and apparent weakness in a chain of command. Lack of public shaming may attract and promote sexual deviants, who may be tasked with publicly shaming members of the public for sexual immorality. Secretly, these employees may consider themselves to be liberated from tradition, norms, and oppression, which they are paid to effectuate. They may believe that the public is unable outwardly to detect their betrayal. Nevertheless, the public's sense of moral obligation to society wanes in response to authority figures' hollow gestures, unfair sexual liberation, and sneaky and anarchistic tactics to tear down morality in society by lacking integrity and personal responsibility (Cass, Levett, & Kovera, 2010). Furthermore, particularly egregious cases, such as police using evidence in sexual abuse cases as erotic material, may be instructive or suggestive to the public as to where society's moral compass actually points, and suggest to criminals which arguments, attorneys, and expert witnesses to use or not to use to be found not guilty when prosecuted.

CHAPTER FOUR

PRISON EMPLOYEES

Penitentiaries illustrate cyclical moral decay. Members of the justice system and people under their control reciprocally devolve from traditional roles into sexual anarchy (Worley, Marquart, & Mullings, 2003). Ultimately, members of the system are responsible for their sexual misdeeds and for permitting wards and their associates in the free world to misbehave. Systemic problems implicating gender, consent, public conduct, and private sexual behavior are evident in prison. The prison environment is so infamously overlooked by overseers, government agencies, and moral crusaders that it may be a flagship for individuals and groups actively attempting to dismantle tradition and corresponding authority to enforce and impose moral behavior.

Immorality occurs at every level in prison (18 U.S.C. §§ 2241-2245, 2016). One study found that sexual abuse and misconduct were distributed among corrections staff: nine percent in food service; six percent in recreation; five percent in education and training; five percent in correctional services; five percent in case management; five percent in inmate services; four percent in religion; four percent in health; four percent in psychological services; four percent in federal prison industries; three percent in mechanical services; two percent in business; two percent in records; one percent in computer services; and one percent in the warden's office (DOJ, 2009). Prison guards may be the most reprehensible and blameworthy because they are directly entrusted to protect, discipline, and control inmates. Their authority is unparalleled, and therefore incomparable with other members of the justice system. However, their position, like other penitentiary employees, represents a clear dichotomy between those, who are in control of sex and power and those, who are not.

Patriarchy may create cycles of abuse that lead to systemic decay and cover-ups of serious and injurious abuse, which simultaneously masculinizes and degrades inmates while it reinforces the importance of power and control in anarchical scenarios (Cusack, 2013; Vronsky, 2007; Walker, 2016). "Institutionalized patriarchy demands that women conform to their subservient gender roles and be subjected to controlling behavior by those officers with power" (Blackburn, et al., 2011, p. 357). Female staff may also be victims of patriarchy within penitentiaries.

Patriarchy has been described as a key tactic for promoting unbeneficial traditions and sexual inequality.

> Patriarchy, as a cultural force, determines gender role socialization for men and women. Generally, patriarchy leads to the conception that the male gender role is superior to that of a woman's gender role, which then leads to the perceived belief that control of women by men is acceptable. A patriarchal system justifies violence against women. Institutionalized patriarchy combines with masculine gender socialization to control women inside prison. Policies used to control men in prison work to attack and strip male inmates of their manhood by creating dependence, domination, deprivation of heterosexuality, and ability to compete. The same policies used to govern men's prisons also govern women's prisons; so, women inmates are subjected to a similar system of control designed by men for men (Blackburn, et al., 2011, p. 357).

Female inmates are not only subjected to institutional policies established for male inmates, "but also the oppressive treatment of women by those with authority that is seen outside prison walls" (Blackburn, et al., 2011, p. 322). Either gender may welcome the benefits of *quid pro quos,* but suffer from "unwelcomed consequences associated with these types of relationships that may affect different segments of the prison population differentially" (Blackburn, et al., 2011, p. 322).

The Department of Justice (DOJ) found that most allegations of sexual abuse in prison, 55%, were non-injurious; however, it often involved threat or force; and 35% involved sexual touching (DOJ, 2009). Inmates consider use of force to be a clear indication of sexual assault, whereas other forms of coercion are less clear (Fowler, et al., 2010). Injury, such as "road rash" from oral sex, and physical resistance may indicate sexual assault and lead other inmates to support victimized inmates (DOJ, 2009; Millwood-Jones v. Holder, 2016). Being turned-out, for example repaying a debt with sex, may not be considered violative because it was precipitated by a voluntary bargained-for exchange.

Sex and gender are factors in sexual conduct, abuse, and reporting. Male inmates are likelier to discuss victimization by inmates as being problematic; and less likely to volunteer information about victimization by staff (Fowler, et al., 2010). Between 60% and 75% of alleged sexual misconduct reportedly involves male staff members (DOJ, 2009). Descriptive statistics and the records from which they are derived may likely be unreliable because inmates may likely underreport sexual contact with males. Tradition dictates that males should be ashamed of same-sex aggression, pressure, or contact; and because they may believe that male authority figures are entitled to impose their sexualities. Therefore, they may be unable to acknowledge inappropriate sexual contact and may be prevented from reporting it due to internal and external controls. Approximately only four percent of male staff members have been alleged to have participated in sexually abusive behaviors; and only two percent in same-sex misconduct. Homosexual and bisexual inmates are less likely to report victimization to authorities (Fowler, et al., 2010). Homophobic attitudes may correlate with broader definitions of "sexual assault," which is why homosexual assault may be underreported. Although prisons may encourage inmates to report homosexual assault by staff, and may be sympathetic and punish staff, traditional morality correlating with homophobia is one basis for prison policies. Victimized heterosexual, bisexual, transgender, and homosexual inmates may be exposed to homophobic consternation and social rejection in the process of disclosing assault and pursuing justice (Fowler, et al., 2010; Sista Souljah, 2006).

Research may be skewed to undermine the extent of same-sex abuse and male staff members' abuse. Anecdotal evidence suggests that more than four percent of male guards participate in sexual contact with inmates (DOJ, 2009). However, the statistic claiming that only two percent of male guards have committed same-sex misconduct follows traditional beliefs that homosexuals comprise only two percent of the general population. Like inmates and staff, whose beliefs and actions may enforce traditional perceptions of immoral mechanisms by "obfuscating" moral decay, research methods may contribute to the same problem (Sutton, 2002).

Rape-supportive beliefs exclude more activities from definitions of "sexual violation" (Fowler, et al., 2010). Researchers have intentionally provided male and female inmates with differing operationalizations (e.g. hypothetical scenarios) in order to achieve results that demonstrate gender differences (Fowler, et al., 2010). These results skew institutional attitudes and could influence how future researchers and justice members identify perpetrators. In addition to testing attitudes toward hypothetical scenarios, many studies rely on self-reporting or official records, not undercover investigations (Cusack, 2015). Each data collection method is unreliable particularly when the subject matter is sensitive and the population is vulnerable (Fitzpatrick, Sanders, & Worthen, 2011). Furthermore, government agencies studying sexual misconduct assess the total number of violations without analyzing the relevance of multiple allegations made against the same staff member (DOJ, 2009). Deleterious and intimidating effects of institutional ambivalence toward a person repeatedly accused of sexual misconduct are unstudied by the government when they conclude that there is a relatively low incidence of male-perpetrated sexual abuse inside prisons. Multiple allegations made by an inmate against the same staff member only count as a single incident when measured by the agencies attempting to determine the percentage of staff involved in incidents. This lends support to the idea that the framework for these studies implicitly overlooks and explicitly ignores the relevance of the behavior to institutional patterns by minimizing the appearance of sexual abuse. A corrosive spiral is evident because victims of sexual assault in prison are less likely to report sexual abuse by prison employees (Fowler, et al., 2010).

Contributing to entropic decline is an intensifying conflict between development of gender equality in the penitentiary workforce and researchers' growing propaganda specifying that female staff are the main weakness in prisons' abilities to control sexual deviance. For example, an eight-year study by the DOJ found that 8,600 females and 23,908 males were involved in sexual misconduct (DOJ, 2009). This figure is disproportionately high for female staff members. Allegations of opposite-sex abuse by female staff were proportionally and numerically the greatest problem. However, other studies demonstrate similar rates of victimization between incarcerated males and females (Fowler, et al., 2010). The DOJ's findings promote derogatory aspects of traditional beliefs, for example that females are morally weak and males are sociosexually dominant. Their study corrodes gender equality without admitting to the likely possibility that complaints against males made by males may be underreported while complaints against females could potentially be exaggerated by male inmates attempting to brag about, harass, intimidate, control, and threaten females. Even if the DOJ's results are accurate, the study implies a traditional belief that females are a firewall for sexual morals. Research methods and findings may also distract from the seriousness of misconduct perpetuated against female staff (i.e. "slut shaming") by male and female staff and inmates.

Consistent with traditional gender role enforcement and moral boundaries, female officers often work in non-contact positions at male penitentiaries (Cheeseman, Mullings, & Marquart, 2001). Non-contact positions may not benefit male inmates because heterosexual male inmates may be likelier to identify same-sexual contact as sexual assault (Fowler, et al., 2010). While one study found that female inmates are less likely to identify same-sex contact as violative, another found that female inmates are significantly degraded by same-sex violations.

> Sexual contact in the line of duty occurs when officers abuse their powers or overstep their professional bounds. Strip and pat searches are routine

> practices in prison, and both have the potential to be major sources of degradation for inmates. Women inmates in particular report experiencing powerlessness and humiliation, even when the searches did not have sexual overtones. Officers, even officers of the same sex, can sexualize women and use pat and strip searches as a method of control through degradation. Each search involves the potential for inappropriate officer–inmate contact, and contributes to an environment where the women inmates feel sexualized and powerless (Blackburn, et al., 2011, p. 358).

However, a positive outcome of task-oriented segregation is that male inmates reportedly view female staff as being equally or more competent than male counterparts.

Weakening power is a cause and an effect of decaying morality, which manifests over time. Cultural changes promoting tolerance and paradigmatic shifts in consciousness are evident in prison, but may mask ongoing and worsening misconduct (i.e. boundary violations). The prison environment —a model for trends in other justice environments—demonstrates that inundation affects perception of sexual deviance. For example, serving more than six years in prison correlates with likelihood of boundary violations (Dial & Worley, 2008). Having served fewer than five years significantly decreases likelihood of past or current boundary violations. One study found that as time served increased, the chance of reporting sexual abuse by guards decreased; however, another study found that time served was not a factor (Fowler, et al., 2010). As likelihood of boundary violations increases, likelihood of reporting decreases. One explanation is that new inmates maybe less familiar with prison rules, for example expectation that unpaid debts will be repaid with sexual favors; and may be unaware that initiating consensual relationships with guards may result in continuing coercion (Fowler, et al., 2010).

Familiarization with the prison environment may correlate with decreased reporting. Another study found that amount of time served was not significant with women. Time served did not correlate with increased or decreased analytical separation of sexual assault from being turned-out (e.g. debt repayment). Prison environments may make more sense to male inmates, may offer fewer remedies to males, or provide greater incentives for compliance. Age may affect inmates' willingness to participate in deviance and support reporting. Younger inmates are more supportive than older inmates of blurred lines between staff and inmates (Blackburn, et al., 2011). Staff members, who commit sexual misconduct, tend to be younger than those, who commit sexual harassment (Beck, et al., 2014). One-third of staff, who committed misconduct, were younger than 29 years-old, but only 15% of sexual harassment was committed by members of the same age group. In 37% of sexual harassment cases and 25% of sexual misconduct, staff were older than 45 years old. They are most at-risk for institutional deviance during their first year (Dial & Worley, 2008). Therefore, while staff's likelihood of deviance may decrease over time, like inmates, their likelihood of boundary violations may increase over time.

Gender, relationship status, and sexuality influence perceptions of control and conformity. Sexual assault may be a form of social control. Overall, inmates, like people in the free world, are likelier to have narrower definitions of "sexual assault" when they also have rape-supportive cultural beliefs and attitudes. Though feminist philosophy says that groups of men, for example fraternal organizations, are likelier to have rape supportive attitudes (e.g. victim-blaming), this gender-specific trend is not necessarily evident in prison (Cusack, 2013; Cusack, 2015; Reddington & Kreisel, 2009). In research contexts, males are likelier to discuss prison culture that demands sexual favors in exchange for unpaid debts. Females may be less likely to discuss it generally, and may underreport. Female inmates tend to contextualize sexual violence with intimate partner violence and post-break-up fallout (Fowler, et al., 2010). They are more troubled by sexual victimization by staff than sexual violence by inmates; and female inmates may be less supportive than men of officers' violations (Blackburn, et al., 2011). Single female inmates are likelier to have narrower definitions of "sexual assault," but not single men (Fowler, et al., 2010). This may be one reason why female inmates may be likelier to recommend that victims report abuse (Fowler, et al., 2010). Females with narrow definitions, who believe that an inmate has been abused, may view abuse as being a serious offense of official concern. This may be one reason why female inmates may be likelier to recommend that victims report abuse (Fowler, et al., 2010). "[T]he social control of women inmates" may be likened "to a male batterer's social control of female victims because batterers use intimidation, isolation from others, male privilege, exploitation of children, economic control, threats of violence, and physical violence, making it a challenge for women to control their bodies and sexuality" (Blackburn, et al., 2011, p. 357; Koss & Goodman, 1994). "[F]emale offenders are subjected to a general climate of control, isolated from external support networks and children, and subjected to discipline and violence" (Blackburn, et al., 2011, p. 357). For example, one guard began relationships by discussing the Bible and inmates' children, then escalated to compliments and hugs until he fondled an inmate and asked for a *quid pro quo* (McLaughlin, 2016). He threatened to prevent her from seeing her children and to block her request to transfer to a facility near her children. The same guard repeatedly raped and sexually assaulted other victims while threatening their status and ability to visit their children (Cusack, 2003; McLaughlin, 2016). This behavior may be a reason why females contextualize sexual violence and control with intimacy.

Women in prison are far likelier to have been victims of physical and sexual abuse than male inmates or females in the free world. Victims of abuse may seek dysfunctional or exploitive relationships in order to replace or replicate early experiences with lovers and relatives. A study of 436 female inmates found that 68% of the sample had experienced sexual victimization; and 17% had been victimized while incarcerated (Blackburn, Mullings, & Marquart, 2008). Three percent had been raped in prison. Research has found that approximately two-thirds of sexual victims will likely enter cycles of sexual abuse.

Environmental factors that contribute to lawbreaking may increase likelihood of abuse in prison; for example, family conflict; physical, sexual, and substance abuse; socioeconomic problems; and powerlessness or marginalization (Blackburn, et al., 2011). A combination of patriarchy, trauma from sexually humiliating events (e.g. pat-downs and strip searches), and vulnerability may cause women to internalize and willfully participate in the institutionalization of gendered abuse. They may acquiesce from fear, ignorance, complacency, and environmental pressures, such as callous grievance processes. This may explain why lifetime sexual victimization is not a significant contributing factor for non-supportive attitudes toward reporting.

Government authority may be used arbitrarily, capriciously, and intentionally callously, but not evidently in contravention of the Eighth Amendment, which may intimidate and discourage inmates from reporting and turn-out inmates. For example, women may be "subjected to more punitive treatment by correctional officers, with increased chances for being cited for offenses and receiving more severe punishments for the same offenses as men" (Blackburn, et al., 2011, p. 357). They may be likelier to have specific rules enforced against them even though those rules are not enforced against male inmates while official policies may appear to provide women with gentler environmental conditions, for example access to more items in the commissary (Cusack, 2015). This may heighten women's perceived needs or willingness to trade sex for toiletries and other items. They are led to believe that they are entitled to necessities (e.g. menstrual items), but then items are withheld from them on the basis of sexual discrimination in comparison to male inmates. "This practice is especially troublesome when officers trade items used for basic human needs in which inmates have restricted access, like toilet paper" (Blackburn, et al., 2011, p. 358). In this type of boundary violation officers have the power to create a debt in which repayment is a sexual favor, which makes this form of sexual relationship between officer and inmate exploitive. "This commoditization of sex can lead to the worldview that the free exchange of sex for everyday things becomes an accepted practice" (Blackburn, et al., 2011, p. 358). In some facilities, it may result in staff forcibly prostituting female inmates to male prisoners.

Definitions of "sexual assault" may correlate with traditional and non-normative sexualities (Blackburn, et al., 2011). Male heterosexual inmates are likelier to blame victims of same-sex assault than homosexual inmates. Homosexual and bisexual inmates may be more sensitive to perceived same-sex abuse. Correctional staff's homophobic attitudes may result in increased victim-blaming, and narrowed definitions of "sexual assault" (Blackburn, et al., 2011; Cusack, 2015). Homophobia may result among female inmates due to limited definitions of "sexual assault," but not necessarily cause limited definitions. Socialization in prison may engender inmates to learn to avoid homosexuality and the appearance of homosexuality in order to deter and prevent sex abuse. Homophobia may result in aversions to victimization. All of these factors contribute to perceived boundaries and boundary violations by staff and inmates; and yet, institutional policies singularly define boundaries and violations, which may differ from perceived violations. Boundary violations blur and diminish professional distance from the served population.

American society is experiencing increased disruptions and fading of boundaries in general, and particularly in justice professions, such as penitentiaries. "[T]he public is inundated with stories of sexual boundary violations. Boundaries in prison can be blurred due to the proximity in which officers and inmates interact and by the staff's need to control inmates" (Blackburn, et al., 2011, p. 352). The number of boundary violations continues to increase as the justice system expands with unprecedented caseloads, increased numbers of prisons, new departments and agencies, and more bureaucracy (Gerth & Mills, 1946; Greeley, 2004). Prison environments continue to worsen with overcrowding, violence, and overt institutionalized sexual deviance. Increased drug addiction in America also contributes to increased numbers of boundary violations because inmates and guards have greater incentives to trade contraband for sexual conduct.

Reciprocity becomes the norm when staff overlook minor infractions in exchange for compliance and some assistance. Reciprocity, which may involve privilege, personal gain, and reward, blurs official prison boundaries and may blur perceived boundaries and prison customs. Boundary violations, not only involve minor breaches, they "undermine the legitimacy of the officers' professional expectations and include the physical or sexual abuse of inmates, bringing contraband into the prison, or ignoring inmates altogether" (Blackburn, et al., 2011, p. 354). "While official statistics do point to incidents of boundary violations, it is recognized that official reports may underestimate the magnitude of these violations perhaps due to the lack of official reporting by inmates and/or to the lack of evidence in cases that are reported" (Blackburn, et al., 2011, p. 355). Inmates may behave as turners, who intentionally manipulate boundaries, using heartbreak, exploitation, and hell-raising. Hell-raisers conduct "psychological warfare" "to cause trouble and create hell for the prison system" because they are "rebels with a cause," who are "consumed with the idea of creating havoc and trouble for an institution for the sake of it" (Gerth & Mills, 1946; Lerman & Page, 2016, p. 189). Interviews with 32 male turners demonstrated that staff were likelier to be turned when they had non-shareable problems, such as "social isolation, relationship failures, wild social lives, financial problems, and job-related problems" (Blackburn, et al., 2011, p. 356).

Boundary violations are not limited to sexual abuse (Blackburn, et al., 2011). They include discrete actions as well as proactive attempts to cause egregious violations, which must be reported. Lenient policies, based on liberal worldviews, for example those that permit anonymous payments to trust funds, may signal to staff and inmates that games may be played (Lerman & Page, 2016). Games may begin with confidential notes or romantic letters being passed between inmates and staff members; development of personal friendships between staff and inmates; and encouraging inmates to build friendships with other staff members. When female staff aggressively violate boundaries with male inmates, they alter the traditional gendered victim-aggressor paradigm in justice environments (Jones, 2015). Society may use a traditional patriarchal view of female staff members to treat them as victims (e.g. manipulation). Therefore, boundary violations may be perceived differently for male staff. Harmless boundary crossings and exploitative boundary violations may be defined differently for male and female staff.

A portrait of female prison staff was depicted by a female researcher, who worked within the corrections system for more than 30 years.

> I held positions ranging from an entry-level officer to a prison warden. In those positions, I experienced working as a coworker, as a supervisor, and as the warden with many women who left employment because of relationships with male inmates. In my early years, I was one of the many

> who looked on these women as traitors or as outcasts of a noble profession. As I matured and my experiences were broadened, I began to question this view (Jones, 2015, p. 367).

She said that it is important in correctional culture for employees to refrain from discussing boundary violations apart from stipulating the rules. Superiors are typically unwilling to discuss their experiences, mistakes, and temptations because they do not want to appear weak and invite pejoration or rejection. To share in such a fashion would be to admit to weakness, and in correctional culture, this type of disclosure would be met with disdain and judgment. Omissions isolate staff, who may be tempted, and suggest that they independently must grapple with their problems and recognize potential threats without instruction or support. "Female leaders in corrections agencies not only remain silent on this issue and fail to share their vulnerable and human side, they also frequently proclaim that the negative actions of other women hurt all women in this field" (Jones, 2015, p. 373). This pressure is an intense and consequential impediment for male and female staff because it deters intervention, defines gender, and reinforces culture (Dressler & Garvey, 2012). Therefore, culture change that reduces shaming and perceived judgment is critical to upholding the law and maintaining moral environments. However, leaders and colleagues cannot willfully or negligently exploit those seeking counsel by focusing on tawdry details in an arousing or degrading manner (Dugard, 2012).

Cultural shifts that value and reward adherence to training programs as well as relatively relaxed, safe, secure, and genteel environments are necessary. Role models are key for organizational and systemic transformations and maintenance. They may be particularly instrumental in therapeutic environments where transference and emotional development are pivotal. Although society presently uses reports about boundary crossings in justice environments as learning tools, change must manifest through discussions about prevention and remedies in the way that does not glamorize or sensationalize deviance.

As morals deteriorate and government influence and demands weaken, temptations may increase; however, reciprocal compassion and systemic understanding, flexibility, and training are necessary counterbalances. Employers may anticipate temptations, provide training, and be open to discussing and regularly intervening into potential crises and boundary breaches. Justice system employees and superiors must guard against temptation and train employees to detect patterns (Dressler & Garvey, 2012). Staff must buy-into a culture of disclosure and intervention rather than maintaining atmospheres of secrecy, collusion, or consternation.

Intervention must include approbation and possible reassignment to positions that do not adversely affect or inconvenience employees, at least in the short-term before returning to regular positions, in order to quell tempting situations.

Research shows that when supervisors are unsupportive, institutional deviance increases. A study of 501 correctional officers found that those with higher incidences of deviance had unsupportive supervisors, even when they had supportive peers (Worley & Worley, 2013). When officers believed that their jobs were more dangerous, they were less likely to be deviant; however, females are less likely than males to work in dangerous positions. Normalization among peers of institutional deviance facilitated perspectives accepting of deviance. The effect of poor leadership is inappropriate bonding among staff that implodes moral morale. A study of inmates revealed that they believe that supervisors are leery of female staff because of possible embroilment with inappropriate relationships (Worley, Tewksbury, & Frantzen, 2010). Perceived and actual ostracization may lead to marginalization and relegation to a network of peers and inmates causing, benefiting from, and suffering the effects of deviance. "It's pretty stupid for a boss lady to get involved with a convict. Nine times out of ten, she'll get burned by the convict she's having a relationship with. If a convict gets in a jam over something else, he might give the boss lady up in order to wipe the slate clean. This can mean her job" (Worley, Tewksbury, & Frantzen, 2010, pp. 352-353).

Unprosecuted or unpunished relationships recognized, tolerated, or supported by multiple inmates could cause severely damaging views about preferential treatment and absence of institutional collaboration and teamwork, which may bolster hostility in an undesirable working ambiance. An inmate explained this cycle.

> It's unprofessional because these relationships make officers fight with each other over who's dirty and who's not. It makes employees feel paranoid even if they're not doing anything wrong. Also, because dirty officers act unprofessionally and break the law every time they bring in contraband or have sex with an inmate, this sets a bad example for all of the other offenders (Worley, Tewksbury, & Frantzen, 2010, p. 351).

Supervisors may turn to inmates for information about deviant staff members, but "[t]here is no doubt that using inmate informants is a questionable practice" (Skolnick, 1994; Worley, Tewksbury, & Frantzen, 2010, p. 351).

Undercover investigations subject inmates to sexual abuse, which officials may feel is a necessary evil in order to substantiate allegations

(Santo, 2015). For example, a graphic recording allegedly made by Clements Unit in Texas depicts Domenic Hidalgo asking a male inmate to allow her to perform oral sex or masturbate him in exchange for scheduled drugs. The documentation seems to contribute to or satisfy exploitive penchants because it is freely available on the Internet. Yet, it serves a "retributive" purpose, even though publication of the investigation and incident may compound and perpetuate the inmate's pain and humiliation (Dressler & Garvey, 2012, p. 224). In a similar situation in free society, people may develop paranoia about incentivized privacy violations. This may worsen the effect of transforming the public sphere into a place to air dirty laundry and savor sordid details of private affairs. Inside prison and in the free world, snitches may suffer serious consequences. Revelatory activities may link to crimes of passion, as well as peeping, hacking, catfishing, stalking, and other intrusive behaviors that blur public and private realms (Cusack, 2014; Cusack, 2015; Cusack, 2017).

Unfortunately, deviant correctional environments may only self-correct with violence. Deviance decreases as perceived danger increases, and danger may become more imminent as violations increase and enforcement decreases (Worley & Worley, 2013). Because inmates are likelier to engage in boundary violations as the level of security increases, lack of supervision is particularly dangerous (Dial & Worley, 2008). This process is evident in the free world as well, where paralyzing tension correlates with austerity, criticality, and oversight; while lack of oversight may result in anarchical or hegemonic inequality, risk-taking, and marginalization. A spiral may result (Cusack, 2014). One inmate extrapolated, "These relationships are dangerous. If a convict has a boss on his payroll, he can go around and victimize other inmates without getting in any trouble" (Worley, Tewksbury, & Frantzen, 2010, p. 352). Male inmates, who initiate sexual contact, are likelier to intimidate, blackmail, and threaten physically to harm staff (Dial & Worley, 2008). This group is also significantly likelier to "gun" at female guards (i.e. masturbate) to test female guards' professional and emotional weakness (Lerman & Page, 2016). They may suffer from courtship disorders and believe that female guards want to view their penises and participate in sex acts (Cusack, 2012). For example, an inmate later married a former staff member for whom he gunned (Lerman & Page, 2016). "Before I married my wife, I used to always jack off for her and do a little show whenever she walked her runs. She used to love it too" (Lerman & Page, 2016, p. 191). Their behavior is dangerous because there is a high comorbidity between public masturbation and worse "paraphilic disorders" (APA, 2013, p. 333; Cusack, 2012).

Bureau of Prison (BOP) statistics suggest that non-security staff may be easier targets than guards, which may increase opportunities for threat and violence because non-security staff may be less willing to take control and defend themselves (DOJ, 2009). These kinds of inmates target personnel, who are not guards. This may demonstrate that staff's immorality is just as important to institutional integrity as guards', even though society frames immorality as a control issue when guards use their power over inmates. Inmates may see that deterioration occurs in the prohibited sexual relationship, not the abuse of power (Lerman & Page, 2016, p. 191). "In one interview, the respondent claimed to have had several sexual relationships with non-security employees, including both a chaplain's secretary and warden's wife" (Lerman & Page, 2016, p. 191). Inmates consciously seeking to destroy the institution may be likelier to suggest that females work in institutions to "find a man" (Lerman & Page, 2016, p. 191).

One inmate identified perceived correlations between the female gender, institutions, and welfare dependence. "Women guards work here, so they can look at a bunch of dicks. That's one of the main reasons why they come here. That and the fact that they can't get welfare" (Lerman & Page, 2016, p. 191). Gunning encourages an atmosphere of sexual liberation and opportunism; and it impedes reform. It is a form of sexual harassment that female guards may not report because it is degrading; may cause them to appear to be incompetent; and because they fear reassignment (Cusack, 2012). Male superiors may not ignore complaints about gunning; however, they may rationalize the behavior. This endangers female staff and other inmates. Danger indirectly correlates with lack of institutional cohesion and enforcement. It directly results from the activities; for example, inmates may be high on cocaine overlooked or supplied by a staff member.

Repercussions for staff, who become involved with inmates, is an unlikely outcome. In 52% of substantiated cases of sexual harassment, staff were fired; and 43% were disciplined, demoted, or transferred (Beck, et al., 2014). Six percent were arrested or prosecuted. In 85% of instances of sexual misconduct, staff were dismissed; and they were arrested or prosecuted in 56% of instances.

When inmates are castigated, it may have a variety of effects; for example, it may deter inmates, arouse hell-raisers, and spread gossip, which raises suspicion and weakens the appearance of institutional integrity.

> Several inmate boundary violators…[explained] that an offender who is involved in a relationship with a staff member is subject to many severe

> disciplinary sanctions, including the loss of good time, being sent to a less desirable facility, and having negative information placed in his or her official records. Also…offenders can lose their contact visits and access to college classes if they are apprehended and punished for having inappropriate relationships….[O]nce they had been labeled as having been involved in an inappropriate relationship they were quickly ostracized by correctional staff members (Worley, Tewksbury, & Frantzen, 2010, p. 352).

Even when inmates are not disciplined, gossip may put-off officers and staff. This reaction demonstrates that traditional morals are present in government workplaces, but may not be rigorously implemented. Group mentalities that consciously oppose immorality may be reactive rather than openly visible, unambiguous, and proactive.

Rules in some justice professions, such as corrections, may be perceived as being strict mandates; however, some staff may believe that rules are meant for safety, and if rule breaking is not the proximate cause of physical harm, then boundaries may be bent or broken. Violence may be diffused from prisons into staff members' private lives. Relationship problems then factor into institutional deviance. It may give staff a strained appearance, which further isolates them from their peers and superiors, who want to give them space or do not want to experience their mood or emotional aggravation. Isolation lends to increased emotional and physical vulnerability as well as opportunity for staff to be deviant and for inmates to target staff. If staff seem to be off-putting, then superiors may attempt to befriend inmates, which is risky because staff may be threatened and coerced more easily when inmates believe that they have achieved status. When superiors befriend inmates, staff may be unable to report boundary violations and infractions to their employers. Inmates' are not the only people to capitalize on status conferred by affiliation; for example, judges and politicians have been alleged to violate their oaths by capitalizing on prestige and placing themselves and their staff members on higher legal ground than other citizens (Gerth & Mills, 1946).

Inmates have suggested that to deter boundary violations and change culture, cross-gender supervision should be eliminated or only used when necessary (Worley, Tewksbury, & Frantzen, 2010). From a rehabilitative point-of-view, this policy could be problematic. Inmates may require cross-gender socialization before being reintroduced into society. However, mixed gender environments could be arranged so that opposite-gender staff are present, but not in direct or sustained contact with inmates. Sex-based segregation is not possible in other justice fields; however, the salient principle is applicable. For example, female victims of sexual abuse may be interviewed by female staff. Yet, in some fields, for example law, female defense attorneys and prosecutors may be equally insensitive to or exploitive of female victims. They may harass or psychologically demean victims because their own traumas have been triggered.

In many institutions, male officers are not allowed to pat-down females, but this level of segregation may not be effective enough. The BOP found that in 15 of 16 occupations, increased exposure to inmates correlated with higher likelihood for sexual misconduct and abuse (DOJ, 2009). The likeliest employees worked in food services, recreation, education, and vocational training, which are all traditional pink collar fields. More than half of allegations, 65%, involved criminal sexual abuse, not misconduct. Females represent 27% of prison staff, but were alleged to have committed between 30% and 39% of sexual abuse and misconduct involving inmates. Approximately half of sexual misconduct and abuse allegations were made against prison staff, not inmates; and this is despite the fact that there are many more inmates than staff (Beck, et al., 2014). Approximately, 10% were investigated and substantiated. Therefore, there may be greater systemic tolerance, collusion, and encouragement of male staff sexual assault and fewer significant opportunities for inmates credibly to prove misconduct by male staff.

Some research analyzes disproportionate impacts of women committing sexual deviance in prison without acknowledging the role of patriarchy in investigations and substantiation (Mastropasqua, 2015; Smith & Loomis, 2013). Research accepts that investigators (e.g. administrators) equally, rigorously, and in good faith investigate complaints against females and males made by inmates of each sex. However, this may not be the case. Investigators may be more willing to investigate females or believe males for institutional, societal, cultural, or personal reasons. For example, a societal reason may be that they seek to enforce traditional norms against allegedly sexually weak females, who wield professional power over men, so that they can depict men as seducers, not victims. Of investigated and substantiated infractions, 84% allegedly were committed by female staff and 37% were committed by male staff (Beck, et al., 2014). Males abused their power and were physically coercive in 20% of instances, but females only did so in 1% of instances. Cross-gender sexual misconduct involving female staff may be voluntary is 84% of instances (Worley, 2016). Female inmates comprise 7% of sentenced inmates, but are the victims in 33% of cases of staff misconduct in prisons (Beck, et al., 2014). In jails, 13% of inmates are females, yet represent 67% of inmates victimized by staff. Female staff were likelier to commit sexual misconduct in prisons; whereas male staff were likelier to victimize inmates in local jails. Female staff perpetrated 54% of sexual misconduct; and 26% of sexual harassment was perpetrated by females. Males committed 46% of sexual misconduct and 74% of sexual harassment. Sexual harassment and misconduct in state and federal penitentiaries were committed by males in 67% of cases; female victims comprised 67% of victims, but only 80% of violators were male staff. Female inmates were violated by female staff in 20% of cases. Female staff may violate women for power or because of the institutional mindset. They may deviate against women because they feel powerless or weak as a result of having violated boundaries with men (Dial & Worley, 2008). They may appear to be weak to female inmates, who select them for relationships.

Female officers are perceived by male boundary violators as being fearful and a source of sexual tension (Dial & Worley, 2008). Perceived sexual tension may cause them to negotiate with inmates; and inmates may appear to offer protection to women, who seem to lack physical strength in comparison to male inmates (Cusack, 2012; Cusack, 2012). Boundary violators have claimed that female officers are less capable of controlling inmates than male officers; therefore, female officers may threaten security (Dial & Worley, 2008). Female officers may experience strain because they are attempting to assert their independence and gender identity within a system designed for men by men. As a result, boundary violators are likelier to detect or perceive that guards are flirting and seeking attention; and in return they manipulate and deceive. This explains why they discuss relationship problems with female staff. Conversation may be used to manipulate and gather information about rivals.

Despite substantial literature on boundary violations, research almost exclusively discusses it in terms of institutional and societal costs, not morality, tradition, or prohibitions against sexual deviance. For example, boundary violations resulting in termination are viewed as wasting money to recruit and educate new trainees (Dial & Worley, 2008). Literature also focuses on administrative and emotional harm. Researchers and guards may subtly believe that innocent gestures by inmates to achieve friendships, sympathy, or perhaps additional supervision for protection are not truly deviant sexual boundary explorations. Even when institutions are acutely attuned to the seriousness of boundary violations, their main concern may not be morality, but deterrence, prevention, enforcement, and safety.

> One former prison employee said, 'I witnessed many of my fellow guards chastise and even threaten to write up inmates who offered them snacks. Whenever this happened, the inmate would act as though his feelings were genuinely hurt because the employee had rejected his open display of

> friendship. But this is only one of the many games that inmates like to play. An inmate offering a staff member a cookie, a magazine, a small bag of Cheetos, or anything can best be viewed as what described as an exploratory gesture…to gauge the intentions of others (Worley, 2016, p. 1218).

Exploratory gestures may not be immoral, but they correlate with misconduct.

> I remember one occasion when several officers, both male and female, secretly worked in cahoots to make sure that a female guard who had designed a homemade bracelet and given it to a male offender was reprimanded and punished by the unit warden. Although this may seem harsh to outsiders, the social norms of the prison organization permeated the belief that if a staff member gave an inmate minor, nuisance contraband, it would only be a matter of time before he or she was smuggling dangerous contraband such as drugs, money, cellphones, or weapons into the facility, which could put everyone at risk (Worley, 2016, p. 1221).

Researchers disagree about whether guards tolerate, collude, reject, or protect when fellow guards violate boundaries, but all the possibilities seem likely to occur at an institution at any given time. Therefore, some guards will readily report their colleagues' failure to flag exploratory gestures as an indication of acquiescence and boundary crossing. Reporting all boundary explorations, for example accidentally simultaneously grabbing the same door handle, may seem fanatical, impossible, and akin to power-mongering. However, accidental touching is considered to be equal to intentional unauthorized contact. "Unauthorized contact [is] considered such a serious infraction of the rules that no distinction was made between intentional and accidental contact between an inmate and correctional officer. In other words, even if an offender accidentally bumped into a staff member, he still ran the risk of being written up and disciplined for this offense and could easily lose privileges and even good-time credits" (Worley, 2016, p. 1223). "[L]everage that the inmate" may acquire during "a lapse" "due to a combination of low morale and inadequate supervision," could stage "*the economics*, which descends into "a *crossing over*," if an "inmate's gesture of friendship" is validated or not punished (Worley, 2016, p. 1223).

Guards may be unwilling to view unauthorized contact as a moral issue because fundamentally the prohibitive principle is the same underlying all forms of conduct, including accidental, harmless, voluntary sexual, and abusive forcible contact. The troublesomely diminishing force is the role, not the morals. The question of whether it is equally immoral for an inmate to coerce a guard as it is for a guard to seduce an inmate under his or her control is usurped by institutional and legal viewpoints indicating that it is a far worse breach of rules and society's expectations for a guard to engage in sexual conduct with an inmate than for an inmate to manipulate or coerce a guard. Nevertheless, all boundary violations, whether moral or immoral, threaten safety and institutional integrity.

In some cases, when inmates and staff continue romantic relationships after they have been disciplined, some members of society may view their relationships as being cleansed of their immoral and wrongful beginnings. For example, one guard smuggled tobacco and marijuana into a penitentiary for her lover. After she was terminated, she cohabited with his mother (Worley, 2016). Members of society may disagree about whether staff marrying inmates reconstitutes morality within the union and legitimizes relationships (Turner v. Safely, 1987). Inmates and staff possess a fundamental right to marry, which is recognized in many state statutes making exemptions to sexual assault statutes. In federal court, it is an affirmative defense established by the preponderance of the evidence that an inmate and staff member were married while they engaged in sexual conduct (18 U.S.C. § 2243(c)(2), 2016). However, dating an inmate while a staff member is employed is strictly forbidden.

Like cases from the 19th century in which women were promised legitimization and then were seduced by suitors, inmates may discuss marriage strictly for personal gain (Neal, 2009). Discussing marriage is a boundary violation. In a study of 32 inmates, who had turned staff members, eight were labeled by researchers as heart-breakers, who engaged staff in long-term relationships (Lerman & Page, 2016). Of the heartbreakers, 63% claimed to have married a former correctional staff member. Heartbreakers may treat staff as dependents inside and in the free world.

> As one male inmate explained: After we got busted, she went and lived with my family for a little while. But then she left, and now my mom is mad at her. I guess my mom just figured she was freeloading, but I really loved that girl. In a related example, another informant made the following statement: Right now my old lady is shacking up with my parents and her two kids[, b]ut as soon as I get out we're gonna [sic] get our own place (Lerman & Page, 2016, p. 183).

Boundaries between romance, usury, stability, and mind games may be uncertain and blurred by both parties.

One example demonstrates how deviance may be bound within presumably moral intentions, blossoming love, and marriage. Similar to examples of romance in free society, this example of duality attests to the difficulty of institutionalizing morality and implementing rules (Cusack, 2016). A female guard and male inmate met inside prison (Marie, 2014). The inmate believed that he eventually would pair with the guard. At first, she maintained a professional demeanor with the inmate. She recounted collusion and rule-breaking that facilitated their romance.

> I got fired for something totally unrelated. When I left I sent back thank-you notes to five guys who were still there. A lot of times women are used to calm men down in the prison system, but I also gained a lot of wisdom from the guys. I just thanked them for being who they were and I wished them well in life. The lady in the mailroom got the letter for Robert and pulled him in and let him read it. It had my phone number in it and then she destroyed the letter. He remembered the number and took it to the prison chaplain and the chaplain let him call me….The chaplain knew I was a good person and I wasn't fired for anything of ill nature. He basically was friends with Robert and wanted Robert to have a good life and if Robert wanted to call someone—and that's the first time he ever asked to call anybody—he was gonna [sic] let him do it (Marie, 2014).

The inmate and former guard pleaded with a chaplain, who represents a nexus between religion and the state in a marriage, which privately and publicly binds marital parties. Before the inmate reentered society, he called the former guard twice; and they planned to meet near a highway. "My mom took me there, and when I got out of the car, we kissed and off we went" (Marie, 2014). Traditionally, parental figures represent alliance and approbation.

The couple explained why their marriage is not founded on traditional morality.

> Given the fact that he had to kind of grow up in prison from 24 to 34, there were probably a lot of things in life he didn't experience, you know, sexually, and I gave him that freedom to express that. I was always open to any experiences he wanted as long as I was involved. So we did do a few things that he wanted to do outside of our relationship. I facilitated him having sex with one of my best friends; we've been to some swinger parties. Sex didn't work out there, it just didn't feel right for either of us. We utilize sex toys and we're into erotic novels and stuff like that. We keep a lot of things to ourselves, but I allow him to experience other things as well (Marie, 2014).

She dismissed monogamy as being precipitated by jealousy, not morals. "My motive has always been friends first and as his friend—not his lover or his girlfriend, [but] as his friend—I wanted him to experience all that life has to offer and I was by no means going to stand in his way" (Marie, 2014). "I'm just not a jealous person. You don't get jealous with someone if you're secure with yourself" (Marie, 2014).
He distinguished his body from their marriage and objectified himself.

> There's a difference between me being with her and me being with somebody else. She not only has my heart and my mind, she's got everything else that goes with that. The other person, they're only getting that body for however long it takes for them to do what they gotta [sic] do and then it's over. With her, I want to cuddle and hug and kiss and lie there and go to sleep. With them, I want it to get done and go home (Marie, 2014).

His comment may reveal that while in prison he became accustomed to dissociating his inner person from his body (e.g. pat-downs); and that he may be unable to distinguish their relationship from his time in prison. Reentry caused him emotional difficulty. Early in their marriage he became an alcoholic and was arrested from driving under the influence.

Despite their divergences, the former guard said that they shared a bond that sparked when they first met. "I just remember looking at him and feeling weird. It wasn't like, 'Ooh, he's hot,' it was like, 'Huh, what was that?' Like a bolt of lightning hit me[; b]ut I knew that a lot of rumors centered around female corrections officers in male prisons. So given I felt some kind of vibe, I kept my distance. There was no discussion" (Marie, 2014). She portrayed their bond as the being the basis for their open marriage. "He expressed interest because we were friends[; a]nd he didn't have to say, 'I don't mean this to hurt your feelings.' I knew where his head was. He was my best friend I wanted him to have everything he wanted" (Marie, 2014).

They emphasized this bond when coping with her desire to become involved with another man.

> So one day somebody caught my eye and I felt like, if my heart wasn't open, then I wouldn't have caught this person's eye. So we struck up a friendship and there was an interest there and I came back and I told my husband, 'There's an interest here and I'm really thinking about it.' He thought about it for a few days and he came back and said, 'If this is something you really wanna [sic] do, you really wanna [sic] be with this guy, I'm gonna [sic] give you 30 days. Do whatever you gotta [sic] do. We'll get back together in 30 days and decide whether you want to stay

> with me and stay married or you want to let it go'….I was like, 'Well, I don't want you to leave me. I don't wanna [sic] let you go. This is just something I'm thinking about. I haven't even done anything.' I don't want to jeopardize my marriage for one thing just because I'm curious. It would've been different if the guy had a girlfriend and they were interested in a swap, then we could have a discussion, you know? But I just decided it wasn't worth my marriage (Marie, 2014).

She drew attention to the value of time. "I said, 'The reason my attention fell on somebody else was that I really wanna [sic] spend time with you.' So he rearranged his schedule. But I needed to communicate with him instead of letting him go do his thing" (Marie, 2014). He did not comment on the significance of serving time while under her supervision; how her presence reflected on his reentry and rehabilitation; or whether his new freedom to arrange his schedule had affected his judgment or desire to spend time with her.

The former inmate also discussed how he was instantly drawn to marry her. "I was standing there with my brother and a close friend and I looked at her and we kind of met eyes and I told those two, 'That's gonna [sic] be my girl one of these days.' They were just looking at me like, 'You don't even know her name'" (Marie, 2014)! Serving time with his brother could have contributed to his desire to marry her.

The couple's awareness of traditional familial roles may be evident in their relationships with their parents. For example, they justified having deceived her father about how they met. "He thinks that I was at the gate and he worked with a company that came in for prison ministry. If he knew the truth, he wouldn't be here now. He's already prejudiced as can be" (Marie, 2014). Her comment demonstrates the importance of his approbation. She described the significance of respect and how mothers may shape their children's relationships. "My advice to my daughter is that when you get interested in a boy, the first thing you do is see how he acts with his mother. If he has a good relationship with his mother, then he'll have a good relationship with you. If he argues with his mother, then he's gonna [sic] argue with you. If he shows disrespect toward her, then he's gonna [sic] show the same thing toward you" (Marie, 2014). Subordinating their relationship to standards set by their parents may relate to the fact that an institutional setting sparked their romance; and institutional deviance (e.g. the chaplain lending his phone) appeared to them to be approbation, which facilitated their love and encouraged their unification. Institutional deviants and inmates paradigmatically may associate their surroundings with a traditional higher power or family-life.

Boundary violations may be a symptom of their willingness to treat their work environments like home.

Subtle environmental and familial influences may be etiologies for "transcendent" problems (Thoreau, 2013, p. 218). Cognitive and verbal recognition of "spiritual" problems is increasingly difficult in non-religious, public environments (Durkheim, 2008, p. 259). Inmates and staff members may experience inclinations to deviate because they are influenced by unseen forces; for example, memories and unconscious suggestions (Proust, 2003). Inmates and staff may experience compelling emotions, ideas, or desires, which are subtly detectable to others, but not acutely explainable, transmutable, or identifiable. Receptive individuals suffering from weak identities, who accept group mentalities, may be influenced. Neurological, social, and psychological sensations causing one to experience psychic directives may result in deviance. It may appear as an "Aha!" solution to interpersonal problems in the free world; instinct; intuition; or a useful way to participate in social economics (Heine, 2004, p. 128; Heine, 2005; Lao-Tzu, 1996). This phenomenon, which may be ubiquitous, is difficult to explain and has been relegated by scholars to discussions about ethos, contagion, and possession, even though it may be a common occurrence in everyday life. This thrust, based on a belief of social support or unexplainable guidance, may have catastrophic effects.

"[T]he intrusion of the supernatural in the life of a" prisoner "that provides a necessary instruction leading to a breakthrough from some impasse rooted in ignorance and attachment" has "reinforced" "exorcism" (Heine, 2004, p. 128). For example, subtle inclinations to participate in prison culture may be derived from Biblical lessons learned at chapel. Socializing may "evoke the quality of morality tale literature" whereby "a person is transformed and enlightened by learning a crucial moral lesson through a heightened moment of encounter with otherworldly forces" (Heine, 2004, p. 128). "These forces manifest at a crucial moment or key turning point and reveal an important truth that cuts through illusion and alters the person's perspective forever" (Heine, 2004, p. 128). However, the lesson available to inmates in prison may not violate boundaries. Being an inmate and a deviant requires "shapeshifting" to "represent a seduction, temptation, or betrayal that heightens the sense of illusion until" the inmate "comes to" his or her "breaking point that allows the truth to be revealed in a compelling fashion" (Cusack, 2010; Heine, 2004, p. 128; Marcellus, 2009). Yet, the truth may be forbidden by the institution; for example, the inmate may be in love with a staff member; an addict, who cannot rehabilitated; or a hell-raiser. Spiritual "breakthrough[s]" are "double-edged swords in that they represent the forces of protection and redemption as well as seduction and delusion" (Heine, 2004, p. 128). In this sense, the "structure of morality tale" "is strikingly paralleled to the function…in which there is frequently an experience of a breakthrough to another dimension of spirituality," "which is free from man and yet which continuously victimizes" (Durkheim, 2008; Heine, 1985, p. 3; Heine, 2004, p. 128).

> It is as if time were in pursuit of man and capable of overtaking him should he relinquish his hold on the present—so he attempts to seize it all the more firmly without realizing its fabricated nature. Despite man's fixations, he always seems to be losing time or he can never get enough of time as he watches it speed by him. The movement of time seems to be remote and unreachable; no matter how diligently he chases after it or how accurately he measures it, man cannot prevent or dissuade, subdue or forestall the irreversible sequential tide. In fact, it is just these attempts which further remove man from a genuine experience (Heine, 2004, p. 128).

In the spiritual realm, men and women are the objects and God is the subject, but not in prison. Time passes too slowly for ignorance to absolve them from fate. Therefore, they must contemplate their own existences and why God has left them. In this state, they conjure commands from their cohort, which may potentially be overcome through formal training (e.g. education or religion), but rarely is due to the onslaught of socialization (i.e. near total cohabitation with fellow inmates and staff).

> The fact that man is constantly measuring time and trying to refine his sense of calculation, and then lets himself be controlled by this reckoning, as if it were absolutely real, indicates how he feels victimized by time, taking it for granted as something given and not subject to inquiry without ever really understanding it or trying to become aware of the source of his bondage to it (Heine, 2004, p. 128).

An inmate is "caught in an entanglement of seeking more time while losing his grasp on what he has, and of taking one particular moment to be appropriate or not for reasons dictated by external circumstances, man conceals from himself primordial time in insidious yet all-pervasive ways" (Heine, 1985, p. 3). "The dimensions of...interpretation of impermanence" "throughout" "include the exhortative, poetic-naturalistic[,] and ontological" (Heine, 1985, p. 3; Keenan, 2013). A religious "hero," through morality lessons and "autobiographical works" "offers numerous parables, anecdotes and homiletic injunctions to inspire his disciples with a sense of immediacy and urgency in the soteriological quest for the Way of non-self so that they will train as if their lives were directly at stake with each decision and effort" (Ausband, 2000; Cusack, 2016; Glenn, 2004; Heine, 1985, p. 92; MacLaine, 2012; Northup, 2006). His time "blooms ever anew" each day "to illustrate the" government's "interpretation of" society through an inmate's "life and death, arising and desistence in each impermanent and insubstantial self-generating moment" (Heine, 1985, p. 92). "Aging, dying[,] and destruction...do not indicate some negative condition—as it is understood in the derivative view of impermanence—but point to the ever renewable and selfless possibilities of evanescence" (Heine, 1985, pp. 92-93).

Training may be invaluable in prison for breaking bonds that arise from "primordial" desires to love and follow a group (Heine, 1985, p. 3). For example, training may help guards and inmates to identify susceptibility and build solid identities (Worley & Worley, 2011). However, substance abuse, trauma, and an atmosphere of subordination deteriorate identity. Prison guard subculture is like police and attorney subcultures in that teammates never "rat" on colleagues to the authorities. Whistleblowing is discouraged. Identity within the profession may rest in part on a team mentality, which increases susceptibility and decreases opportunity to relinquish negative influences and absorbed tensions. The cycle is evident in theft and brutality against inmates (Copeland, 2016). Training must overtly discuss subtle cues, not merely focus on self-esteem. Because employees, who feel cared-for by their institutions, are not less likely to be deviant, "brotherhoods" or "sisterhoods" and sensitive approaches may not help to institute moral identities in individuals and groups unless training directly targets difficult topics, such as how to identify temptations, seek counsel, and make better decisions once unexplainable cues begin to manifest as thoughts, solutions, or interests. Training should describe to staff how behavior is observed and communicated before staff are turned (Allen & Bosta, 1981; Cheeseman & Worley, 2006). Susceptibility to manipulation may be evident in their mannerisms and body language; their overt and subtle responses to mundane situations and conversation; distractibility; willingness to comprise; emotional stability; and personal identity. Conversations about politics or religion may seem harmless or edifying, but may explore boundaries and weaknesses. Religion and political opinions may have polarizing effects that breakdown institutional strength and supernaturally bond inmates and staff.

Immorality inside prisons directly corrodes morality on the outside because it interferes with tradition.

> [A] female prisoner had this to say, I started talking real nice to the officer where I worked, in the laundry. He was married but I told him how his old lady didn't pay him enough attention. You know that if he was my man how I would treat him. He started writing me notes and cards. Pretty soon I got him to bring in eyeliner, perfume, and some cigarettes. I sold the stuff. Oh it was fun to talk to him and stuff but I never let it get any further. I mean I never let him touch me or anything. I used him to make my life easier in here. Why not? You'd do the same thing. To obtain contraband, 'exploiters' develop a 'lever' or 'hold' over security officers. Levers…were ploys that offenders use to manipulate staff members into violating organizational policies and procedures (Lerman & Page, 2016, p. 186).

Officers may distribute "jack books" (i.e. pornographic pictorials), which may be offensive to their families and communities (Cusack, 2012; Cusack, 2013; Lerman & Page, 2016, p. 187; Miller v. California, 1973).

In many cases, morality prevails and neither staff nor inmates participate in sexual deviance. One inmate explained his moral point-of-view.

> My cellmate used me as a contact with a female laundry officer. He and I were working together to bring tobacco in and were making good money. I was just happy to be involved and didn't want to do anything stupid to bring down any heat. Also, at the time, I was married to someone in the free world and didn't want to mess that up either (Lerman & Page, 2016, p. 188).

His business savvy overcame temptation triggered by interpersonal, emotional, social, and financial turmoil. His comment demonstrates that money was a strong motivator, but that he understood interpersonal and social consequences of sexual deviance.

Inmates having sex with wardens' wives demonstrates how institutional deviance corrodes tradition and the law's ability to enforce morality in the free world.

> When asked to describe his most recent alleged relationships, the offender offered: I've had sex with the wives of two different wardens. One night around Christmas, I went over to the house of one warden and his wife asked me to put her son's bicycle together. You know it was a Christmas present. Then she cooked dinner for me and we had sex right there in the kitchen, on the floor. I can talk my way into any woman's panties. I did it 'cause [sic] I could. You know what I am saying? Man when they busted me for that, all hell broke loose. It was hilarious. Yeah, I lost my outside trusty job but it was worth it 'cause [sic] I embarrassed the shit out of that

warden and his family. I still can't stop laughing 'bout [sic] it (Lerman & Page, 2016, p. 190).

Deviance between inmates and people in the free world may wound the system by demonstrating that anyone can be "anti-social and very detrimental to the institution" (Lerman & Page, 2016, p. 191).

Fig. 4.1, Federal Correctional Institute (FCI), Tallahassee, Florida.

Inmates may be linked to people in the free world through staff members. Spiraling deviance may result from gang activity and multi-party conspiracies. For example, five prison guards, including Gregory Dixon and Alan Moore, at the Federal Correctional Institute (FCI) in Tallahassee, Florida conspired to barter tobacco products, bras, perfume, chewing gum, jewelry, and cosmetic products (Almodovar, 2011; Clarke, 2007). Relatives using money orders outside the prison bribed and paid guards by U.S. mail. Some were intimidated and threatened by guards, who were sentenced in federal court to a term of one year incarceration or detention plus three years supervised release. Six agents were indicted; however, the sixth agent died when federal agents attempted to arrest him at FCI. The guard used an unlawfully possessed personal firearm inside the prison to kill one agent and wound another. As a result, guards are now searched before entering FCI, a procedure opposed by the federal prison employee union. To defend their position, the union has admitted that bribery and sexual abuse is currently investigated at hundreds of prisons; and therefore, searches have been ineffective. This case of rape and bribery apparently was notable because guards used the federal mail (Strickman, 2008). However, female inmates at FCI have alleged rape and sexual harassment by guards for decades.

Boundary violations are common; yet, extreme examples are illustrative of how multiple individuals must fail in their professions and collude to permit abuse. For example, Sergeant Leshawn Terrell at the Denver Women's Correctional Facility inhumanely raped inmate Amanda Hall so frequently that she compared herself to a sex slave (Hall v. Colorado, 2008; Hunter, 2009). Hall was injured by Terrell's violent abuse; and underwent surgery for a torn rectum. Hall sued in federal court and settled for $250,000 in attorney fees and damages. The corrections department agreed to install additional security cameras, which seems to be a popular response to alleged abuse by police and parole officers, but may not be feasible in other justice professions. Terrell was prosecuted, but only pleaded guilty to the misdemeanor of unlawful sexual conduct, and received 60 days incarceration, five years probation, sex offender treatment, and sex offender registration (Hunter, 2009). Many plea deals permit former prison staff "to walk away quietly" without registering as sex offenders or forfeiting their abilities to work with inmates (Krause, 2016). A secretary at a federal prison with a supermax worked for the prison system for 14 years before it was discovered that she had oral and vaginal sex with Eric McClain. Janine Sligar was sentenced to six months incarceration and five years probation.

When guards rape inmates, they do not act within the scope of their employment; and yet, the government uses law to distance itself from justice members' actions (AELE, 2007). For example, a federal court ruled that the government was not liable for intentional sexual assault committed by a male federal guard against a female inmate. The assaulter may have requested the inmate after midnight so that he could have an opportunity to rape her. It was an issue of material fact as to whether two guards may have taken the inmate and left her unattended with the assaulter, who had been assigned to transport her. Their actions may have violated prison regulations. Because there was an issue of material fact, the plaintiff's motion for summary judgment was denied under the Federal Tort Claims Act (FTCA) (28 U.S.C. § 1346, 2017; Davis v. U.S., 2007). Under FTCA, the guard's intentional wrongdoing immunized the government for claims against negligence, such as negligent hiring, training, supervision, and management. FTCA allows for recovery based on negligence (Martinez v. U.S., 2004). For example, superiors will be found to be negligent and will not receive qualified immunity when they permit inmates to be left in the care of guards, who have been accused of committing sexual misconduct against them in the past, and then new substantiated claims of sexual misconduct arise (Gonzales v. Martinez, 2005).

Personal liability may not be imposed on superiors (e.g. superintendents) for the intentional actions of subordinates unless they were directly involved; demonstrated deliberate indifference to a known risk of harm or were grossly negligent in supervision; or had notice, including actual or constructive knowledge of previous abuses that they failed to correct (Morris v. Eversley, 2003). Recidivism may impute knowledge and demonstrate negligent supervision. For example, one guard was accused of assaulting and harassing at least thirty female inmates and a staff member. He was sentenced to the remainder of his life in prison and the state paid approximately $2 million to the victims (Hunter, 2009). Though it would be unjust to hold non-negligent employers to be culpable for employees' intentional criminal actions, the law is structured so that employers may tidily sever particular incidents from institutional culture and uninvestigated or unsubstantiated deviance. By meeting the given elements, employers need not answer for how culture may have contributed to unchecked boundary testing and breaking at several points before the crime culminated.

When particular guards have a relevant history of deviance, superiors may be found to be liable for negligence. For example, a female was awarded $15,000 in compensatory damages and $5,000 in punitive damages against the director of prison security because she was assaulted by a male prison officer. The victim was awarded $25,000 in punitive damages against the warden. They had noticed that the guard posed a substantial risk of serious harm to female inmates (Riley v. Olk-Long, 2002). Evidence that supervisors successfully investigated to substantiate and punish sexual deviance demonstrates that they did not act with deliberate indifference. However, willingness to investigate and substantiate certain claims may be political and formulated in order to demonstrate a track record that acts as a safety net for supervisors, who intentionally ignore or participate in some forms of institutional deviance. For example, in one case female inmates accused multiple guards of sexual misconduct (Heggenmiller v. Correctional Institution, 2005). Officials demonstrated that they had investigated six incidents and dismissed five guards in four years. This evidence persuaded the court because they showed that they also rigorously prohibited contact between guards and inmates and had trained guards. For a civil rights claim to prevail, deliberate indifference, not merely negligence, must be shown (Scott v. Moore, 1997). Deliberate indifference indicates that actions must have been severe; for example, it is the standard used in Eighth Amendment claims for cruel and unusual punishment (Cusack, 2015). This exceedingly high standard barring thousands of inmates from recovery is not limited to recovery for sexual assault claims made by inmates. It is evident in civil rights claims for sexual harassment made in the free world against employers. The standard has been described by attorneys, judges, and victims as upholding traditionally sexist beliefs that women ought not to work, complain about sexual attention, or criticize males' sexual agendas. Similar to a claim for intentional infliction of emotional distress under state law, conduct must be proven to be outrageous or extreme, and damages must be severe (Smith v. Cochran, 2002). Females may learn to submit to males, while male victims may adhere to a patriarchal code of silence. Therefore, both may internalize, mitigate, and deny the severity of their injuries and fail to document and prove damages.

The American Civil Liberties Union (ACLU) worked on a case in which a female inmate had been seriously abused, but the court dismissed her case before considering the merits (ACLU, n.d.). A senior guard solicited from an inmate sexual conduct in exchange for food and toiletries. When she refused, the guard threatened her, withheld 50% of her food, and denied required hygienic supplies (e.g. toilet paper). The ACLU acknowledges that male guards sexually abuse female inmates "with almost total impunity...., but that the full extent of the problem is unknown because many women prisoners are reluctant to report staff sexual misconduct" (ACLU, n.d.). The inmate was unsure of where or how to report his conduct without being disregarded or labeled a troublemaker and compromising opportunities for parole, visitation, or other privileges. She was also afraid of being placed in solitary confinement. Institutional pressure served its purpose; and the inmate failed to disclose the abuse. Like many prisoners, the inmate was attacked in a laundry room without video surveillance (ACLU, n.d.; Cusack, 2014). He convinced her that she would be labeled a liar if she reported having been forcibly raped. The inmate sustained Post Traumatic Stress Disorder (PTSD) as a result of past abuse, "worthlessness," and "despair" (ACLU, n.d.). She was repeatedly rejected from mental health services. When the prison attempted to prescribe a psychotropic drug, Thorazine, she refused to take it because other inmates had volatile and suicidal reactions. "Despite their greater mental health needs, women in prison often get lower quality mental health care than their male counterparts. Very few prison systems provide counseling. Women attempting to access mental health services are routinely given medication without any opportunity to undergo psychotherapeutic treatment" (ACLU, n.d.).

The inmate reported the rape to a mental health counselor, the prison superintendent, and an investigative officer; however, she was totally ignored (ACLU, n.d.). Reporting to a mental health counselor or physician may be risky because they may view the victim as being weak and then attempt to sexually assault the inmate (Heilbrum, 2009). For example, Flo-Mari Crisostomo, a counselor, exchanged candy for sex with a minor inmate; and Doctor Brian Bohlmann molested several inmates during routine examinations (Hunter, 2009). One year passed before she filed a grievance (ACLU, n.d.). Although her grievance was ignored, she joined a lawsuit against the guard. The case was dismissed, and the guard maintained his employment. Female inmates continued to file complaints about abuse and harassment with the state investigative office. Under the federal Prison Litigation Reform Act (PLRA), an optional piece of legislation adopted by states in exchange for federal funding, inmates may bring suit in civil court after they have complied with and exhausted administrative complaint procedures (e.g. appeals) and remedies (42 U.S.C. § 1997e, 2017). However, "the psychological and emotional effects of custodial sexual abuse make it unreasonable to expect women to be mentally and emotionally capable of following strict grievance procedures that require prisoners to not only report a problem, but also to identify the means and procedures to remedy it" (ACLU, n.d.). Injury, but not harassment or psychological abuse, may be compensated (42 U.S.C. § 1997e(e), 2017).

Institutions may adhere to and facilitate grievance procedures, but inmates and trustworthy guards may be outnumbered by deviants, who intimidate inmates and conspire to cover essential facts that stymie investigations. An inmate, who used an oxygen tank, was repeatedly raped by a "rape squad" (Doe v. Denning, 2007; Hunter, 2009). At night, guards forced her into the guards' restroom. After she reported several of 29 total sexual assaults, she was segregated from the general population; and her letters to the press and her attorney were destroyed. She was impregnated, and said, "You can't fight them because they grip you from behind the neck….You don't know if they're going to kill you" (Hunter, 2009). After reentering society, she delivered her child and sued the warden and assistant warden, two officers, and eight guards.

Inmates are vulnerable to attacks from contractors, who may share institutional rape culture or have rape supportive attitudes that are not present inside institutions. Prisons may be liable for their conduct in some cases. In one case, Shaun McFadden, an employee for a private company, TransCor, illegally transported two female inmates to a hotel. He allegedly gained access to the inmates by claiming to jailers that inmates, who he had transported to the facility, required physicals at a local hospital (Hunter, 2009). The guards released the inmates, who had sex with McFadden, and then notified police that they exchanged sex with him for alcohol and cigarettes. Although TransCor claimed that the events were intentional and unreflective of their corporate operations, no fewer than five other victims had made complaints against TransCor guards. Transport makes inmates vulnerable, because they may be handcuffed, shackled, isolated, kidnapped, and trapped. Entitled guards, who view sex and deviance in relativistic terms, may use patrol vehicles as sex dens. For example, Dewayne Wood kept pornography, condoms, erectile dysfunction medication, and appetite suppressants in his patrol vehicle. He was sentenced to two years incarceration and eight years probation for sexual assault and controlled substance violations.

Harassment is a pervasive social disease. Laws compensating victims are pro-defendant. Guards not only harass inmates, but also decay the work environment by harassing their colleagues (Saunders v. Hunter, 1997). Attorneys may readily and authoritatively paraphrase dicta as a holding, for example "sexual harassment law is not a civility code" for "overly sensitive plaintiffs," in order to discourage victims from suing powerful defendants (Julien, 2016). They may believe that plaintiffs will not survive summary judgment if they have publicly discussed sex, for example writing about birth control on the internet (Thibaut, 2016).

In Saunders v. Hunter (1997), the court showed how swiftly it applies rules to dismiss claims and how attorneys may intentionally or negligently improperly make claims to the detriment of their clients. A corrections officer made claims under Florida's Whistleblower's Act and Fair Labor Standards Act (FLSA) (29 U.S.C.S. § 201, 1997; 42 U.S.C.S. § 1983, 1997; Fla. Stat. § 112.532, 1997; Saunders v. Hunter, 1997). She became an instructor at the academy, where coworkers and supervisors made "profane" and sexual remarks and used gender-biased language (Durkheim, 2008, p. 259; Saunders v. Hunter, 1997). She alleged that the cumulative effect was a hostile work environment permitted under color of law by her supervisors. The lower court agreed; and found that they had constructive knowledge of sexual harassment and knew that their decision to maintain the hostile environment was not lawful. The court nodded at moral reasoning when it maintained her claim against her employers because they are "policy makers," "who with their decisions, created policies and customs" (Saunders v. Hunter, 1997, p. 1245). Their influence on institutional deviance and the public could not be undermined. Their dicta merely seemed to nod at, not acknowledge, morality. "A local government may be sued under § 1983 when execution of a government's policy or custom, whether made by its lawmakers or by those whose edicts or acts may fairly be said to represent official capacity, inflicts the injury the government as an entity is responsible under § 1983" (Saunders v. Hunter, 1997, p. 1246). Because the employers failed to take action against harassment and retaliation, they could be sued under § 1983 (42 U.S.C.S. § 1983, 1997).

The court was unpersuaded that the totality of her facts demonstrated a First Amendment violation; and she was barred from a FLSA claim through a § 1983 claim for deprivation of constitutional rights (Saunders v. Hunter, 1997). Judge Elizabeth A. Kovachevich of the Eleventh Circuit Court of Appeals agreed and dismissed Fifth and Fourteenth Amendment due process claims. The appellate court agreed that claims should not be dismissed by the district court, unless it seemed beyond any doubt that the plaintiff would not be able to prove material facts. The court will view facts in a light most favorable to the plaintiff; but, to survive a motion to dismiss, the plaintiff must show sufficient facts, not merely label a claim or imply the facts. This threshold ought to be low; but, plaintiffs' claims are scrutinized at the summary judgment stage in federal court, and effectively the burden is exceedingly high. The appellate court repeated sexual harassment claim jargon explaining that under Title VII claims, a hostile work environment is proven by facts demonstrating severe or pervasive conduct. Courts rarely find that facts meet this standard. The plaintiff's claim was not brought under Title VII, it was brought under 42 U.S.C. § 1983 as a deprivation of her First, Fourth, Fifth, and Fourteenth Amendment rights. The Title VII standard may have been mentioned by the court to indicate that their decision was made to be consistent with pro-defendant federal court judges frequently dismissing Title VII claims. A plaintiff must demonstrate that deprivation of a constitutional right was committed under color of state law. To act under color of law is "acting with the power possessed by virtue of the defendant's employment with the state" (Saunders v. Hunter, 1997, p. 1242). Therefore, complaints made against non-supervisors must be dismissed because non-supervisors lack "supervisory authority to create a hostile work environment" (Saunders v. Hunter, 1997, p. 1242). The court treated the plaintiff's colleague's "de facto authority over her" as a conclusory and vague allegation (Saunders v. Hunter, 1997, p. 1242). Her allegations may have been reasonable because in some institutions responsibility may be "diffused throughout the office" (Easley v. Apollo Detective Agency, 1979, p. 521; Minuti, 1988; Saunders v. Hunter, 1997). However, the court dismissed her claim.

Supervisors may act as private individuals, not under color of law, when the violations that they commit are not committed using the state's power (Saunders v. Hunter, 1997). In Saunders v. Hunter (1997), the facts alleged about the plaintiff's supervisors demonstrated that, if true, then they acted under the color of law to maintain a hostile work environment that unreasonably interfered with work performance, intimidated, or offended the plaintiff. For example, she was held by male guards and hosed-off while her supervisors watched. In the court's opinion, only her supervisors may have acted under color of law. Superiors acting under color of law may be immunized if the law was not clearly established at the time the rights were violated. If they believed that their failure to act was lawful, then they will be entitled to qualified immunity. The court found that the employer could not have believed that in light of clearly established law it would have been acceptable and lawful to ignore sexual harassment and discrimination.

The appellate court applied a four-part test to determine whether employers retaliated against protected speech (Saunders v. Hunter, 1997). The first prong considered whether the employee exercised the First Amendment on a matter of public concern. The employer may argue that the employee's speech was private, and not of public concern. Yet, pervasive sexual harassment under color of law would be a matter of public concern. However, if the plaintiff was speaking as a private citizen when she complained, and not as a citizen complaining about official conduct, then her personal interest would not satisfy the first prong. In the second prong, the test balanced free speech interests against the state's interest in promoting public services. If the plaintiff's interest outweighs the employer's interest, then the third prong requires the court to determine whether the plaintiff's speech played a substantial role in the employee being discharged or demoted. The fourth prong allows the state to prove by the preponderance of the evidence that regardless of the plaintiff's speech, the employee would have been demoted or dismissed.

The plaintiff's First Amendment claim was dismissed after the court analyzed the first prong (Saunders v. Hunter, 1997). The court positioned itself to side with defendants by judging the content and context of sexual harassment complaints made to government employers. The court may look for evidence to finely distinguish between a complaint made in the interest of the public and a complaint made to alleviate unwanted working conditions maintained under color of law. Employers may destroy or fabricate evidence, for example in this case a time sheet (McLaughlin, 2016; Saunders v. Hunter, 1997). A complainant must have evidence that she complained to the employer in the public interest, not to benefit or protect herself; "however, the fact that the topic of employees' speech is of public concern is not the deciding factor" (Saunders v. Hunter, 1997, p. 1243). The court found that because the employer did not harass and retaliate against other employees, the employer's conduct did not demonstrate a matter for public concern; and therefore, her speech was a private complaint. The employee did not allege that sexual harassment was pervasive against other employees and contributed to a hostile work environment. In fairness, the court could not find for the plaintiff; however, had the law considered whether morals intended to be upheld by the state were violated by persons acting under color of law, then the plaintiff undoubtedly would have prevailed.

The court noted that the plaintiff was unable to produce any binding or persuasive case law demonstrating that the Fourteenth Amendment should be applied to an employment-based violation (Saunders v. Hunter, 1997). The court said that when she was hosed, her liberty had not been deprived similarly to arrest; and therefore, her Fourteenth Amendment claim was not viable. A Fifth Amendment claim may apply when the federal government is the defendant; however, she was employed by a state agency. Claims against state employers may be made under the Fourteenth Amendment when a plaintiff can demonstrate that she was deprived without due process of life, liberty, or property. Her allegation of deprivation arose when the administration failed properly to forward her request for a professional opportunity after she complained to her employer about sexual harassment. She was questioned about her complaint during an evaluation. The underlying facts were not of public record, and the court tidily dismissed her claim. The court did not dismiss her equal protection claim under the Fourteenth Amendment.

Courts are reluctant to consider sexual harassment by women against males or females. An allegation that a harasser is a lesbian, who harasses women, is a relatively new and somewhat untested exception to this form of judicial advocacy whereby judges deny that sexual harassment exists; that women are capable of it; and that harassers and employers, who maintain hostile work environments, should be held responsible (Dilman, 2016; Julien, 2016). In prisons, gossip culture may be one reason that female guards are not confronted by employers when they commit sexual deviance with staff and inmates (Williams, Giuffre, & Dellinger, 1999). They may participate in gossip culture; tolerate rumors and complaints as a form of gossip; or believe that rumors of lesbianism are stereotypes about guards that should be ignored in the interest of equal protection. The may not be able to distinguish between gossip and "an open secret" (McLaughlin, 2016). However, studies show that female officers are as likely as or likelier than male guards to have sexual relationships with female inmates; and increasing anecdotal evidence demonstrates that women (e.g. mothers of young children) are equally responsible as males for all types of sex crime perpetration. Female guards are as likely as male guards to lose their jobs because they had sex with inmates. Rumors may also persist because dozens of inmates may be assigned to a single dormitory supervised by a single guard for an eight-hour shift, unlike panopticon designs (Foucault, 1995; Williams, Giuffre, & Dellinger, 1999). In these contexts, dichotomies, such as married/single, heterosexual/homosexual, and deviant/normal evaporate.

Gary L. Heyward described his career as an officer at Riker's Island (Heyward, 2015). He explained the inner-workings of prison black markets and corruption; as well as sexual immorality between guards, within the inmate population, and between guards and inmates. For example, pillow talk between officers may serve as pipelines for information from higher ranking officers about how officers will be investigated and disciplined for criminal activity (Gerth & Mills, 1946). In his biography *Corruption Officer*, Heyward graphically depicts sexual liaisons between guards, who fornicate, participate in adultery, and conceive children out-of-wedlock within the prison during work hours (Cusack, 2014; Heyward, 2015). More than one female guard earned supplementary income from working as a "copstitute" (Heyward, 2015, p. 184).

A female officer explained her prostitution scheme to Heyward and then roped him into her crime ring.

> 'I started with a few officers in here that have been all in my face trying to sex me. They were always offering to buy me things and take me on trips and all that. S[o] I just converted all that shit to cash….The first one, I just told him that I needed a bill paid and he did it for a two-minute slurp session.' She makes a slurp sound with her mouth and says, 'Right there in area two top….Honestly speaking, most of these chicks around here are giving it up for free, and besides me I know of only two others that are rocking like me, but they are bum bitches and be settling….A chick like me is making school tuition and mortgage money.'…She leans back again so that I can see her cunt lips through her pants and pops it twice (Heyward, 2015, pp. 141-142).

Their business expanded to include inmate clientele. Heyward would keep watch for the female officer while she fornicated with males in utility closets and other locations throughout the prison.

> I had the other inmates glued to the television on both sides because I had put a porno show on the tube….While they watched the DVD, I checked up on her and [the inmate] to make sure that he wasn't killing her ass in there. I cracked the door open a little and saw that he had her bent over holding onto some dirty pipes while he was on his tippy toes hitting it. I chuckled as I heard her badge keep hitting the metal pipes. That was what was making the *tink*, *tink*, *tink* sound….[A]fter the porno went off they all went to their cells and locked in, putting up the towels so they could make love to themselves in private (Heyward, 2015, pp. 184-185).

Some immorality was consensual, but often it was used sadistically to inflict punishment and retaliation. It came in the form of sexual harassment and contact. In one case, a female officer manipulated the system falsely to portray an inmate as a homosexual in need of special housing arrangements because he insulted her by saying "THAT BITCH CAN SUCK MY DICK IN MACY'S WINDOWS AT CHRISTMAS" (Heyward, 2015, p. 121)! Even though she retaliated against the inmate by "getting really disrespectful with the inmate, telling him he is a bum nigga for being in jail and how some other man is butt-fucking his girl right now, and so on," the inmate continued to harass and insult the female officer (Heyward, 2015, p. 121).

> Bitch, you better respect J-Murder, you ugly fat bucktooth orangutan-in-the-face-looking-bitch! Look atcha [sic] self. I wouldn't fuck you right now if you begged me, and I've been down some joints. You know you ain't no dime on the streets. Hell, you ain't even average! Don't let these niggas in here fool you into thinking you're somebody, 'cause you're not. They just trying to get their dicks sucked! You're just a thirsty ass cock-gazing bitch, always creeping up on a nigga when he gets out the shower trying to get a peek. You ain't getting no dick on the streets but walk around here like you the Queen of Sheeba [sic] or something (Heyward, 2015, p. 122).

The female officer began to cry, but the inmate relentlessly harassed her. "'Don't worry, bitch. I'm a nice guy. I'll let you lick it later on when nobody's around.' Then he step[ped] back and expose[d] himself" (Heyward, 2015, p. 122). She defended her plan to destroy the inmate by claiming that females must use their minds, not brawn, to level the playing field. First, she used a network of prison officers to distribute the inmate's commissary number to drain J-Murder's commissary account balance. Then, she forged a form signed by the inmate claiming that he was a homosexual, who wanted to be relocated to protective housing. The officer claimed that because the inmate exposed himself, her supervisor would accept the forged document, which effectively sentenced the inmate to violent sexual assault in the homosexual housing wing.

Language used by inmates toward officers allegedly instigated immoral retaliation; however, officers used similarly terse and immoral language toward inmates (Cusack, 2013; Cusack, 2015; Heyward, 2015). For example, Heyward described language typically used during strip and cavity searches during which inmates are ordered by officers to display their genitals, tongues, and hands (Cusack, 2014; Cusack, 2015; Heyward, 2015).

> After the clothing is searched comes the most embarrassing and humiliating part for the inmate, the cavity search. An officer orders an inmate to 'open ya [sic] cocksucker (mouth) and stick out ya ball licker (tongue).' The officer says to another officer, 'Half of these punks are fags anyway.'…Then it's, 'Let me see ya dick beaters (hands)'….'Now turn around and bend over and spread ya aasssss [sic] cheeks.' 'Let me see if you're a lover (been having anal sex) or a fighter (been keeping the wolves up off ya)' (Heyward, 2015, p. 126).

In comparison to inmates' grotesque treatment of guards, guards' language describing and perhaps demonstrating immorality seems to be situationally appropriate; but, officers' domination continually prevails inside prisons where they torture inmates with immorality.

Heyward described J-Murders' fate in housing arrangements for homosexuals.

> There was an inmate under the bed wrapped from head to toe in a sheet with nothing exposed but his buttocks, which had blood dripping from them. I also saw something lightly cut into his skin, but I could not make out what it was. I panicked and frantically dragged him from under the bed, hoping he wasn't dead. I heard him moan, which was a relief. Then I rolled him over and noticed that his whole head was wrapped, with just his mouth exposed. I could see dried-up semen all around his mouth and I could only imagine what they used him for (Heyward, 2015, p. 131).

Heyward explained how authority figures abuse discretion and perpetuate immorality to eradicate immoral character traits in inmates.

> I felt that a lot of these young men that come through here really think that jail is some kind of badge of honor and really don't realize that they are in here with people that have been transformed to individuals that no longer live by society's rules....Now he was dressed and lying on his bed in a fetal position facing the wall so that I could not see his face....I personally escorted the inmate out of his cell and out of the area. He had his head down and his belongings in a bag draped over his shoulders. Gone was the young vibrant loudmouth gangster from the other day. Gone was the disrespectful penis-flashing individual and gone altogether was the gang-banging, I-can-live-anywhere thug known as J-Murder. In his place was a different person, someone who would probably have mental problems and nightmares for years to come from what he's just suffered. From now on J-Murder...would assume a new name. He would be called 'Juicy Fruits' by certain individuals. The reason I know this is that it was carved in his back for bend-over purposes—right above his butt cheeks (Heyward, 2015, pp. 132-133).

It seems that the officers used "street justice" to match immoral criminals' behavior in an attempt to achieve compliance because legal processes were ineffective.

Hayward described how moral corrosion permeates prison walls.

> I parked a few blocks down from where I picked her up so that I could get this over with and be on my way. [An inmate's grandmother] handed me the liquor and the cake and before she handed me the money she said, 'Um, the money is a little short.'...She sat back in her seat and said, 'I'll do anything to make sure my baby is alright.' Then she put her thumb in her mouth....She looked around to see who was around then leaned over into my lap and started to unbuckle my belt. Guess what? I did not stop her....It felt eerie seeing her salt-and-pepper hair go up and down[, but it was]...so good that it took me two seconds to upchuck and release my [sperm]....She pointed to my dashboard and my eyes widened when I saw why her performance was so good. Sitting up near my window was a full set of dentures! She had gummed me (Heyward, 2015, pp. 175-176).

Heyward's autobiography demonstrates the difficulty with instituting morality and uniformly enforcing laws and policies to protect society (Heyward, 2015).

CHAPTER FIVE

OFFICIALS

Politicians and public officials regularly become embroiled in political scandal involving sexual deviance and sex crimes (Barayuga, 2006; Fox News, 2014; Kertscher, 2010). Demand by the American public for politicians to behave morally while in office may be in decline. Some members of the public may complain about ethics violations relating to fiscal irresponsibility; yet, overlook relationships between civic duties and morality. Others may be titillated by deviance, acts that defy tradition, and tales of immorality. Yet, many voters may consider the relevance of morality. Numerous politicians' careers have been doomed or bogged by sexual scandal (e.g. John Edwards) demonstrating that although the public may expect politicians to be self-serving, and possibly untrustworthy, they may vote for a candidate, who may be likelier to share and espouse their moral values. For example, conservatives may promote traditional family values, while liberals promote marriage equality; however, candidates seldom are elected by promoting premarital sex and adultery.

Appointed officials may face similar public scrutiny, even in cases when the public may have been unaware of their names or titles prior to a scandal. Although they lose their public careers, their influence on society continues. The public may feel betrayed, and at the same time, be interested in the participants' methods for having affairs, for example by using government equipment. Paula Broadwell and Central Intelligence Agency (CIA) Director David Petraeus shocked America with their clever use of a shared email box in which they left email drafts that allowed them to avoid documenting their affair in transmitted emails. Some immoral citizens or those experiencing weakness, alienation, strain, or decay may be influenced by scandals (Baum, 2006). Some may go so far as to use officials as role models for sex, power, romance, and career advancement. The cumulative effect is association between public and private immorality rather than morality.

Public figures may participate in immoral acts because they feel pressure to conform to their predecessors' traditional behavior in the face of progressive standards. Old guards, such as patriarchs, may have treated sex differently than their contemporary constituents would anticipate moral

Fig. 5.1, Capitol Hill, Washington, D.C.

Fig. 5.2, Site of Fred Lippman's office, Florida Legislature, Tallahassee, Florida.

people should (e.g. gay bashing and sexism). Rumors or unspoken behavioral cues may suggest to politicians how they should behave to signify their status and willingness to participate in longstanding patterns or relevant trends. They may succumb to pressure from subordinates, who are seeking to climb to power using worn paths, including those involving sex, moral corruption, and usurpation. Subordinates may influence, take advantage of, pressure, or set-up their employers in order to blackmail, influence, and use them. They may use their positions as political, personal, and professional litmus paper to test the climate. Some employees may feel that they are required to service politicians or perform *quid pro quos,* while others may relish the opportunity to work on Capitol Hill or in other political arenas.

Fred Lippman was caught in a complex sexual scandal during his tenure in the Florida House of Representatives (*The New York Times*, 1991; Van Gieson, 1990). Other politicians were terrified that their secrecy would be come back to haunt them. Kathie Jennings, Lippman's employee alleged that he fondled and kissed her against her will. The State of Florida secretly settled with her for $47,000 to purchase her silence and prevent her from filing a $300,000 lawsuit against Lippman and Ken Sarvis, another employee acting as House Committee staff director. The terms of their agreement required that she repay $94,000 if she violated the gag clause. As the State Attorney's office investigated, political and public pressure for an investigation by the House of Representatives mounted because the House has refused to release her from the clause. However, a judge released her from the clause to allow prosecutors to investigate, but she was unable to talk with the press. The main pipeline for information had been other politicians and state employees concerned with how the scandal may unfold and reveal their secrets. The rumors about the settlement only emerged after he was elected as majority leader; and her allegations only emerged after she was denied a promised position in corrections. Although the investigation showed that she may have been unqualified for the job, the allegations were serious. For example, she said that Lippman once burst into the bedroom of an apartment that she rented from him and attempted to disrobe her (*The New York Times*, 1991). He allegedly coerced her to work for him as an apartment manager during business hours while she was employed by the state (Van Gieson, 1990). The investigators were determined from "the very beginning" to uncover "official misconduct;" however, they "also looked at the sexual side of it" (Van Gieson, 1990). The payment was not made to restore her dignity or appease their conscience (Dostoyevsky, 2001). Rather, she was paid the equivalent of two years' salary because Lipmann's harassment "'showed substantial potential liability" (Van Gieson, 1990). Other staffers corroborated her allegations against Sarvis; and the government investigated how the House justified the payment. The state's conspiracy to hide the harassment, including "bypassing normal state procedures for settling liability claims," and destroying evidence in its possession, illustrated how moral decay is a cause and effect of the state's incapacity to enforce morality. Dominic Calabro, a political overseer, said "the process leaves a tremendous amount to be desired….I think the attitude (that) the rules are different here is a statement of an era long past. There needs to be some noticeable reform of fiscal management by the Florida Legislature so it's more accountable, more honest to the taxpayers and more responsive and fair to all members" (Van Gieson, 1990). Rationally, his statement could have been restated to describe morality, not fiscal responsibility; but, a moralized call to action may have motivated fewer citizens than a call for fiscal responsibility. For example, *The New York Times* (1991) described the extent to which a sexual scandal motivated the public when it said that the events "proved both titillating and embarrassing," but not empowering or shocking to the public conscience.

A grand jury was "appalled that 20 years after Watergate, there are reasonably intelligent individuals, who have apparently not learned that secrecy compounds all problems and controversies" (*The New York Times*, 1991). They failed to indict Lippman or Sarvis, but recommended that House procedures be improved for dealing with complaints about sexual harassment. Jurors also wanted the House to "help end sexual innuendo in the workplace" (*The New York Times*, 1991). They may have believed in the House's ability to do that for its own employees; demonstrate leadership in that regard; and design strong policies and laws to prevent and punish harassing speech in the workplace. Homages to gender equality may have increased since then, and Florida's sexual harassment and whistleblower laws may help some victims unassisted by the federal court system (Boswell, 2016). However, courts' reluctance to hear cases continues to churn the culture of sexual harassment in Florida workplaces, particularly in legal and legislative places of employment and training programs for justice members (e.g. academies and criminal justice classes). The payment was disbursed one year after the State Attorney's office originally investigated, but did not prosecute, Lippman's obsession with the victim, which led him to offer her "pot," "coke," and "alcohol" to arouse her (*The New York Times*, 1991). He denied that he treated her differently than other employees and referred to his long-term marriage as evidence of his likelihood not to have committed sexual deviance. Perhaps his manipulative display of power over the system, his colleagues, and his wife was like pornography for other legislators and members of the public attracted to eccentric displays of corruption and sexual deviance (LeBlanc, 2017; Sheer, 2008).

Lobbying influences legislators to champion for sexual deviance, for example free speech in pornography instead of traditional morality (Rosoff, Pontell, & Tillman, 2014). These influences may reflect or affect their personal perspectives on sexuality and deviance. Sexual deviance may be a type of "defiance" that fosters "expression of repression and a battle against repression" (Franco, 2010). However, "the one eyed shrew of the heterosexual dollar" may be the driving force behind political support for decriminalization of obscenity and tolerance for indecency (Ginsberg, 1956).

> Each year, an intricate budget-allocation minuet—a dance of legislators, Pentagon officials and corporate lobbyists—is conducted and largely ignored by the mass media, and therefore the public. This annual ritual matters a great deal in the division of spoils, and it is a process deliberately shrouded in mystery by its primary practitioners. Only through a rare window, and usually when scandal erupts, do outsiders catch a glimpse of the system's deep corruption (Sheer, 2008).

Lobbying may be direct, for example by the Free Speech Coalition, a powerful lobby of pornographers (Ashcroft v. Free Speech Coalition, 2002; Cusack, 2011). Indirect lobbying may be as persuasive and revelatory of public figures' personal agendas. For example, Donald Trump and Arnold Schwarzenegger have visited the Playboy Mansion; Schwarzenegger has been interviewed by the magazine; and Trump has appeared on its cover (Dowd, 2016; Gries, 2016). Mary Fallin, who served as Governor of Oklahoma and as a U.S. Congresswoman, became engaged at the Playboy Mansion (Hinton, 1998; *Sooner Politics*, 2015). She allegedly had an extramarital affair with a married state trooper, Greg Allen, who worked as her bodyguard. He admitted to participating in romantic, unprofessional conduct and was permitted to resign. Representative Loretta Sanchez was to speak at the Democratic National Convention in 2000; however, she was denied the privilege, but later reinstated, after she defied an order from Vice President Al Gore to cancel a fundraiser at the Playboy Mansion (Finnegan, 2015). Critics blamed Gore's "moralistic tone" on the religious values of his running mate, Joe Lieberman. Lieberman was described as "an overtly religious moral crusader best known for railing against excessive sexuality" in media and politics (*The Washington Times*, 2000). Playboy depicted Lieberman as being an extreme fundamentalist, who had a negative effect on Gore (*The Washington Times*, 2000). "Playboy has always been very supportive of the Democratic Party;" and yet, it ridiculed Gore by comparing his "harsh" stance to Minister Pat Robertson's position on the "very, very conservative right" (*The Washington Times*, 2000). Gore refused to return campaign contributions from Hugh Hefner and his daughter, Christie Hefner, because donations were not made as part of a fundraiser at Playboy Mansion (*The Washington Times*, 2000). "One could call her actions eccentric, or courageously charting her own path, or bad political judgment;" but, "they're not actions that enhance someone's ability to run a credible Senate campaign" (Finnegan, 2015). Sanchez moved her fundraiser because her conflict with the Democratic Party would not "help with donors….[or] with other elected leaders" (Finnegan, 2015). Heffner is one of the top donors to the Democratic Party in Orange County, a county which is outside Sanchez's district. He claims to support her political agenda. "If that's true then Sanchez is the only individual member of Congress who shares his progressive views, which would be strange since Sanchez—one of the few remaining members of the fiscally conservative and slightly center-left Blue Dog Caucus—is rarely, if ever, accused of being a progressive" (Fleming, 2016). Critics speculate that she publicly affiliates with Playboy because politicians "need to capture the public's imagination;" therefore, "her eccentricities will really help her" (Finnegan, 2015). Sexual "eccentricities" alleged at the Playboy mansion include group sex, homosexuality, a collection of rare obscenity, and bestiality (Allen, 1982; Cusack, 2013; Cusack, 2015; Cusack, 2016; Lovelace, 2006).

The Playboy Foundation annually has awarded recognition to influential persons, such as law professor Bruce Rogow; Hans Arthur Linde, a member of the Oregon Supreme Court; Thomas Andrews Drake, a former senior executive of the U.S. National Security Agency (NSA); and Drake's attorney, Jesselyn Radack (Gries, 2016; Leflore, 2016; McMullan, 2010; Playboy, n.d.).

Gloria Steinem, who began her career in feminism by working undercover at the Playboy Club, discussed intersections between society, *Playboy*, and politics (Begley, 2015; Cusack, 2014). She demonstrated her ideas by explaining that the Playboy corporation necessarily aggrandizes men and objectifies women. Political relationships are rooted in this premise. Steinem described *Playboy*'s decision briefly to terminate their publication of nude pictorials.

> [I]t's as if the [National Rifle Association] NRA said we're no longer selling handguns because now assault weapons are so available. For *Playboy* to change, they would have to change their brain cells, their language, their title, and every thought they've ever had….It's not as violent and sadistic as some other magazines and online pornography, but it's a question of degree, not kind. They seem to have had a rule called

> 'women can't win,' even in fiction. The title alone is absurd, 'playboy' (Begley, 2015).

Her description of the title as "absurd" eliminates any question of whether the editorial subtly encourages women sexually to exploit themselves to seduce, objectify, game, and toy with males (Begley, 2015; Cusack, 2015).

Steinem repeated a sentiment expressed during the Hillary Rodham Clinton-Donald Trump election. Rodham Clinton would have been lambasted far worse than Trump had she said that fame practically entitled her to "grab [women] by the pussy" because she "can do anything," a comment made by Trump and published by the press during the election (Complex News, 2016; Hilton, 2008). Steinem said, "I was thinking about this the other day: suppose Hugh Hefner had never existed, and I as a feminist wrote a novel making up such a man, they would call me anti-male" (Begley, 2015)! She said that in a feminist perspective, Heffner is rendered to be impossibly "ridiculous" (Begley, 2015). Similarly, she explained how Rodham Clinton's marriage to Bill Clinton ought to have legitimized her enough with the old guard; but yet, some Democrats failed to vote for her because of their anti-women perspectives.

> I wouldn't try to attribute motives to people I don't know, but I had the impression then that she was threatening to some women because she was an implicit criticism of their lives. She had done more, despite being a woman. She had a partnership with her husband who respected her intellect and political ability, and they did not….I think in a larger sense, we are all, women and men, mostly raised by women, so we may associate female authority with childhood. It may seem threatening[.] [W]e may even feel regressed to childhood when we see a powerful woman. That happens more to men, I think that's part of the reason that some otherwise very professional male journalists have said some pretty dumb things in 2008 about Hillary, you know, 'I cross my legs whenever I see her,' all kind of crazy things, because…perhaps when they saw a powerful woman, they felt regressed to childhood, even if they didn't understand why (Begley, 2015).

Steinem explained that women do not necessarily vote for their own sex, whereas men may. This may be one reason why sex-based lobbying may work against women rather than for women.

Lobbyers are likelier not only to use the force of pornography to appeal to male interests, but male candidates may be likelier to persuade males and females because there are more male politicians and men are depicted as controlling sexuality in American society. Steinem said that some female candidates do not support women and should not be put into power. "[I]t's about substance and consciousness. However, there is something very important about having lived as a female human being....You know a reality that other people may not" share (Begley, 2015). She commented that women can be "helpful...in political office," a description that seems shamefaced (Begley, 2015). Steinem's word choice may reveal a fear of women's powerlessness that is engrained in American consciousness perhaps through morality literature. For example, the Biblical tale of Adam and Eve depicts Eve as being a helper to Adam; and several stories depict females as being servants (e.g. Abraham and Hagar have Esau) (Cusack, 2016). This worldview no doubt contributes to the moral decay of women seeking power, who are willing to build networks under a glass ceiling "reinforced with steel beams" based on sexual worth rather than moral conviction (Alter, 2016; Valenti, 2007).

Politicians concerned with enforcing morality laws in a manner that permits lawful pornography to be protected as free speech, while opposing permeation of hardcore pornography into society, risk being affiliated with anti-pornography groups and religious organizations, who feel that pornography is like "spiritual prostitution" (Heimbach, 2004; Israel, 2014). Although taking this risk may seem to favor the entertainment industry, it challenges other major industries that have favored "dignity" over profit (NCSE, n.d.). For example, a movement in the hospitality industry has resulted in banning pornography from hotels, such as Intercontinental, Hilton, Hyatt, and Starwood. Other industries have stopped pornography from spreading into the mainstream. For example, sexually explicit applications and advertisements have been blocked from Google despite loss of tremendous revenue.

Neither legal nor illegal pornography may be blamed for the government's disempowerment to enforce morality-based laws, particularly when pornography consumption has been credited with reducing other gender-based sex crimes, such as marital rape (Cusack, 2013; Hickman & Muehlenhard, 2007; Woolley, 2007). These claims allege that pornography helps to alleviate sex crimes in conjunction with relatively new morality-based laws, such as those that prohibit marital rape. However, married women are less likely to report spouse-perpetrated rape than rape violently perpetrated by strangers. Married women may be unaware of how pornography reduces marital rape; and instead, may claim that their husbands are likelier to participate in sex crimes due to pornography use (e.g. prostitution or child pornography). Whether motivated by Humean virtue or Kantian praxis, the teleological goal is to make moral decisions in the public interest (Denis & Wilson, 2016; Schiller, 2004). Both etiologies, criminalization and protection for pornography, may result in the state fortifying its authority to regulate morality and implement its police power.

Public figures may behave in office as they do in their private lives. Failure to hold them accountable in their private lives may train them or entitle them to avoid accountability in public office. A reciprocal affect may also be evident when corrupt politicians are disciplined by society, it may encourage individuals privately harmed by politicians to defend themselves. For example, former Miami Beach Mayor and braggadocious criminal, Alex Daoud, was incarcerated following his conviction for racketeering (Daoud, 2008). After he was released from prison, he continued to exhibit deviant behavior (e.g. exploit strippers) (Teproff, 2014). His daughter eventually sued him. Politicians may continue to be corrupt in office because their proponents fail to protest, even though privately they admonish them. Proponents may respect the voting process and take pride in their power to put candidates into office; and thus, resist criticizing immoral actions, even when those actions take sexual liberties that some supportive voters may prefer were decriminalized for all people. Conversely, consistently moral lawmakers may have a steadying effect on constituents and justice members publicly and privately.

A culture that breeds secrecy, including the legislative process, lobbying, negotiations, and unpublicized outcomes, may foster indecency and deviance in Washington, D.C. (Matlin, 2008). In this climate, lobbyists may indeed become crusaders against sex crime (Ashcroft v. Free Speech Coalition, 2002; Cusack, 2012; Matlin, 2008). For example, *Hustler* Magazine forced Senator David Vitter to admit that he paid for sex. Vitter denied that he was a customer of Deborah Jeane Palfrey, the D.C. Madam; however, records demonstrated that he had called her multiple times and utilized a brothel in New Orleans, Louisiana. Prostitution is rampant in D.C., and sexual services may be supplied by politicians and their staffers. Prostitution was brought to light during Eliot Spitzer's scandal, when he was caught paying large sums of money to prostitutes at the Mayflower Hotel. Representative Mark Foley resigned from the House of Representatives when he was caught having sex with young adults, who worked as his congressional pages. Senator Gary Hart's political career concluded after the *Miami Herald* showed him spending the night at the home of his paramour, Donna Rice. Representative Gary Condit's intern, Chandra Levy, was killed; and her mother claimed that she dated Condit.

Fig. 5.3, Senator David Vitter's office, 516 Hart Senate Office Building, Washington, D.C.

Fig. 5.4, Site of Eliot Spitzer's sex affair with known prostitutes, Washington, D.C.

Fig. 5.5, Site of Gary Condit's residence when he allegedly dated Chandra Levy, 2600 block of Adams Mill Road NW, Washington, D.C.

Same-sex affairs and prostitution are also rampant in politics; and some politicians have alleged that they are less risky because of social shame barriers. For example, Florida Lieutenant Governor Jennifer Carroll and a female aide, Beatriz Ramos, were observed by Carletha Cole in "a compromising position" inside her office (Peltier, 2012). Cole publicly stated that Carroll, who is married, had "misuse[d]" her "office for sexual escapade" (Peltier, 2012). Cole, an Episcopal minister, was then fired and arrested for making unauthorized recordings in the office. Cole, described as "a loose cannon," leaked the recordings to the press (Peltier, 2012). Society may have opted to ignore the affair because it was unappealing.

Legislators suffering from mental defects may engage in illegal activities. For example, former Illinois State Representative Keith Farnham used computers in his office and home to transmit child pornography (Rogers, 2014). He pleaded guilty and faced a minimum sentence of five years for emailing pornographic videos of children, including infants. In his state office and home, he possessed nearly 3,000 depictions of prepubescent children being sexually and sadistically abused. He resigned when U.S Immigration and Customs officers found that he had chatted online about raping a six year-old girl. Farnham claimed to authorities that he had not actually abused a child. Another lawmaker, Harry Morel, Jr., psychopathically harassed, fondled, and participated in *quid pro quos* with dozens of women while reducing defendants' charges, falsifying documents, racketeering, and breaking other laws (Bacon-Blood, 2016; Bacon-Blood, 2016).

Fig. 5.6, Site of Gary Hart's affair with Donna Rice, 517 Sixth St. SE, Washington, D.C.

Fig. 5.7, Mark Foley's residence at the time of his sexual deviance, 137 D St. SE, Washington, D.C.

Fig. 5.8, Florida Lieutenant Governor's office, 400 S. Monroe St., Tallahassee, Florida.

As lawmakers continue to decriminalize immorality and secularize sex, they may continue to exercise their liberty as citizens; for example, by having noncriminal extramarital affairs, which may demonstrate to the public that the state's morality power is irrelevant (Greeley, 2004). Hobbes (2013) explained that when restraints are absent, then people use their power to fulfil whatever desires seem reasonable.

> By LIBERTY, is understood, according to the proper signification of the word, the absence of [external] Impediments: which Impediments, may oft take away part of a [man's] power to do what [he] would; but cannot hinder him from using the power left him, according as his judgement, and reason shall dictate to him (Hobbes, 2013, p. 111).

Though society has benefited from decriminalization of some allegedly immoral acts, such as increased domestic violence protection for same-sex couples and emerging equality in public indecency laws, Justice Antonin Scalia's fear, described in Lawrence v. Texas (2003), is the total loss of legislative authority to prevent immorality, for example crimes against nature, including incest and bestiality (Cusack, 2016; Cusack, 2017;

Davis, 2013; Ring, 2004). Without power to enforce morality, people would have a right to be completely immoral to victims' detriment.

> A LAW OF NATURE, (Lex Naturalis,) is a Precept, or [general] Rule, found out by Reason, by which a man is forbidden to do, that, which is destructive of his life, or taketh away the means of preserving the same; and to omit, that, by which he [thinks] it may be best preserved. For though they that speak of this subject, use to confound Jus, and Lex, Right and Law; yet they ought to be distinguished; because RIGHT, [consists] in liberty to do, or to [forbear]; Whereas LAW, [determines], and [binds] to one of them: so that Law, and Right, differ as much, as Obligation, and Liberty; which in one and the same matter are inconsistent (Hobbes, 2013, p. 111).

A greater danger may be in allowing the law to control sex and overtake fundamental rights to privacy, sex, and family because law condemns individuals, who commit harmless acts that do not disrupt fulfillment of public duties.

The law cannot rigidly be designed to control deviant lawmakers simply to create role models for people, who prefer excessively restrictive laws to autonomy and self-control.

> [B]ecause every Subject is by this Institution Author of all the Actions, and Judgements of the [Sovereign] Instituted; it [follows], that whatsoever he doth, it can be no injury to any of his Subjects; nor ought he to be by any of them accused of Injustice. For he that doth [anything] by authority from another, doth therein no injury to him by whose authority he [acts]: But by this Institution of a Commonwealth, every particular man is Author of all the [Sovereign] doth; and consequently he that [complains] of injury from his [Sovereign], [complains] of that whereof he [himself] is Author; and therefore ought not to accuse any man but [himself]; no nor [himself] of injury; because to do injury to ones [self], is impossible. It is true that they that have [Sovereign] power, may commit Iniquity; but not Injustice, or Injury in the proper signification (Hobbes, 2013, p. 155).

Even when laws are unjust, legal avenues must be used to strike laws and terminate the government's power to enforce laws.

Elected leaders may use persuasion to ask people to follow customs, but in order to use the police to enforce laws, laws must be just. Just laws are enforceable. When elected leaders appear to be conspiring to ignore widespread abuse of the law, their actions infect the sovereign. Although the sovereign may not be punished, the sovereign may lose the appearance of having a legitimate basis for imposing any morality-based restrictions. Like a body losing a pulse, life may not be pumped into the extremities through the blood. "[C]onsequently to that which was [said] last, no man that hath [Sovereign] power can justly be put to death, or otherwise in any manner by his Subjects punished. For seeing every Subject is author of the actions of his [Sovereign]; he [punishes] another, for the actions committed by" himself (Hobbes, 2013, p. 151). The government may lose the appearance of legitimacy, which can only be regained by establishing laws that the people want to obey, particularly those, who are most willing to deviate from norms, but desire structure. Although this may seem ideal, it may defeat the purpose of the law in some regards.

Seldom citizens effectively use morality-based laws to enforce morality against deviant legislators. Some legislators, such as Rafael Mack, refuse to step down and must be removed by court order (Bryan, 2014). Other legislators may admit to sexual deviance, but defend their positions. One county commissioner even asked to be reimbursed for attorney's fees. The court analyzed whether his underlying conduct entitled him to relief. Eugene Danaher, a citizen of Leon County, Florida, filed an ethics complaint against Commissioner Rudy Maloy. The Florida Commission on Ethics ("Commission") convened to determine whether Maloy violated the Florida Code of Ethics for Public Officers and Employees (Fla. Stat. §§ 112.311-.326, 2000; Maloy v. Board, 2007). Danaher alleged that Maloy participated in a bevy of deviant activities, including solicitation and acceptance of gifts; solicitation and acceptance of a *quid pro quo* from his aide Ms. Morris; and misuse of a public position (Fla. Stat. §§ 112.311-.326, 2000; Maloy v. Board, 2007). The complainant alleged that sexual conduct repeatedly caused a conflict between his personal interests and discharge of his public duties. The Florida Department of Law Enforcement investigated; and the Commission found probable cause to believe that Maloy used his position to engage in sexual conduct; and that he intended to influence his professional judgment with sexual favors when he solicited a *quid pro quo* from female staff. "[P]rivate, consensual affairs that Maloy had with two women…occurred both in and out of the office, occurred while one woman was employed by [Department of Traffic] DOT and later by Leon County, and after she left the employ of both, and while one woman was employed by the county, but outside of the office" (Maloy v. Board, 2007, p. 1263). The evidence was brought before the court and analyzed under administrative law. Maloy denied the allegations, prevailed, and requested reimbursement for legal fees under a county policy. The Board of Commissioners denied Maloy's request for reimbursement. He sued in circuit court for reimbursement under county policy and common law; and he sought a declaratory judgment about an official's right to be reimbursed by the public. In this case, the court held that the county enjoyed the state's sovereign immunity; and the commissioner could not sue under common law or seek a declaratory judgment against the state. Maloy's motion for summary judgment for reimbursement under the county policy was denied because "the heart of the ethics complaint did not arise out of and in the scope of Maloy's employment with Leon County while in his official capacity and while serving a public purpose" (Maloy v. Board, 2007, p. 1262). "Nothing in Maloy's duties for Leon County required him to" have sex with other government employees, and doing so "certainly did not serve the public interest or a public purpose" (Maloy v. Board, 2007, p. 1263). Therefore, the county was under no obligation to reimburse Maloy even though that was an option. The appellate court reviewed *de novo* the order of summary judgement. They analyzed Maloy's three claims. First, they analyzed whether public officials may bring claims for reimbursement from public funds. They considered whether sovereigns were immunized from suits brought under common law. They concluded that under the common law *Thornber* Test, Floridian lawmakers are entitled to tax-funded legal representation to defend themselves when they are sued over unfounded allegations arising from the fulfilment of their public duties because service has a public purpose (Thornber v. City of Fort Walton Beach, 1990). This means that although the government is not obligated to pay, sovereign immunity will not bar a legislator from petitioning for reimbursement. Maloy's alleged misconduct did not occur in the fulfillment of his public service. Therefore, his actions did not meet the *Thornber* Test (Thornber v. City of Fort Walton Beach, 1990). Officials' representation may not to be reimbursed if alleged misconduct did not serve a public purpose. Sexual conduct, such as sexual harassment and consensual sex, whether in private or public places, does not serve a public purpose. Therefore, the trial court's order was affirmed. This case demonstrates that society may differentiate between the state's power, an official's duties, culpability, sexual deviance, and immorality. Although the government could immunize officials, who breach their duties, municipalities may refuse to include sexual activity as occurring within the course of official duties. This policy may fortify the public's faith in the Leviathan and their societal, political, and monetary investment in public offices.

CHAPTER SIX

POLICE

States have the power to use police to enforce morality (Barnes v. Glen Theatre, 1991; California v. LaRue, 1972; Caminetti v. U.S., 1916; Carey v. Population Services International, 1977; L'Hote v. New Orleans, 1900; Paris Adult Theatre v. Slaton, 1973; Poe v. Ullman, 1961). Police power is a physical power to enforce upon individuals and groups restraint and prohibition from certain immoral actions deemed illegal by the government, a Leviathan comprised of representatives of the people. As the nation attempts to become more progressive and inclusive, people lobby to change laws that are no longer reflective of their group identities or are discriminatory (Goldfeder & Sheff, 2011; Layne, 2015; Shamir, 2013). Their representatives should consider their wishes, and change laws that prohibit the government from authorizing use of police power to physically control people to act in traditionally moral ways. Yet, as culture changes, traditional standards may continue to be implemented; and therefore enforced (Bond v. U. S., 2011; Ginsberg v. New York, 1968; Lawrence v. Texas, 2003; U. S. v. Windsor, 2013). For example, in some states, adultery continues to be a criminal act, whereas most states now consider it to be a civil matter that may not be treated punitively, but may be weighed by the court in its fair division of assets (Layne, 2015). In states where adultery is criminal, the state may authorize police to arrest adulterers. They may also authorize officers, including jailers, to prevent adulterers from cohabiting in the future (i.e. arrest, seizure, and incarceration). In states where adultery is a criminal act, the government may ignore the law and not use police power. Although the law is enforceable, it is unenforced. For example, before sodomy was decriminalized in 2003, many governments ignored it, particularly among married, consenting, and heterosexual adults (Lawrence v. Texas, 2003).

Police not only act under the color of law, publicly they also bear indicia of power, such as badges, clubs, and guns that denote authority (Slidell Police Department, 2015; Wilson, 2016). Their power demonstrates the state's directives and the people's will. Their presence in the community is heroic and challenging because it is the initial and primary interface between the government and the people. Police encounters may be the extent of most individuals' interactions with the Leviathan; and typically may be the basis for a community's opinions about the government and the local environment (Slidell Police Department, 2015). The impression that police create during encounters is an essential form of communication between the government and the people. In addition to accomplishing superior police work, animals, including K-9 officers, equestrian officers, and other beings, invite community members to accept police work, trust officers, and build goodwill (Cusack, 2015; Cusack, 2015; Cusack, 2015; Cusack, 2015; Cusack, 2016). Police assure individuals, including children and undocumented residents, that the government serves to protect their interests in "life, liberty, or property" (U.S. Const. am. 5). They also protect municipal and state property, nature, animals, other forms of life, corpses (e.g. cemeteries), elements, and intangibles, such as privacy, speech, and space (Cusack, 2016; Orovitz, 2012; People v. Ryan, 1993; Slidell Police Department, 2015; Ward v. Rock Against Racism, 1989).

Police presence is vital for deterring crime and maintaining order (Cusack, 2015; Slidell Police Department, 2015). Police communicate the law and inform people about which laws are relevant. They are responsible for explaining local interpretations of applicable laws, but are neither attorneys nor members of the judiciary. Their explanations of the law are not the same as their legal duties, except in particular situations, such as Mirandizing suspects in custody (Miranda v. Arizona, 1966). Explanations may serve as orders that people must follow or authoritative guidance that they may follow with impunity. Explanations may be a courtesy that they provide to community members. Their knowledge of the community, personal awareness, and professional experiences may subtly or overtly help them to illustrate and articulate how and why enforcement of the law may be relative in culturally interpreted contexts.

Their role as an interface is the key to why it is so devastating to the government's authority to implement and enforce laws when a few police officers commit sexual deviance and harassment. Under color of law, they lead by example. Police reflect the Leviathan, "which is an inseparable corollary of…a priori unconditionally valid practical law[s]" (Denis & Wilson, 2016; Kant, 1788). "A properly trained officer may reasonably be expected to 'exercise a higher degree of restraint' than the average citizen, and thus be less likely to respond" to seduction, temptation, and offers for *quid pro quo* (Lewis v. City of New Orleans, 1974, p. 135; Orovitz, 2012). When they succumb, they may confer power onto particular citizens. For example, "neighborhood violence" is a "predictor of early intercourse;" and "young women" exposed to violence, who date police officers, "may be hoping to attain what is called 'ascribed' status (status conferred by association with someone of higher status)" (Denmark, et al., 2006, p. 69). As deviance destroys order and the government's power to enforce morality, safety, and equality, the women "are achieving neither" "ascribed status" "nor 'achieved' status (status earned on the basis of behavior, expertise or other resources)" (Denmark, et al., 2006, p. 69). A spiral of powerlessness ensues because illusory images, including women's protection and officers' objectivity and authority, replace the Leviathan's interests.

Police culture potentially may subsume officers' willingness to effectuate their duties in a non-sexual manner. Fraternal organizations may express rape supportive beliefs (e.g. sexual derogation, explicit language, and lewd jokes), encourage hypermasculinity, and require collusion to the detriment of good judgment (Cusack, 2012; Cusack, 2015). When multiple officers respond to calls, they tend collaboratively to make decisions. Officers may feel obligated during police encounters to use deductive reasoning that conforms to a group mentality. For example, they may act as if certain complaints should be ignored and other similar complaints should be treated as crimes based on preferential treatment of certain people (e.g. patriarchy or sexual interest). They may deal with crimes by offering advice rather than investigating. To elicit sexual responses or maintain flirtation, police may gather evidence more favorably for one party over another, or gather irrelevant facts to stymie police work. Officers may intimidate, ridicule, and chill people's rights in order to coerce them. Their behavior directly interferes with the Leviathan's interests and ability to regulate people by impacting records (e.g. reported and solved crime statistics). Police records impact individuals' lives; for example, their decisions to buy homes in certain neighborhoods (e.g. hate crime perpetration), overcrowded courts, and rape kit analysis.

Patriarchal influence may cause police to view victims as exaggerating their pain or departing from gender roles. In an attempt to stabilize situations or demonstrate authority, they may subtly demand compliance with or enforce gender roles that render women submissive and men in authoritative or assistive positions. Even sexually liberated men, who may view women as being sexually empowered, inappropriately may perceive supposed sexual empowerment as being threatening or inviting. Some officers may overstep their boundaries to commit sexual deviance by force, coercion, persuasion, or in a bargained-for exchange. Officers suffering from a sense of entitlement may believe that under color of law they may solicit sexual behavior in exchange for discretionary actions.

A few officers may be persuaded that deviance is an essential method for protecting society from serious harm. For example, "police feel there is some point, as a matter of public order, to keeping street-walkers prudent in their actions of solicitation" (Skolnick, 1994, p. 98). Research shows that sexual deviance among this population may correlate with job-related stress and pressure, group culture, and institutional deviance. Stereotypes about officers may wear on officers' self-esteem and individuality resulting in increased willingness to accept solicitations or conform to their environments. Studies about police officers and fraternal organizations suggest that sample populations were likelier to have been unfaithful to their spouses and cheat with other criminal justice employees (Cusack, 2013; Cusack, 2014). Reputations for immoral conduct could contribute to the state's declining control over morality for several reasons, such as public perception of arbitrary enforcement. Another reason may be that lack of respect for law enforcement demoralizes society because law enforcement is the most visible branch of the government. This correlates with anti-authoritarian attitudes. As a result, officers may develop low self-esteem and experience discord within their groups. To defend against negative perceptions, prevent negligence, and avoid liability they may attempt to appear as innocent as possible. This tension and inflated disposition could rile mistrust; and yet, opportunistic civilians may attempt to use apparent vulnerabilities to coerce officers. This breakdown corrodes police power at various levels resulting in evident harms, such violence against police officers, anarchy, police brutality, and unconstitutional police encounters (Pollock, 2013).

Gloria Steinem said that society is "not paying enough attention to the women who have been brutalized by the police. There are crimes against women and probably disproportionately women of color that are sexualized and therefore somehow not counted" (Begley, 2015). "I think we're not looking at the reality of everyone affected by police brutality, but there is a deeper relationship, because among the biggest and perhaps the single biggest determinant of whether someone is violent is whether they grew up in a household with domestic abuse" (Begley, 2015). "[B]y discounting violence against females, you produce men who continue to commit what I think of as supremacy crimes—that is, they're not going to get rich from these crimes, they're about control. So the male dominant impulse to control women and the [W]hite dominant impulse to control people of color are very related in the same people" (Begley, 2015). Steinem observed that low numbers of female officers cause the government to fail to meet communities' needs. She recommended that greater numbers of female officers should respond to violent calls in order to reduce tension and facilitate peacefulness.

> [W]hen we arrive on a scene of violence or a criminal act, our arrival doesn't escalate the situation. The arrival of men sometimes does. I have a friend who volunteers as a mounted police officer in Central Park, a woman, and she was talking about an incident in which her partner, a mounted policeman, was not able to negotiate—he was able to give orders, but not negotiate, and so sometimes increased the tension or the violence (Begley, 2015).

Some police forces may use fraternal culture to discourage sexually integrated groups to preserve traditional morality or the appearance of propriety. Their attitudes may relegate female officers to being sexual silage; discriminate against women; and cause male police officers to develop sexist attitudes, which deprive society of female officers. Fraternal enforcement of traditional attitudes may result in male police officers being more susceptible to homosexual and heterosexual misconduct. The presence of female partners may discourage the public from offering *quid pro quos* to officers; and police officers may be somewhat less likely to commit same-sex misconduct with their colleagues if female officers are present. This dynamic may be particularly cogent when female officers are willing to be sexually intimate with male officers and are polyamorous (Goldfeder & Sheff, 2011).

> Affairs and young cop divorce rates: In the academy, this is blushed over about the stress of police marriages, and most of the students may not be married yet and doze through this topic. Now on the streets, there are these mystical creatures of the night who are attracted to men and women in uniform. There is always a story of a young cop who finds this young lady who is 'midnight pretty' and soon the adventure begins. [Police forces should] [w]arn all of [their] young coppers of the dangers of badge bunnies, holster sniffers, and these other changelings who lurk in the night (Harvey, 2015).

Officers experiencing temptation may feel as if their public roles may be unappreciated and people in their private lives may be emotionally unequipped to accept their adversities.

> With the public constantly criticizing the police in this country, individuals who have no respect or idea regarding the daily grind make an officer feel as if one has minimal value in their community. In addition to the lack of appreciation for their dedication to serve and protect a massive

number of citizens, the absence of positive media interest can turn an officer into a disillusioned individual (Cox, 2014).

Like corrections officers, police officers may feel that they cannot report corruption or deviance.

One officer recommended that officers wishing to report institutional deviance and corruption (e.g. pervasive *quid pro quos*) ought to deliver evidence directly to the press (U.S. Const. am. 1).

> You've discovered serious corruption in your department. If you turn in a fellow officer you face harassment, death threats, even the possible loss of your career. The solution is to get this information to the proper authorities anonymously and in such a way that it can't be traced to you. Your Chief of Police isn't all that interested in hearing about criminal activity in his department; therefore, you must divulge what you know to people who will see to it that the criminals are investigated, exposed and punished. You must send your information to the District Attorney, the State's Attorney General, the [Federal Bureau of Investigation (FBI)], and if applicable the Federal Drug Enforcement Agency. Send copies to the Mayor, City Council and your own Chief of Police. Finally—the most important act—send copies of your report to the newspapers, radio stations and all television news departments in your area. Be very careful to protect yourself. Type the report on a word processor or computer. It's absolutely necessary that you wear plastic surgical gloves because you don't want to leave fingerprints. Beware of DNA tracing: don't lick envelopes or stamps. Make only the copies you need for mailing, no extra copies, not even for yourself. When the information reaches the police department they're going to start looking for you! It's a natural psychological response because they don't want to believe or admit there is anything wrong. Their immediate reaction is to find the person who is saying these terrible things. If they don't know who you are, they can't accuse you or attack you. They'll stop their search once a nosy TV reporter or investigative journalist begins inquiring into the allegations. For bosses, what's worse than the existence of corruption in their departments is the possibility of being humiliated by the truth of the accusations. Put everything you know into the report—names, places, dates, license numbers, and what you think has happened. Spare nothing and no one. It's the job of the agencies you copied to find out the truth, not yours. You have only one chance to tell your story safely. When it comes time to do the mailing, be sure to have the proper postage and a false return address. Do the mailing at night. Pick a mail box that is distant from your precinct and your home—distant, too, from the route you take home from work every day. Then forget about it. You've done your job. If there is corruption, your information will bring it to the surface and expose it to the light of day. What you've done must remain secret forever. Tell no one about it, not your wife or your best

> friend or your partner, absolutely no one! From this point on, you're the shadow. You've gained the ability to cloud men's minds so they can't see you. Criminals have a long memory. You have to be satisfied with having done the right thing at the right time for the right reasons. Leave it at that. Justice has been served (Browne, 1999).

This brave method may expose corruption, but may feed into society's negative perceptions of officers and the public's interest in sensational sex tales. It also affirms negative perceptions that disclosing sexual deviance harms institutions and only serves to enflame sexual curiosity.

Officers may use the state's power to exploit victims (Cusack, 2014). For example, they may claim that they are investigating abuse in order to take inappropriate photos of teens; or they may misuse evidence depicting sexual exploitation. They may exploit victims' testimony by effectively converting it into pornography. Even when they do not intend to exploit the victim, a combination of factors may result in the public perceiving that explicit sexual evidence is the most noteworthy part of investigations and prosecutions, rather than restitution to the victim and retribution against the offender (Dressler & Garvey, 2012). Unable to cope with their own morbid interests, the public may further resent police, courts, and trials. Fearing exploitation, some victims may become unwilling to disclose harassment and abuse.

As more officers' morality is called into question and society lowers its moral standards, the more akin to pornography sensational testimony of victimization and systemic impropriety become (Cusack, 2013).

> [N]ewspapers' sensationalized reports of sexual trials might be masked as public service announcements, communities' prurient curiosity as episodes of chivalry, litigants' sexual storytelling as necessary elements of evidence gathering, and lawyers' bawdy humor as a particularly effective weapon within the legal arsenal (Hayes, 2014, p. 202).

In the face of such decay, immorality previously considered to be serious, such as adultery and fornication, ceases to offend the people and the sovereign loses sight of it.

> As sites for obscenity production, as spaces where the processes of retelling and reimagining past sexual encounters gave these incidents new life, and as loci of local and state authority, courtrooms [have] offered a curious blend of public amusement, oral erotica, and displays of public power at work. Significantly, even as moral campaigns for sexual purity and against obscenity gained adherents, voyeuristic explorations of female sexual agency, male sexual aggrandizement, and bawdy humor flourished

> and commanded authority in an unlikely institutional setting: the local county courthouse. In an enigmatic twist of history, the very institutions that aimed to destroy…erotica thus produced a scurrilous sexual culture of their own making (Hayes, 2014, p. 202).

This process is evident when public knowledge of police affairs or *quid pro quos* focus on seduction, not abuse of authority.

Police activities under color of law may be criminal, but do not grasp the public's imagination and collective will power to the same extent as their sexual trysts. "Most importantly, the" police's "positions as regulatory bodies" lend "legitimacy, even respectability, to the contradictory explorations of female and male sexuality that flourish[] under its auspices. If seduction as a cultural concept" is "meant to discourage young women from coquettish kinds of behavior and to prevent men from" marauding "young women, its applications within" police departments "do not seem to have had the desired outcomes" (Hayes, 2014, p. 202).

When members of law enforcement commit immoral actions and their actions are brought to the public's attention, enforcement of "sexual regulation" has "a number of destabilizing effects" (Hayes, 2014, p. 156). "By authorizing men," who "boast of their sexual exploits," to enforce morality laws, public "conversations about naturally aggressive male sex drives" become justifiers for civil disobedience and deviance (Hayes, 2014, p. 156). Informal "sexual trials" conducted by the press, but not the courts, expand society's "emphasis on the importance of female chastity encouraged" by "the public…debate" about how "to scrutinize female sexual desire, agency, and motives. The legal culture of sexuality thus use[s] an odd medium to convey its impudent messages—seduction—a cultural concept perhaps most associated with" "restrictive guidelines for female sexuality" to "expose[] and fuel[] bolder facets of feminine sexuality even as they popularize[] the more familiar archetype of sexual passivity and vulnerability" (Hayes, 2014, p. 156; Segal, 1999).

Eventually, the public becomes so jaded that only the worst examples are even reported (Fisher, 2012). The most vulnerable victims are shamed and ridiculed by the press and the system under the pretenses of freedom of press and due process. For example, the press focused on a police officer, who entered an apartment in a senior living facility and committed rape, forcible sodomy, burglary, and sexual battery (Mint News Press, 2015). On more than one occasion, he raped a woman. The victim was unable verbally to describe details of the attack because she had suffered a stroke and her speech was impaired. As in this case, most criminal justice employees' DNA has not been entered into databases; and therefore, the perpetrator's identity was unknown. The victim installed motion activated cameras. When police saw the footage, they immediately recognized and investigated the suspect. Police did not exploit the victim, but officers may have taken personal satisfaction in allowing the press to further punish the deviant officer, who betrayed his position in law enforcement. At the sentencing, Judge Ernest Sawtelle called attention to the victim's vulnerability possibly to exploit the grotesqueness of the crime while attempting to seem compassionate and unwilling to scandalize the details of victimization. The judged may have knowingly mocked the victim when he referred to the crimes as being horridly "unspeakable" (Mint News Press, 2015).

Some police may feel confident about judges' insensitivity toward victims. For example, an officer forcibly raped Ashlyn Moreno in his squad car after he told her that he may be able to assist her with federal charges. He threatened to arrest her if she reported the rape; and told the victim that she should "show the judge some nipple" to avoid federal charges (Bonner, n.d.). Federal judges are notoriously insensitive to complaints of sexual harassment and the comment may have reflected officers' opportunistic, fraternal, and collusive character. He told the victim that he was well-connected within the system. Federal prosecutors dismissed her allegations; but, she sought punitive damages because she was subjected to excessive force, unreasonable search and seizure, and sexual harassment (Filming Cops, n.d.).

In Boynton Beach, Stephen Maiorino, temporarily seized a vehicle at a checkpoint (Lawsuit, n.d.). The driver was arrested by another officer, and Maiorino began to sexually harass the victim, who was in his squad car. He forcibly sodomized her and threatened to arrest her for driving under the influence even though she had not been driving. He unholstered his service weapon, pointed it at the victim and demanded that she "get the f–k out of the car" while in a field (Filming Cops, n.d.). He held his gun while raping her on the hood of his squad car; and he threatened to kill her if she disclosed the truth. Complaints had been filed against Maiorino in the past, which gave the city notice that he should be disciplined and needed additional training and supervision. Because the victim was violated and Boynton Beach Police Department was deliberately indifferent, she sought compensatory damages for negligent hiring, supervision, retention, and training; a civil rights violation; and intentional torts, including battery, assault, false imprisonment, and intentional infliction of emotional distress. Maiorino's attorney said, "the only thing" Maiorino "was guilty of was showing bad judgement when he decided to have consensual sex on the job with a woman other than his wife"

(Farberov, 2015). His attorney suggested that immorality was apparent and the basis for the allegations. Supposing that his statement was true and the defendant had consensual sex with the woman, then it appears as if the woman and the officer used the state's power, the court, and the media to carry out a harmful, dangerous, and obscene sex game (Blackhurst & McGinn, 2016; Knox, 2014; Sollecito & Gumbel, 2012).

In another case, Jose Rigoberto Sanchez admitted to raping the victim, but initially treated his crimes as if they had been consensual, and asked for the victim's phone number so that they could "mess around" again (Brandl, 2014). Two days after raping the first victim, he solicited a *quid pro quo* from a female suspected of driving with a suspended license while intoxicated. She rejected his offer for a *quid pro quo*, so he forcibly orally, vaginally, and anally raped her on the hood of his squad car. Misuse by police officers of police vehicles (e.g. motorcycles), service weapons, and other state resources is similar to prison guards, who use handcuffs, their offices, cells, vans, and other state assets as rape "tool kits" (Brandl, 2014). The press described him as being confident that he would not get caught. Sanchez registered as a sex offender.

Recidivism perpetrated by Daniel Holtzclaw captivated the public's attention, but failed to stir the public's conscience sufficiently to initiate reform or activate political discussions about morality (Brandes, 2016). Police knew that the first victim complained months before Holtzclaw victimized seven other women while acting in an official capacity. One victim's attorney, Benjamin Crump, described him as "a serial rapist with a badge" (Brandes, 2016). Police opened an investigation after the second complaint was filed, yet thirteen women testified that he coerced and forced them to perform sex acts on him. Holtzclaw "unlawfully detained" the victim while she was "visiting her terminally ill daughter at a hospital" (Brandes, 2016; Price Foley, 2009). He "slammed her into a brick wall" at a restaurant and "rubbed his genitals against her before handcuffing her and driving" his police car (Brandes, 2016). He let her go after she excreted on herself.

Officers, who abuse children, not only violate cultural norms, they shock the conscience thereby numbing the public, and possibly the laws' effect on them. One example is Stephen Young, a "good cop," who raped approximately 20 infants and toddlers (Filming Cops, n.d.). Another officer sexually assaulted a pre-pubescent child (Filming Cops, n.d.). A former Police Chief, Steve E. Bodine, raped prepubescent children for 40 years. Eduardo Cornejo was arrested for pimping (Eustachewich, 2016). While on bail he attempted to challenge and weaken the legal process by posting messages online, such as the following: "I got a bag for the lawyers like, 'What's your charges?' Hop out the courtroom like #WhatCharges? Big p***in' on you court steps. CASE YOU AIN'T NOTICE, I AIN'T LOST YET" (Eustachewich, 2016)! He violated the conditions of his bail by pimping at least ten women, including at least one female minor, and was remanded into custody. Alberto Randazzo participated in virtual child abuse when he asked a woman to exhibit sexual abuse of an infant on the internet (Vankin, 2015). He repeatedly solicited from her real-time depictions of an infant being verbally degraded and sexually molested. Randazzo gave the woman explicit instructions about how to molest the child. He violated the terms of his conditional release while awaiting trial.

Egregious examples are highlighted, but violations are typical; and one reason may be that although conditions of police employment are delineated in police manuals, which specify rules of conduct, examples are neither given nor discussed. They may give officers notice and provide accurate job descriptions to inform the public of police responsibilities (UCMJ art. 134, 2017). Florida Department of Law Enforcement's *Law Enforcement Officer Ethical Standards of Conduct* provides examples of typical, plainly written rules prohibiting immoral conduct (FDLE, n.d.).

> 4.4 Police officers, while on duty, shall not commit any act which, as defined under Florida law, constitutes sexual harassment, including but not limited to, making unwelcome sexual advances, requesting sexual favors, engaging in sexually motivated physical contact or other verbal or physical conduct or communication of a sexual nature.
> 4.5 Police officers, while off duty, shall not engage in any conduct which the officer knows, or reasonably should know, constitutes an unwelcome sexual advance or request for sexual favor, or unwelcome sexually motivated physical contact or other unwelcome verbal or physical conduct or communication of a sexual nature.
> 4.6 Police officers shall not commit any acts which, as defined under Florida law, constitute sexual assault or indecent exposure. Sexual assault does not include a frisk or other search done in accordance with proper police procedures.
> 4.8 Police officers shall not, in the course of performing their duties, engage in any sexual contact or conduct constituting lewd behavior, including but not limited to, showering or receiving a massage in the nude, exposing themselves or otherwise making physical contact with the nude or partially nude body of any person, except as pursuant to a written policy of the Department.
> 6.4 Unless required for the performance of official duties, police officers shall not, while on duty, be present at establishments that have the primary purpose of providing sexually oriented adult entertainment. This rule does

> not prohibit officers from conducting walk-throughs of such establishments as part of regular assigned duties (FDLE, n.d.).

Some rules, such as prohibitions against lewd behavior seem redundant because lewd conduct is criminal. The inclusion of such rules demonstrates the state's willingness to require, not only enforce, morality. It also proves that some deviant officers would defend against allegations of misconduct by claiming that requirements for moral behavior had not been specified.

CHAPTER SEVEN

PROSECUTORS

Some prosecutors have been known to circumvent the law in order to achieve allegedly just results; however, several prosecutors have participated in immoral acts and practices in order to advance their careers and accommodate their libidos. Others intentionally have violated policies and laws to defy a restrictive system. Some seek personal liberation. Others intend to defy and quietly divest the state of its power to regulate personal matters. Although this may cause them incompetently to consider probable cause or prosecute morality-based charges, these prosecutors may continue hypocritically to prosecute immoral actors (Gordon Mullane, 2014).

When prosecutors' behavior raises red flags, but the system fails to respond in a timely manner, the public may blame the system and suggest that authorities overlooked clear indications of problematic behavior because they are not interested in discovering immorality within the government or are complicit. For example, John David Roy Atchison was a prosecutor of federal civil property and forfeiture cases before he committed suicide while awaiting trial (Cusack, 2014). During an undercover sting, he allegedly believed that he chatted online with a mother in Michigan, who promised to allow him to rape her five year-old daughter. He purchased gifts for the child, who he believed would serve as one of his prepubescent girlfriends. Months before his arrest, he requested training in an area of law dealing with child molestation, which should have raised authorities' suspicions (Cusack, 2014). However, an isolated incident may not have amounted to an indication of wrongdoing. Yet, one of his neighbor's attitudes seemed to embody a pervasive spirit of apathy toward foreseeable sexual misconduct (Goodnough, 2007). She said that although a screening process for coaches could possibly have discovered Atchison's alleged penchant for raping children, "Coaches put in tons of time, [so], [h]ow can you ask them to take a psychological evaluation on top of that" (Goodnough, 2007)? Her words demonstrate widespread acceptance and pretext for community leaders (Goodnough, 2007). The local sheriff said that he was unsurprised that a prosecutor had been accused of this kind of crime because prosecutors are not less likely than other people to exploit children (Cusack, 2014).

Prosecutors may poorly assess risk (Heilbrum, 2009). A sample of public defenders working with sex offense registration demonstrated that prosecutors do not consistently assess risk (Lanterman, Boyle, & Ragusa-Salerno, 2014). They may under-classify offenders' risk, which results in compromised public safety. This deficiency may be intentional or because they are unable properly to assess risk because of their deviant frames of reference. They may also use classifications as political tools to participate in a systemic culture of deviance.

Prosecutors may exploit defendants' sexualities and their prosecutorial authority by bringing to light scintillatingly sordid or obscene evidence and testimony. Prosecutors may star as the directors of pornographic investigations and trials, sometimes hyping gender stereotypes to frame facts most favorable to the state and appeal to prurient interests or morbid curiosities (Hayes, 2014, p. 181).

> The sexual accounts told by prosecuting witnesses (and torn down by defendants and the lawyers who argue[] cases for them) epitomize[] a reputable kind of prurience, one that offer[s] titillation without the seedy connotations of pornography. In other words, the location that house[s] these lurid conversations matter[s] a great deal. In the courts, quasipornographic tales of…sex manifest[,] not as…faithful presentations of the facts of a case. However much legal participants [have] enjoyed listening to and watching young women painstakingly detail their sexual experiences, in a courtroom setting, prurient sexual pleasure might be transformed into a kind of unfortunate incidental: a byproduct that [has] not inhibit[ed] the true purpose of such litigation, which was to find and deliver justice (Hayes, 2014, p. 184).

They blend dramatic facts with pornography scripts and traditional gender roles to concoct emotionally persuasive, if not seemingly plausible, narratives that alchemize convictions.

In spite of their success, prosecutors may resent and envy the legitimization of public disclosure. They may take excessive risks and make poor decisions because the consequences of being caught not only fail to deter them, but may appeal to them. Prosecutors may err and rise above their own indiscretions by parading sexually deviant defendants before the court and public.

> Recounting sexual experiences before eager listeners…[is] a practice outside the courts as much as inside the legal system…because [they spend] considerable time gossiping with one another about particular

> episodes of sexual transgression, engendering prurient curiosity in these scandalous goings-on in the weeks or even months before proceedings….Although…gossip networks dr[a]w both male and female participants, particular aspects of sexual storytelling have a decidedly masculine cast. Just as voyeurism [goes] hand in hand with the sexual disclosures of female litigants, the intimate storytelling of defendants and male witnesses function, in many ways, as extensions of male camaraderie rituals (Hayes, 2014, p. 184).

When prosecutors become defendants, their implicitly braggadocios win-win position announces to the public moral legislations' weakness, the governments' powerless, the pointlessness of prosecutorial deterrence, and the glorious infamy of defying governmentally instituted conventions. They become local, and sometimes renowned, albeit infamous, celebrities (Cusack, 2013). They may receive celebrity justice (e.g. sweetheart deal). Though they evade justice, they may be drawn in by the "culture of sexual storytelling" and prepare for and rationalize the possibility of prosecution by talking to colleagues about their sexual experiences (Hayes, 2014, p. 185). Female prosecutors may also participate in this by talking (e.g. "ventilation"), listening, and failing to complain (Reddington & Kreisel, 2009, p. 103).

> When sexual escapades [have] brought…[prosecutors] under the purview of the courts, they [have] continued to draw on this culture of male bonding. Defendants, for example, often depend[] upon sexual conversations they had overheard to identify acquaintances and friends able—or at least willing—to testify…as one conceivable way for defendants to exonerate themselves. Significantly, the sexual revelations disclosed by defendants' witnesses…[may be] some of the most scandalous given over the course of sexual trials, because such narratives play[] up young women's flirtatious behavior and active roles in sexually compromising situations….It also constitute[s] one way for men to publically confirm membership in a sexually aggressive breed of manhood: a categorization that [does] not always bode well for those seeking exoneration from sexual offenses. Whereas rehashing actual intimate bouts to comrades or spinning yarns about desired/imagined erotic encounters to one another constituted a male cultural tradition followed by men in a wide variety of settings and periods….men in pursuit of erotically charged subject matter [do] not have to rely only on the conversations those in their peer networks generate[] (Hayes, 2014, p. 185).

Prosecutors may carefully lead double lives, but then disclose salacious details demonstrating the iconicism of their disregard for the risks they have assumed and the power of the government to punish them. Though educated in law, many readily incriminate themselves.

> [R]egardless of the truth or falsity of the factual matters asserted within the quoted statement, the attribution [or]....self-condemnatory quotation may carry more force than criticism by another. It is against self-interest to admit one's own criminal liability, arrogance, or lack of integrity, and so all the more easy to credit when it happens. This principle underlies the elemental rule of evidence which permits the introduction of statements against interest, despite their hearsay character, because we assume 'that persons do not make statements which are damaging to themselves unless satisfied for good reason that they are true' (Masson v. *New Yorker Magazine*, 1991, pp. 511-512).

Even when prosecutors would rather plead not guilty, and remain silent, such as Atchison who hanged himself before trial, the press may invoke the First Amendment to sensationalize coverage thereby circumventing obscenity laws to graphically depict sexual abuse in manner that possesses redeeming value and supposedly fails to appeal to prurient interests (Miller v. California, 1973). When the people hear the coverage, it acts as "rocket fuel," and makes them feel like "winners" in comparison to the victims and prosecutors being lambasted (*Huffington Post*, 2008).

News coverage may seem to condemn the prosecutors' abuse and betrayal of society while capitalizing on, and essentially promoting, events surrounding it. For example, one media outlet discussed Atchison.

> Ruth Spencer: New at 5 [PM], a disturbing case of perverted justice! He's sworn to uphold the law; to prosecute those who commit crimes, but tonight, this man, a Justice Department officer, is charged after being caught in an internet sex sting involving children.
>
> Rhonda Walker: Good Evening Everyone, and thank you so much for joining us. We do want to tell you that we should caution you. What you are learning tonight is very disturbing.
>
> Ruth Spencer: Yes, an Assistant U.S. Attorney from Florida finds himself on the wrong side of the law tonight. He's accused of going after a five year-old girl from right here in Metro Detroit.
>
> Rhonda Walker: The intended victim is from Macomb County. The Florida lawman is from the town of Pensacola down in Florida, but at this hour he is being held in a local jail cell. Local 4's Steve Garagiola is live in downtown Detroit with more on how this case came down.

> Steve Garagiola: Oh, it is just incredibly disturbing. Not only is this guy an Assistant United States Attorney, but he's also president of a youth sports association in the city where he lives near Pensacola, Florida. So, he's got a lot of contact with young children. Now, this was a sting operation, so there is no actual victim in this case; but what is truly frightening is that, based on statements from the accused, there are very likely many real children out there, who are victims. John David Atchison arrested yesterday at Metro Airport upon arrival from Florida, made his first appearance in Detroit federal court today. According to a deposition from the FBI special agent in charge of the investigation, Atchison told the undercover detective to tell her daughter that 'You found her a sweet boyfriend who will bring her presents.' The undercover detective expressed concern about physical injury to a five year-old girl engaged in sexual activity. The suspect responds, 'I am always gentle and loving; not to worry.' Most disturbing to investigators is the suspect's third response when the detective asks, 'How can you be certain there will be no injury?' The suspect responds, 'Just gotta [sic] go slow and very easy. I've done it plenty.' Atchison is 53 years old; an Assistant United States Attorney in Pensacola, Florida, who described himself online as a family man. So, Atchison remains in federal custody right now. A detention hearing happens tomorrow at which time a judge will entertain questions about bond.
>
> Rhonda Walker: Oh Steve, this is so disturbing. Can you tell us, what was the connection to Michigan? Does this Assistant U.S. Attorney have any special connection here to Metro Detroit?
>
> Steve Garagiola: Actually, no. He has no special connection to Metro Detroit; and here credit has to go to the Macomb County Sheriff's Department and their MACE Unit, which is Macomb Area Computer Enforcement Team. They set up the online sting, and in fact, they have arrested three out-of-state suspects, who have tried to engage sex with a minor. So, the work of the Macomb County Sheriffs is really paying off, that work their doing online.
>
> Rhonda Walker: Oh yeah, well we've reported on their successes many times with that unit, many times, Steve. We're glad it worked in this case (Youtube.com, 2007).

The reporters used the most shocking and perverted details to entice viewers in a manner that they acknowledge may offend the local community. This language, for example, could not appear on billboards without being scrutinized. News coverage also reports graphic details about how Atchison possessed Vaseline when he was arrested (Cusack, 2014). Although they described how he wanted slowly and skillfully to penetrate a victim to avoid harming her, they never discussed the harm, which is obviously one reason that sexual abuse is a very serious crime. Atchison's chat with undercover officers was not protected under the First Amendment because it was an obscene conspiracy, not an erotic fantasy; however, the press could repeat it *ad infinitum* without repercussions.

Interplay between corruption and sensationalism is evident in the trial of Amanda Knox. Perhaps Italian prosecutors felt that an immoral American, such as Knox, should be castigated and subjected to a humiliating debacle; and he believed that American prosecutors similarly have exploited defendants and victims (Sollecito & Gumbel, 2012). Knox's then-boyfriend and co-defendant, Raffaele Sollecito, described the court's indecency.

> The single most atrocious moment of the appeal came when Francesco Maresca, the lawyer representing the [victim's] family, flashed brutally graphic photographs of the crime scene in open court, including images of Meredith [Kercher]'s near-naked body and the ghastly wounds to her neck (Sollecito & Gumbel, 2012, p. 240).
>
> [Rudy] Guede crept into her room and grabbed her from behind under the chin and yanked his hand up over her mouth to prevent her from crying out. He held his knife to the right side of her neck as he issued his demands, presumably for sex. In the ensuing struggle, he jabbed her twice, causing blood to spurt out. Our best guess was that he didn't set out to kill her, but at some point decided he'd caused so much damage he had no option but to finish her off. He tried to plunge the knife in farther but could not find the right angle. So he switched sides and stuck the blade a full eight centimeters into the left side of her neck, hacking back and forth in an effort to sever her carotid artery, which he missed. As Meredith struggled for her life, her lungs filling with blood through the perforation he had made in her throat, Guede lost his right shoe and his foot started slipping around in the growing pool of blood. He waited for her to die, but her agony, according to the medical experts continued for more than 10 minutes....Guede may have masturbated over her body (Sollecito & Gumbel, 2012, p. 242).
>
> Amanda and I instinctively turned away, not because we had not seen such images before—we had—but because the moment seemed to be in such unforgivably bad taste (Sollecito & Gumbel, 2012, p. 240).

Prosecutors may accuse defendants of participating in fiascos to blame the victim for rape.

> Maresca had spent years accusing us and our defense teams of exploiting Meredith's death and soiling her memory, but here he was doing the very thing he was so fond of condemning in others. 'Meredith was butchered, like victims of Mafia killings are butchered, in revenge for some wrong,' Maresca thundered as the gallery gasped and the press photographers snapped away. 'I'm showing you these photos so you can see how she suffered as she died.' These images had been shown by the prosecution during the evidentiary phase of the first trial, but when they did it, they at least cleared the public gallery and gave due warning (Sollecito & Gumbel, 2012, pp. 240-241).

Former FBI agent Steve Moore attended the trial and described the graphic onslaught as being "without warning, without dignity, without any apparent concern for Meredith or her grieving family, without decency" (Sollecito & Gumbel, 2012, p. 241).

Some prosecutors may sensationalize courtrooms with heavy-handed justice, but may secretly participate in the deviant crimes that they prosecute. For example, Stuart Dunnings III was elected in 1996, and by 2016 he earned more income through the county than any other elected official (i.e., $132,000 annual salary) (Holley, 2016). With that income, he paid for sex hundreds of times. In 2001, he aggressively "cracked down" by impounding vehicles of sex buyers and implementing a three-strike rule that charged recidivist sex-sellers and buyers with felonies (Holley, 2016). By 2004, he had impounded more than 50 vehicles and charged 19 people with felonies. Investigators discovered evidence as far back as 2010 that he contacted prostitutes through websites, such as BackDoor.com, and met them at hotels or through pimps. He used escort services to date women, pay for sex, and pay their living expenses and drug treatment. Dunnings had ongoing relationships (e.g. five years) with some prostitutes; and told some prostitutes that he was a prosecutor (Eggert, 2016). He shared sex services with his brother, who was also an attorney. He was "outspoken" against sex trafficking (Holley, 2016). He "never intervened to help victims he said were 'brutalized, assaulted, manipulated, provided drugs, [and] imprisoned'" (Eggert, 2016). He not only breached his duties to enforce the law and report crime by soliciting sex for money, he also assisted a woman with a child custody matter in exchange for sex. His pandering was a felony. The mother, who was a domestic violence survivor, declined his offer, but feared that he would use his influence and power to harm her if she did not have sex with him. Members of the justice system and his former colleagues felt that his crimes were "a huge betrayal" of their "trust, his oath of office, his service to the people" (Holley, 2016). Although there was "chatter" about his lifestyle, no one questioned it until the FBI investigated human trafficking in 2015. His excuse was “that the attorney general’s motivations were political in nature” and promoted by “titillating-type accusations” (Holley, 2016). The attorney general countered by saying, “We live in a time where people wonder if government actually works” (Holley, 2016).

> People wonder if the system is rigged. People wonder whether we have a ‘wink and a nod’ justice system where the chosen few skate and escape punishment because of who they know or because they hold an important position in government….Well, let me be very direct and crystal clear….The system in Michigan is not rigged. Not on my watch (Holley, 2016).

Despite his duplicitous prosecutorial scheme to enforce morality laws, his exploitive lifestyle slyly signaled personal anarchy and approbation of immorality under color of law. The state’s attorney’s words, designed to counter this affect, may have assured some people and reinstated some trust and authority in the government.

CHAPTER EIGHT

PUBLIC DEFENDERS

Public defenders may work for the state or may be private attorneys, who voluntarily work as public defenders. "In the United States, most public defenders are those private practicing attorneys, who are on a list of public defenders accepting cases from the state docket" (Rattner, Turjeman, & Fishman, 2008). Private practitioners have a duty to the public, and represent the government. Because they are less involved with the government than state employees, they may feel that they are entitled to a lower degree of scrutiny and social responsibility. Yet, their presence in the system may have reciprocal effects on the public and state employees with whom they share influence, doctrines, legal analyses, culture, and resources.

In conjunction with their duties and inculcation in legal culture, they may be deviant; for example, they may partake in adult entertainment or participate in adultery. "Sometimes peers [have] used this male pattern of sociability to encourage the men engaged in out-of-wedlock intimate conduct to face the consequences of their actions. These attempts [are] not always unsuccessful, and they offer glimpses into…men's sometimes cavalier treatment of" their jobs, women, homosexual conduct, family law, criminal defense, and sexuality (Hayes, 2014, p. 187). One private attorney, who worked as a court-appointed attorney and assisted indigent defendants, used erotic dance venues to meet individuals with pending criminal and family matters (Cusack, 2016; Gerth & Mills, 1946; Marcellus, 2009). He ate lunch and mingled with clientele while casually networking with a new client base. "Public defenders play an essential role in the criminal justice system by helping to connect financially needy criminal suspects to the legal services they need" (Cohen, 1995). Many of these clients were marginalized or oppressed by race, economic disadvantage, histories of abuse, and other issues that made the public defender an influential and essential link to society and governmental power.

Stress experienced by public defenders may arise from their role as counsel for alleged perpetrators of sexual assault. Although they may personally oppose sex crimes (e.g. pedophilia), they may harbor political and social attitudes that promote egalitarian values, and as such, they may experience inner conflict, which leads to job stress. Conflict may arise from socio-psychological differences between public defenders and members of the justice system. For example, public defenders are less social dominance-oriented than police officers (Sidanius, et al., 1994). A study of 382 undergraduates, 59 police officers, 56 public defenders, and 116 jurors demonstrated that social status, social attitudes, and political attitudes may be shaped by social dominance-oriented personality characteristics that demand hierarchy and are amenable to zero-sum competition. Public defenders, particularly those in private practice, may be less capable than other justice members of impacting the legal environment.

Stress may correlate with job dissatisfaction. Job dissatisfaction may cause public defenders to feel entitled to deviate sexually to relieve tension, violate boundaries, and attempt to reclaim control (Cohen, 1995). Job dissatisfaction affects client representation, "and is often blamed for the high turnover rate" of public defenders (Cohen, 1995). A sample of 411 public defenders in Connecticut, Massachusetts, New York, Pennsylvania, and Philadelphia found that work orientation and sensitivity may affect job dissatisfaction. Stress and sensitivity may negatively correlate with thrill seeking or risky behavior.

Because criminal defendants take risks, breach norms, and often beat the system through plea bargains or exoneration, defense attorneys may idolize criminals or view them as antiestablishment heroes (Frank, 1973; Kamick, 2003; Katz, 1988; Kooistra, 1989; Lynch, 1999; Prager, Moran, & Sanchez, 1996). Within the legal field, public defenders seem to have reputations for participating in deviant behavior, such as drug-use, selling drugs, driving while intoxicated, domestic violence, infidelity, and patronizing adult establishments (Dickson, 2016; Franklin, 2016). Some may have experience with manipulating the system; for example, evading domestic violence investigations when police respond to noise complaints (Pribble, 2008). They may use their knowledge of the law and their experience with clients and the legal environment to exhibit a demeanor during interviews and investigations that appeases, tricks, or deters police.

When immorality is exposed it may taint the public's perception of public defenders' role as administrators of justice and members of the court, who have good intentions; and it may call into question their integrity and trustworthiness. It may also justify deviants' behavior and suggest that the Leviathan, as a force, or as a collection of deviant individuals, will inherently or intentionally fail to protect victims and may facilitate abuse.

Exploitation may be part of legal culture, inextricably embedded into the profession, and partially attributable to gender. Moral collapse may have the beneficial effect of exposing this problem; and yet, weaken the state's ability to enforce morality in society. One study found that males were more morally disengaged than female students (Carroll, 2015). This is in spite of the fact that females and males attend law school at similar rates; and males are likelier to practice law and judges are far likelier to be male (Cusack, 2015; Walter, 2008). The same study demonstrated that females were likelier to possess empathy and self-transcendent values. In comparison to males, they were likelier to be open to value changes. This may cause several phenomena to manifest. For example, women may be likelier to want to retool society to minimize deception and make social practices compatible with accepted standards. They may want to discard traditions that call for the public to repress sexual activity rather than allow an oligarchy to flout the rules while oppressing the people with instituted strongholds. Value changes may have two effects. They may alleviate women and men from some types of oppression (e.g. disparate indecency legislation); and yet, may disempower women by decriminalizing or instituting acceptance for other types of harmful immorality (e.g. uncivilized locker-room talk). Furthermore, morally disengaged males with duplicitous sexual practices make take advantage of self-transcendent and empathetic females while continuing to use courts to stage vendettas against their jobs, the government, and other citizens.

Some female public defenders may be willing to transcend their personal experiences to forge a better system; and therefore, whitewash the reality of shared experiences and pain inflicted by the justice system.

> One of our key assumptions is that no organization that serves the public can be an island unto itself. Once one digs beyond symptoms of any problem that distresses the community, one finds that the needs that must be addressed do not neatly correspond to categories of service delivery and are not the purview of any single agency that does service delivering. The only legitimately insular problem-solving activities may be those that have to do with problems that are internal to an organization and call for improvements in its functioning[; but,] even internal reforms must keep external constituencies in mind (Toch & Grant, 2005).

Balanced, progressive, and sensitive reforms could be initiated by full-time public defenders; but few students are committed to public interest law and may be unwilling to activate reforms.

Many law students become public defenders in hopes of gaining experience and moving onto private practice. "With the expansion of the right to legal counsel and the state's need to provide legal counsel, public defenders came to be viewed with suspicion and mistrust. The widely shared image by the public was that lawyers who became public defenders were those unable to succeed in the private sector" (Rattner, Turjeman, & Fishman, 2008).

A study of 122 public defenders between 1927 and 1971 demonstrates how implementation of governmental authority may have been developed by practitioners, who advanced culture, policies, and practices, which influenced the system and interpretations of laws as well as society's perceptions of public defenders (Platt & Pollock, 1974). "During the 1950's, motivation and careers of the attorneys began to follow a general pattern: most recruits were male, [W]hite, from working and lower-middle class origins, and Protestant and liberal political backgrounds. The [public defender's office] PDO was regarded as a place to develop technical skills, and few attorneys planned to make their career in the PDO" (Platt & Pollock, 1974, p. 1). Inferences may be drawn about the "[i]mplications of the relationship between the state government, the legal profession, and public service, and factors in the disillusioning atmosphere of the PDO which discouraged many lawyers who planned to enter public service" (Platt & Pollock, 1974, p. 1).

Only a small fraction of students with the interest and capacity to practice public interest law and initiate changes will commit to full-time employment with the state. One study found that of 153 respondents, more than half demonstrated some interest, but only 68 worked for legal aid, a non-profit organization, or a public defender's office (Erlanger, et al., 1996). Legislators may overestimate the degree of citizen support for public defenders; and fail to provide incentives (e.g. programming and scholarships) to attract moral actors, who are willing to defend the systems' efficaciousness, accountability, and greater purpose. Admissions committees may intentionally accept and retain applicants, who are likelier to fit-in with the legal community; for example, tolerate corruption and participate in deviance. Systemically, patriarchal outlooks may be used to foster males' careers and decision-making to render females compliant players; yet, hide sexual deviance from women, while encouraging women to think like men, but not reward them for it or permit them to institute progressive changes that generate and facilitate equality.

Female public defenders may feel more bothered by conflicts with clients and prosecutors because of male-centric support networks; being assigned more work; perceiving that they are assigned a greater volume of work; attitudes within legal culture; harsher responses from judges; and fear of being viewed as weak or emotionally incompetent (Lynch, 1997).

Empowerment to improve the system may be perceived as defensiveness against the system (Garcia, Darley, & Robinson, 2001).

> The challenge of providing high-quality public defense services continues to be a concern at federal, state, and local levels. Some scholars have alluded to a potential solution in client-centered representation, but research in this area is sparse at best. Such a lack of understanding leaves in its place speculation, particularly as to the potential importance of client perceptions in shaping broader system legitimacy (Campbell, et al., 2015, p. 751).

Even if public defenders' offices were revitalized with improved client relationships, job satisfaction, gender equality, and increased interpersonal integrity and sexual decency, their performance in the courtroom may still reflect sexist courts and the public's demand for salacious details.

Trial procedures may harm society and victims. Rhetorical arguments may hint at or explicitly articulate vulgarities and tragic details to shock a jury's conscience, disarm their morals, distract their thoughts, and compromise impartiality (Clason, 2009). One example is that public defenders may fight for their clients' rights to confront alleged child victims (Maryland v. Craig, 1990). In the process, public defenders may insensitively seek to have children present in courtrooms with alleged violators because defendants have a Sixth Amendment right to confront their accusers. Other public defenders may require children to testify by camera in open court (Hall, 2014). Appearing on camera, which may be two-way cameras or may only be visible to the defendant, may further traumatize victims. For example, victims of pornographic exploitation may be traumatized when they are seen on camera by an abuser. Although some children may not be traumatized, public defenders may fail when strategizing to weigh potentially important factors, such as "social cognitive abilities, executive function skills, and attachment profiles of aggressors, victims, and defenders" (Monks, Smith, & Swettenham, 2005). This problem may be impacted by public defenders' sexual deviance (e.g. pedophilia) (McMahon, 2016). One example of a pedophilic public defender illustrates how their deviance may affect legal processes on multiple levels. Richard Comenzo, who specialized in medical marijuana law and internet law, was accused of soliciting sex from minors online (e.g. Tumblr and Craigslist) and distributing child pornography online (WCVB, 2014). A judge from another district arraigned Comenzo because the judge in Comenzo's district had worked with Comenzo several times.

At trial, public defenders attempt to raise reasonable doubts about child victims' credibility (Cusack, 2013; Cusack, 2015; Saunders, 1988). Despite rape shield laws, they may attempt to depict victims as being deviant and use subtle and particular verbal cues and gestures to intimate deviance to the jury. They may also give subtle indications to child victims that they are somehow culpable for having participated in sexual deviance involving children; and therefore, society is deceptive; the system is unfair; victims have been corrupted; and child victims should be shamed, disempowered, disbelieved, and remain voiceless.

Public defenders may also contribute to the perception that morality is rapidly corroding because they pressure and advise innocent clients to take plea deals admitting to sex crimes. For example, one man accepted a plea deal on child pornography charges even though he maintained his innocence; demonstrated that he accidentally downloaded child pornography; proved that he deleted the images as soon as he realized his mistake; and could not possibly have accessed the deleted files, which were the only evidence found by the government on his computer (Greenfield, 2009). He pleaded to serve three years in prison rather than go to trial. Critics of his case suggested that due to his upbringing and class, he was unlikely to have needed a public defender, but may have been pressured by the government. One critic asked, "Is this an example of a public defender pushing a client to plead out rather than fighting the accusation?...[G]iven the appearance of his parent's house in the news video, which appears to be a very nice middle class home, why is he represented by a public defender at all" (Greenfield, 2009)? He was required to register as a sex offender thereby giving the impression to his community that he actually downloaded child pornography to satisfy aberrant sexual desires in violation of morality-based laws designed to protect children from corruption, harm, and exploitation.

Public defenders participate in moral corrosion by zealously advocating for clients, who they know to be guilty. This is not only unethical, it is harmful and dangerous. Some public defenders may ignore confessions, for example in capital cases, because they are interested in attaining positions in the judiciary.

> Law enforcement officers have the obligation to convict the guilty and to make sure they do not convict the innocent. They must be dedicated to making the criminal trial a procedure for the ascertainment of the true facts surrounding the commission of the crime. To this extent, our so-called adversary system is not adversary at all; nor should it be. But defense counsel has no comparable obligation to ascertain or present the truth. Our system assigns him [or her] a different mission. He [or she] must be…interested in preventing the conviction of the innocent, but...we also insist that he [or she] defend his [or her] client whether he [or she] is innocent or guilty. The State has the obligation to present evidence. Defense counsel need present nothing, even if he [or she] knows what the

> truth is. Defense counsel need not furnish any witnesses to the police, or reveal any confidences of his [or her] client, or furnish any other information to help the prosecution's case. If he [or she] can confuse a witness, even a truthful one, or make him [or her] appear at a disadvantage, unsure or indecisive, that will be his [or her] normal course. Our interest in not convicting the innocent permits [this]….Undoubtedly there are some limits which defense counsel must observe but more often than not, defense counsel will cross-examine a prosecution witness, and impeach him [or her] if he [or she] can, even if he [or she] thinks the witness is telling the truth, just as he [or she] will attempt to destroy a witness who he [or she] thinks is lying. In this respect, as part of our modified adversary system and as part of the duty imposed on the most honorable defense counsel, we countenance or require conduct which in many instances has little, if any, relation to the search for truth (U.S. v. Wade, 1967, pp. 256-258).

One public defender commented on how this problem affects society.

> Why do [former public defenders,] ["]ex-PDs["] make such uniformly bad judges. I mean, there are good judges who were PDs (or private lawyers, for that matter), but so many of the best judges I know were either District Attorneys or worked in the federal system….One theory is that as a [p]ublic [d]efender, we've heard all of the bullshit that our clients put out and we no longer buy it. [However], that would mean that only the most cynical [p]ublic [d]efenders make it to the bench (something that doesn't seem impossible, in light of the political process it takes to make it to the bench)….Another theory is that only the most politically adept PDs make it to the bench, so that when they get there they have thoroughly sold their soul[s] to make it there, and they can't do what their conscience asks them to do when they hit that spot for fear of a backlash by the people that put them there….Another, along the same vein, is that as ex-PDs[,] they are under a greater microscope looking for perceived pro-defense bias (something that will really get you bounced from the bench, in contrast to overt pro-prosecution bias, which will get you a sweet gig within the judging ranks, unless you go completely overboard and totally piss off every PD in the county, something that's hard to do). This holds more water, and sort of goes in line with the previous thought. By promising this independence from their prior profession to everyone under the sun, they at least **feel** as if they are being closely scrutinized for possible bias, and want to cover it up (Public Defender Dude, 2007).

Another attorney commented that criminal defense attorneys would never trust a public defender to defend them in a legal matter. One reason is that attorneys are assigned on an assembly line, which explains mistrust for the "public defender system" contaminated with "hacks" (Cernovich, 2010;

Marx & Engels, 1988). "The talented public defenders do not weed out the hacks" and conniving, "rank amateurs" (Cernovich, 2010; Glenn, 2004, p. 128). Hacks may be incompetent or fear aggressive prosecutors' power to punish their clients, so they fail to file motions, meet with their clients, or sufficiently represent clients in order not to "tick off" prosecutors (Cernovich, 2010). "Aren't public defenders who allow incompetent colleagues to take on clients...allow[ing] evil to flourish by doing nothing" (Cernovich, 2010)? "The general defense of public defender is to ignore the individuals, while attacking the system" (Cernovich, 2010).

Defenders are not a homogenously motivated group (Weiss, 2003). Different motivations create a symphony in which good faith actors may institute and help to uphold morality (Halberstam, 2016; Julien, 2016; Minnick, 2016). However, each motivation may coalesce with immoral agendas (Weiss, 2003). A study of 48 public defenders generally divided them into two groups: those, who were motivated by pragmatic concerns, and those, who were politically motivated. Pragmatic motives included gaining trial experience; desire to practice without overhead; and "lifestyle opportunities for government lawyers" (Weiss, 2003, p. iv). "The political motivations of public defenders, on the other hand, represent a distinctively ideological worldview that defenders are unlikely to share with prosecutors; they often encompass cynical perspectives about the social structure in general and the criminal justice system in particular" (Weiss, 2003, p. iv). Political motivations include constitutional motivations (e.g. justice); altruism toward vulnerable populations experiencing legal and personal problems; culturally implemented antidisestablishmentarianism; anti-authoritarianism (e.g. anti-police, anti-prosecutor, anti-judge, and anti-corrections motivations); and fighting systemic unscrupulousness. To satisfy their drives, they deal with "mediocre salaries, heavy caseloads, unpleasant work environments, uncooperative clients, and the moral stigma" (Weiss, 2003, p. iv; Whitehead, Blankenship, & Wright, 1999).

Due to factors such as job dissatisfaction, sexual deviance, ambition, and culture, defense attorneys may transform courtrooms into sexual showgrounds. Both sides may unleash "provocative imagery and rhetoric in their courtroom pontifications" (Hayes, 2014, p. 194). They may feel validated and empowered by "coarse sex talk" (Hayes, 2014, p. 194; WTOL, 2010). Some civil defense attorneys claiming to represent victims of harassment sexualize their interviews with potential clients and clients; for example, by insisting that clients descriptively emphasize same-sex harassment (e.g. "tell me again about the lesbian stuff"), even though courts are reluctant to consider same-sex harassment, particularly between women, as evidence of a hostile workplace (Dilman, 2016). "Sometimes sexually graphic lines of questioning" are delivered using informal "slang" (Hayes, 2014, p. 194). For example, a defense attorney asked a prosecutrix to describe "how far" the defendant "got his old Joseph into" her (Hayes, 2014, p. 194). "If the prosecuting witness signifie[s] anything other than bewilderment or incomprehension, she might endanger her case. From the standpoint of contemporaries, female familiarity with and comprehension of indelicate vernacular [may] not exactly denote sexual innocence or naïveté" (Hayes, 2014, p. 195).

Explicit language is sometimes substituted for unambiguous "eroticized" "insinuation" (Hayes, 2014, p. 195). "Attorneys…join[] litigants and witnesses in addressing the court in a language decidedly" inappropriate (Hayes, 2014, p. 195). The idea is to give jurors "'spoonfuls of eroticism to help the legal medicine go down'" (Hayes, 2014, p. 195). "[B]riefs directed to appellate and high court judges" have demonstrated for more than a century that "lawyers anticipate[] that justices…welcome their efforts to incorporate bawdy humor into their legal arguments just as audience members" and jurors have "appreciated legal talk imbued with a healthy dose of ribaldry" (Hayes, 2014, p. 195; Cusack, 2016). "The fact that actors at every level of the judicial hierarchy [have] participated in coarse sexual talk and jesting, and that such language [has] infiltrated all facets of the legal process demonstrates just how critical vulgarity" has become to the legal process (Hayes, 2014, p. 196).

"[D]efense lawyers might use the opposite tactic in brief writing, and instead bemoan the voyeuristic, crude aspects of civil sexual suits" and prosecutions (Hayes, 2014, p. 196). "Drawing on middle-class notions of sexual decorum and respectability, they lament[] the graphic—and to their minds—licentious evidence such" matters "force[] the court to consider, or worse yet, to visualize" (Hayes, 2014, p. 196). "Of course towing the line of Victorian sexual ideology allow[s] defense teams to take the moral high ground, a tactic intended to secure acquittals for defendants," who are "forced," like judges and jurors to hear "stories of intimate debauchery" (Hayes, 2014, p. 196; Mirow, 2014). Distinctions may be drawn between a "public pretender" and "critiques about the system," which conscripts "overworked" attorney (Cernovich, 2010). Yet, if they participate in institutional, cultural, or interpersonal sexual deviance, then neither motives nor "cognitive dissonance," will alleviate "unironic" "critiques" about how "totally non-self-aware" the government has become in its attempt to enforce morality (Cernovich, 2010).

Some defendants have "framed their participation in sexual proceedings as disagreeable, particularly the necessary task of eliciting and articulating scabrous sexual accounts" (Hayes, 2014, p. 196). In this purview, defendants appear to be morally appalled by "brazen accusations of an immoral" liar; yet, the system may confront witnesses, who admit to familiarity with sexuality (Hayes, 2014, p. 196). For example, in a sexual harassment matter involving a university professor, one attorney said that jurors were totally unlikely to sympathize with researchers, who had written on the topic of sex (Thibaut, 2016). To prevail would require a victim to put the "whole university on trial" (Ross, 2016).

Systemic disregard and callousness, repetitiveness, injustice, and humor may dissolve defense attorney's moral perspectives resulting in personal weaknesses that evidence pervasive immorality in society; governmental ambivalence toward regulation; and conformity due to lack of deterrence and constant exposure to inconsequential or state sanctioned obscenities.

CHAPTER NINE

JUDGES

In one of his final dissenting opinions, Justice Antonin Scalia said, "[W]hat really astounds is the hubris reflected in today's judicial Putsch" because the majority's opinion is "couched in a style that is as pretentious as its content is egotistic" (Obergefell v. Hodges, 2015, pp. 2629-2630).

> Hubris is sometimes defined as o'erweening pride; and pride, we know, goeth before a fall. The Judiciary is the 'least dangerous' of the federal branches because it has 'neither Force nor Will, but merely judgment; and must ultimately depend upon the aid of the executive arm' and the States, 'even for the efficacy of its judgments.' With each decision of ours that takes from the People a question properly left to them—with each decision that is unabashedly based not on law, but on the 'reasoned judgment' of a bare majority of this Court—we move one step closer to being reminded of our impotence (Obergefell v. Hodges, 2015, p. 2631).

His word "impotence" describes the judiciary's inability constitutionally to interpret morality laws when members of the court, including judges, maintain immoral lifestyles and institutionalize immorality (Obergefell v. Hodges, 2015, p. 2631; Whitman, 1855). They become involved in and become the center of entropic collapse. This collapse may reflect their childhood inabilities to defend themselves during crises (e.g. molestation, incest, and rape). It may demonstrate sympathy for offenders; playout a socio-psychodrama disempowering authority; justify deviance; cloak homosexuality; reconcile violations involving transgender individuals; or condone adopted predilections that manifest trauma (Bolivar, 2005; Cusack & Telesco, 2012; Singhal, 2013; Telesco, 2013). Judges reminded of their past hurts may weakly interpret protective laws and evaluate evidence in favor of violators (Dun & Joseph, 2015).

It is clear that some victims are traumatized by the system because members have patriarchal attitudes (Gruber, 2008; Kohn, 2010). Research has repeatedly uncovered deep dissatisfaction with how judges and personnel treat victims in a condescending, impersonal, dismissive, intimidating, or humiliating way (Kohn, 2010). This could lead to further trauma and dissociative reactions (Walker, 2016). Male and female victims may feel that to exercise agency against the patriarchal system, they must choose taboos, such as abortion, homosexuality, or staying in admittedly abusive relationships; these people are especially degraded by the legal process and justice members (David & Mehlman, 1993; Martinez-Garcia & Guerra-Pujol, 2012; The Smiths, 1985; Walker, 2012; Walker, 2016). The reason that it defies patriarchy to stay in an abusive relationship is because the victim has openly admitted to the abuse. The shame of being abused is supposed to deter victims from disclosing abuse.

Research has shown that victims engage in a cost-benefit analysis of losing personal power to the system versus the extent that the system can assist them in evading harm and danger (Cusack, 2013; Kohn, 2010). Many victims refuse to engage the system because they are doubtful that it will offer any aid, and will only infuriate the aggressor while disempowering the victim (Kohn, 2010). Victims find that an attempt to enforce their rights makes them feel disempowered; and making a judgment call to involve the system will lead to the elimination of or expose their agency in the matter (Kohn, 2010). They may experience surprise when they attempt to enforce rights that have teeth, but no bite; or realize that socially accepted perceptions of rights are impracticable or illusory. This explains why research shows that only women, who feel in control, will report overall satisfaction with the system (Walker, 2016).

On one hand, some judges are survivors of abuse and harassment, and they are influenced by their experiences. They may feel that alternative forms of justice are available to help all victims, including defendants, whose crimes evidence trauma or demonstrate that they attempted to seek help and end cycles of abuse (Nielsen & Zion, 2005). On the other hand, some judges are like slaves to cycles of abuse and willingly assist abusers, ignore victims, and seek to abuse vulnerable people. For example, one judge allegedly solicited from defendants, nude photographs and sex acts; conspired to threaten witnesses; attempted to bribe witnesses; and reduced sentences when defendants agreed to *quid pro quos* (Lauer, 2016). He also paid attorneys over whose cases he presided. He began sexually abusing men and participating in sexual misconduct when he was a prosecutor. Dozens of victims came forward, and many claimed that he paid them to receive spankings with a paddle and to photograph their injuries. He paid for others' court fines in exchange for nude photographs. At the time he resigned from being a judge, he allegedly possessed more than 4,600 photographs of nude men or men in a state of undress. Some deviant judges' behavior may be so flagrant that members of society question whether judges knew that they would be caught, but intended to flout shame and boast of their evasion and lifestyles.

A top-heavy and consumptive oligarchy oppresses people on lower rungs of the legal and social ladder (e.g. left realism) (Siegel, 2010, p. 265). At the base of society are powerless individuals, who fear that if they do not tolerate pressure from the top to ignorantly, furtively, and continuously support their agendas, then they will be attacked under color of law, denied privileges, prevented from exercising liberty, persecuted, and perhaps incarcerated. They are confined to their status at the bottom and are conscripted into the service of immoral oligarchs. People with power (e.g. judges) may feel that moral verbosity may seem revolutionary or futile, which would be unacceptable and pointless. Therefore, they may acquiesce, submit to pressure, and participate in making bad decisions on behalf of an unofficial commitment to self-preservation, reciprocity, and *status quo*.

Survivors may also maintain the *status quo*. Unjust immorality laws, albeit well-intended, may confuse victims. For example, a woman who is prostituted by an abusive pimp to whom she is legally married may fear that she will be shamed as an adulterer and prosecuted for sex crimes if she presses charges. Confusion may disempower the system from being able to help survivors. For example, a minor who has voluntary sex with an adult may feel afraid to disclose sexual abuse perpetrated by a parent because she fears that the system will investigate her life and prosecute the adult with whom she voluntarily had sex. Knowing this systemic and personal debility may allow the abusive parent to take advantage and gain control. The parent may harm other children and continue to abuse the victim into adulthood. The abuser may articulate and reinforce this control to the victim. When victims become judges, they may repeat the cycles and rely on them, perhaps unconsciously, to guide them.

Generationally, the effects appear to have worsened, but the problems "did not change" "the conditions that created America's" sexual corrosion "in the first place" because "the institutions" have "represented explicit manifestations" of sexual deviance for centuries (Lanphear, 2015, p. 97). When corrupt judges are investigated and prosecuted, it has "provided" the people with "some evidence that institutions" are "now fair to all," but also demonstrates that unfairness in that courtroom had been "inherent" in "undermining" the "institution[]" (Lanphear, 2015, p. 97). For example, relentless pursuit by Judge James Turner of a courthouse employee resulted in both parties undergoing psychological evaluation. The doctor found that the judge, who had become attached to the employee and appeared uninvited at her work desk and in public places, was "self-centered" and lacked "insight" (In re Inquiry, 2011, p. 905). These characteristics reflect traditionally oppressive attitudes possessed by judges, who in the past have enforced unjust laws (e.g. miscegenation) (Loving v. Virginia, 1967). A panel of judges dismissed the licentiousness of his conduct by agreeing with the following favorable psychological evaluation:

> [The judge was] an individual who prefer[ed] to be in control, with a need to please others, and might push boundaries and rules to meet some of his needs. His lack of psychological insight, or simply put, sometimes he does not get it, might lead to poor judgment behavior whose intent is to receive attention, social approval and to fulfill the need to help others. His social behavior might be seen as audacious and uninhibited (In re Inquiry, 2011, pp. 905-906).

The judge had expertise in employment law, but the panel found that the judge "was oblivious to the fact that his superior position would exploit" his colleague's "need for a job and reluctance to anger or upset him" (In re Inquiry, 2011, p. 906). The panel seemed oblivious because they found that "there was no" overt "sexual component" to the judge's "actions," which they said "were nonetheless unwarranted and unwelcomed and thus constituted an inappropriate intrusion into [her] personal and family life" (Cusack, 2017; In re Inquiry, 2011, p. 906). The panel justified its characterization of the case at bar by explaining that in 1994, it had removed a female judge for sexually harassing her judicial assistant. They removed another female judge in 1997 for misusing her authority to intimidate and dismiss employees.

The panel minimized Judge Turner's sexual harassment by recounting a bizarre event that they said demonstrated general indecorum.

> [W]hen faced with a juvenile defendant who had failed to pay his court costs, Judge Turner arbitrarily selected an item of the juvenile's personal property—a fake diamond earring—and determined its value based upon a short conversation with the juvenile, offsetting the juvenile's court costs in exchange for the earring. The courtroom is not a forum in which defendants may be required sua sponte by a judge to trade items of clothing or personal property in order to offset the costs assessed against them pursuant to our rules of court (In re Inquiry, 2011, pp. 909-910).

The "cumulative" effect of his "impropriety" "undermin[ed] the decorum of the judiciary" (In re Inquiry, 2011, p. 910). The public may see the judiciary as lacking or being unwilling to institute an appropriate amount of decorum when evidentiary standards are too high or panel members are excessively objective and unwilling to interpret evidence by making inferences about human conduct rather than viewing evidence in relation to gender inequality, history of sexual dominance in America, and oligarchical deviance (Aiken, 1962; In re Inquiry, 2011).

Judicial Qualification Committees (JQCs) may favor judges and allow judges to select the most convenient forms of discipline rather than impose harsher reprimands (Inquiry Concerning a Judge, 2006). For example, Judge Brandt C. Downey sexually harassed attorneys, but was permitted to retire with a public reprimand due to his "long, unblemished record of service as a county and circuit court judge from 1984 until 2002" (Inquiry Concerning a Judge, 2006, p. 648). The JQC said that until the case a bar, his record had been "unmarred" (Inquiry Concerning a Judge, 2006, p. 651). The court found that the judge did not have a history of sexual harassment—although there may have been other silent victims, who were too intimidated by his position and were disempowered by nonexistent or weak enforcement of sexual harassment laws. Furthermore, the JQC felt that because there was no concrete evidence that sexual harassment had influenced his capacity to interpret the law, his misconduct, which they described as "judicial error," but not "misconduct," "did not demonstrate a present unfitness to hold office" (Inquiry Concerning a Judge, 2006, p. 648). He denied sexually harassing female attorneys, but admitted to "improper" "communications" (Inquiry Concerning a Judge, 2006, p. 648). "He admitted to habitually viewing pornography from his computer" at work (Inquiry Concerning a Judge, 2006, p. 651). The JQC failed to impose sanctions because the judge "voluntarily sought psychological counseling" and "was remorseful" (Inquiry Concerning a Judge, 2006, p. 648). The judge requested that he be allowed to retire at the end of his term without any sanction. He lamented that by doing so, "he would forfeit approximately $600,000 worth of benefits" (Inquiry Concerning a Judge, 2006, p. 648). He said that even if the JQC forced him to leave his position, then he could run in another election. However, he would relinquish that right permanently if they accepted his terms. The JQC restricted him to civil, non-criminal matters, and permitted him to continue to serve as a judge because he had "shown sincere remorse" (Inquiry Concerning a Judge, 2006, p. 651). "He admitted to habitually viewing pornography from his computer" (Inquiry Concerning a Judge, 2006, p. 651). The judge stipulated to public reprimand and permanent retirement from the judiciary.

The JQC found no evidence that Judge Downey's misconduct had affected his judicial office. "Although the allegations of sexual harassment" were "extremely serious and very disturbing to" the JQC, they "note[d] that this count *as charged* has been denied and remain[ed] unproven" (Inquiry Concerning a Judge, 2006, p. 651). Although any judge submersed in legal culture rife with sexual harassment may be framed as a scapegoat, "[h]e admitted to habitually viewing pornography from his computer," which is a private activity indirectly related to the pressures of participating in public life (Inquiry Concerning a Judge, 2006, p. 651). They reconciled the fact that they allowed him to choose a mild punishment (i.e. work until retirement) by saying that retirement was a much "harsher sanction than a public reprimand and apology" because it "result[ed] in the loss of significant income otherwise available to him" (Inquiry Concerning a Judge, 2006, p. 651).

Like Judge Downey, who "habitually" used a government computer to view pornography, a chief judge in Texas sent sexual text messages (i.e. "sexting") while serving as vice chair of the State Commission for Judicial Conduct (SCJC) (Inquiry Concerning a Judge, 2006, p. 651; Jenaé, 2016). The judge wrote thousands of explicit messages using social media; and one woman's evidence of it was investigated by a private investigator specializing in digital technologies. The former law enforcement officer said that he took the case *pro bono* because he "personally wanted to know…'Is this our county judge? Is this truly our elected county judge that's doing this?…What is he willing to do? How far is he willing to go?'" (Jenaé, 2016). His client had never met the judge, who allegedly sent her explicit sexual messages. Evidence demonstrated that he sent messages during business hours while attending judicial conduct hearings and while at tax-funded conferences. Although the complainant accelerated the judge's solicitations by replying with sexual photos, the judge independently chose to sext from a SCJC hearing. When the scandal became public, the judge denied the allegations, and said that she had attempted to "destroy his family;" but, he never said that his judicial capacity was compromised by impropriety (Jenaé, 2016). The Texas judge said, "I realize that it is vital that I restructure my life so that I and my family can become whole again. I have suffered a great amount of stress, anxiety, depression, and grief. These issues have affected me and my reaction to all the external pressure has almost caused the destruction of my family" (Jenaé, 2016). SCJC members were responsible for considering whether conduct was sexually inappropriate; and whether this judge's conduct violated the Texas Constitution and Judicial Code of Conduct or publicly brought discredit to the judiciary when he "exercised poor judgment" (Jenaé, 2016). The judge resigned before the committee took action (Morning, 2016).

Cases of judges fornicating, raping, and harassing victims, employees, witnesses, defendants, and attorneys in their chambers and other official locations demonstrate a systemic breakdown. Hobbes (2013) believed that the government's power rose and fell according to how judges meted justice and decided cases.

> [He], whose [error] proceeds from the authority of a Teacher, or an Interpreter of the Law [publically] [authorized], is not so faulty, as he whose [error] [proceeds] from a peremptory [pursuit] of his own principles, and reasoning: For what is taught by one that [teaches] by [publically] Authority, the Common-wealth [teaches], and hath a resemblance of Law, till the same Authority [controls] it; and in all Crimes that contain not in them a [denial] of the [Sovereign] Power, nor are against an evident Law, [Excuses] totally: whereas he that [grounds] his actions, on his private Judgement, ought according to the rectitude, or [error] thereof, to stand, or fall (Hobbes, 2013, p. 244).

The public may not be held responsible for their immoral actions if judges were to acknowledge that even the most deviant members of the judiciary lead by example. However, judges may unintentionally wield power to achieve personal psychosexual comfort, but unintentionally set a tone of harassment and sexual misconduct.

Due to their authority and power, judges may lack self-awareness or may begin to believe that their impropriety defines or relates to the success of the justice system in their local communities and workplaces. For example, Judge David W. Lanier was a powerful pillar of the community, who felt that coercive sexual relations helped to bond his entourage and keep under his control otherwise powerless victims and helpless women, such as Vivian Forsythe, one of the victims, who he forcibly sodomized in the judge's chambers (O'Brien, 1996). He invited the victim to apply for employment and then sexually abused her because she was a disenfranchised woman viewed as being reckless, if not immoral, in the eyes of the community. He may have believed that his acceptance legitimized and sanitized her; and to some extent it did, even though his forcible sexual encounters were an open secret among some members of the justice system, who revered him. He was eventually brought to justice; and sentenced to 25 years' incarceration for sexual misconduct with several court employees.

Judges may not objectively observe their sexually inappropriate behavior because of gender bias and traditional occupation of male judges as enforcers of traditional family values. Perhaps to balance what they perceive is a misunderstanding of their roles as social patriarchs, judges may attempt to overlook sexual indiscretions perpetrated by others. They may feel that ignoring some impropriety alleviates people from oppressive oversight and over-enforcement and makes them popular.

Members of the judiciary personally may feel that sexual deviance is not wrong when it is harmless (Carline, 2011). They see that laws and regulations should be interpreted to uphold governmental authority, protect people, restore victims, and punish and deter bad faith actors. They may personally interpret relevant morality laws in a manner that does not apply to their conduct. Regulations and laws interpreted to prevent consensual hedonism or deviance may seem incorrect or unconstitutional to some judges. They may focus on rectifying and punishing concrete injuries rather than presiding over other people's emotions and micromanaging their professional and interpersonal relationships according to idealistic, sexist (e.g. misandrist), or outdated ethical and legal standards.

Judges are entrusted with power to make just decisions in cases and behave ethically inside and outside the courtroom; but, their perceptions of justice, ethics, and sexuality are subjected to inappropriate and unfair cultural, social, and environmental influences that they may endure, and at times, may perpetuate (Fox News, 2016). Respondents in one study rated ethicality of interactions between males and females, who were portrayed in 19 scenarios as clients and counselors (Schwabach, 1994). Respondents' moral development and orientation, sex role schematics, and social role interpretations were examined for gender differences. Male and female respondents differently measured unethical behaviors. Women were likelier than men to respond conservatively to counselor-client sexual scenarios, except when clients and counselors were depicted as both being men. In those cases, men were as likely as women conservatively to view the ethical implications because men may have felt that male clients only could be victimized by other men. Perceptions of ethicality were also predicted by academic ability, moral development and orientation, and sex role identification. Although judgeship may often demonstrate academic ability, the other qualities are only perceptible by observation and to those, who are informed. This information may not be made available to appointers and voters. This study also found that moral development and orientation did not affect judgment about ethicality, further supporting the idea that judges may be happily oblivious to specific unethical behavior that conforms to their perceptions of gender, sex, social roles, power dynamics, etc. Their perceptions of sex differences may be expected by other members of the court to manifest as gender role acceptance.

Perceptions aside, their behavior may prove why law is more important than morality for mediating sexual deviance. Although, with public figures perception is reality. Mediation of sexual deviance may not be based on morality; effective regulations may be based on the state's police power to protect health, safety, and the general welfare (Cusack, 2013; Cohen, 2015). Yet, using other police power circuitously to regulate morality may be unjust. Cesare Beccaria postulated that punishment, other than when absolutely necessary, is tyranny. One study examined relationships between immorality and criminalization of 11 deviant behaviors, such as victimless sex crimes (Fradella & Vogel, 2009). Personal conduct violating social norms and criminal statues appeared to be more immoral. This study found that criminal sanctions were perceived as being necessary in response to immoral actions, but not necessarily for sexual conduct that was consensual. Morality may be perceived as being necessary to mediate deviance when criminal sanctions are inappropriate.

Deterrence theory, whether analyzed as situational crime prevention, specific deterrence, cost, differential association, or in terms of control and social learning, may be interpreted to apply purely to moral sanctions even when those sanctions only involve shaming or stigmatization, but not penological consequences. However, when culture, environment, and workplace politics are supported or led by judges' inappropriate attitudes, judges arc unable to be deterred by external controls because they do not relate. They do not foresee consequences that only apply to underlings, which they fail to apply to defendants through their attitudes and actions with subordinates and their equals.

Morality may be used where law is grey, unapplied, or muted. Without the law representing to be based on morality, immorality may become more pervasive and lead to greater systemic corrosion because "'doing the right thing' depends, in large part, on morality vis-à-vis both the perceived moral legitimacy of the law itself and the perceived execution of fair processes" (Fradella & Vogel, 2009, p. 207). Victimless crimes, whether perpetrated by judges, such as prostitution and transmission of obscenity, may be viewed as relatively moral even when morality is viewed as being elemental to the state's law and power. One study examined legal forms of sexual deviance, such as fornication, same-sex and opposite-sex sodomy, and pornography. Respondents discussed their perceptions of immorality, criminality, and personal history. People identifying as having Asian, African, Native, or Latin American heritage, juveniles, conservatives, and religious people were likelier to label this deviant behavior as being immoral (Cusack, 2015; Fradella & Vogel, 2009; Griffin, 1961). Though judges may be religious and conservative, all are adults and most are European American males (Fradella & Vogel, 2009). This study found that gender did not correlate with immoral labels for fornication or heterosexual sodomy. Males were almost twice as likely as females to label homosexual sodomy as being immoral. Females were twice as likely to judge pornography purchases as being immoral. At 22 years-old, people were less likely than juveniles to view the conduct as being immoral. This study's findings also support the proposition that judges' personal experiences relate to whether they believe that sexual behaviors should be criminalized. Judges ought not to use their personal perspectives to judge cases or the constitutionality of laws; however, they may, like the majority of respondents in the study, believe that the law ought not to regulate pornography, sodomy, or fornication and view cases with bias. Furthermore, 55% of 286 respondents judged premarital sex to be immoral, but had participated in it. Thus, personal experience, judgment of immorality, and perception of criminality were not necessarily related for these respondents and may not be related for judges. Ultimately, when judges are punished for egregious crimes, the public may feel vindicated; but many members of society may feel that the law does not apply equally to everyone.

The people have been explicitly informed that the judiciary does not represent them demographically; and therefore, may be unable to carefully consider the importance of judicial restraint (Cusack, 2013; Cusack & Waranius, 2015; Liptak, 2016). In Obergefell v. Hodges (2015), dissenter Antonin Scalia complained that the justices had stolen power from the people to vote on same-sex marriage. Justice Scalia explained that it was due to their elitist and selective backgrounds.

> Judges are selected precisely for their skill as lawyers; whether they reflect the policy views of a particular constituency is not (or should not be) relevant. Not surprisingly then, the Federal Judiciary is hardly a cross-section of America. Take, for example, this Court, which consists of only nine men and women, all of them successful lawyers who studied at Harvard or Yale Law School. Four of the nine are natives of New York City. Eight of them grew up in east- and west-coast States. Only one hails from the vast expanse in-between. Not a single Southwesterner or even, to tell the truth, a genuine Westerner (California does not count). Not a single evangelical Christian (a group that comprises about one quarter of Americans), or even a Protestant of any denomination. The strikingly unrepresentative character of the body voting on today's social upheaval would be irrelevant if they were functioning as *judges*, answering the legal question whether the American people had ever ratified a constitutional provision that was understood to proscribe the traditional definition of marriage. But of course the Justices in today's majority are not voting on that basis; *they say they are not*. And to allow the policy question of same-sex marriage to be considered and resolved by a select, patrician, highly unrepresentative panel of nine is to violate a principle even more fundamental than no taxation without representation: no social

> transformation without representation (Obergefell v. Hodges, 2015, p. 2629).

He also claimed that "[t]he predominant attitude of tall-building lawyers with respect to the questions presented in these cases is suggested by the fact that the American Bar Association deemed it in accord with the wishes of its members to file a brief in support of the petitioners" (Obergefell v. Hodges, 2015, p. 2629). His indignation clearly describes how an oligarchy usurped the people's power to weaken the government's ability to regulate morality.

CHAPTER TEN

MILITARY

The U.S. military has suffered poor public relations recently due to an onslaught of press coverage about sexual harassment and impropriety, including adultery and prostitution. "Essential to any form of American business is the blame game. It is never one's own fault—but always the fault of others" (Morrissey, 2013, p. 205). Simultaneously, they have revised codes prohibiting sodomy, transgenderism, and same-sex marriage benefits (Balduzzi, 2013; Cox, 2016; Lamothe, 2016). Before Don't Ask, Don't Tell and subsequent changes, "honesty ignited irrational fear in an America where men were draped with medals for killing other men yet imprisoned for loving one another" (Morrissey, 2013, p. 196).

The military prohibited the sale of pornography on military bases. For decades, proscriptions against pornography have been the subject of high-powered battles, for example involving Bob Guccione of *Penthouse Magazine* (*New York Times Magazine,* 1997). Recently, the Army stopped selling magazines depicting nudity because they claimed that sales were low, even though "morality groups and the brewing sexual assault scandal in the military have raised the temperature on issues such as the availability of pornography to the troops" (Zoroya, 2013). Their asserted rationale may be supported by a general decline in the sale of nude pictorials. For example, *Playboy* briefly discontinued the sale of nude magazines claiming that softcore depictions had become *passé* when so many hardcore images were freely available online (Cusack, 2017; Snider, 2017). The magazine returned from "sabbatical" demonstrating demand for stylized depictions of nudity despite the prevalence of free obscenity (Glenn, 2004, p. 117). The magazine said, "*Playboy* will always be a lifestyle brand focused on men's interests,...but as gender roles continue to evolve in society, so will we" (Snider, 2017).

Sex and gender continue to be a source of conflict in the military. The U.S. military has opened combat roles to women, who are now attending training previously reserved exclusively for men. Progressive changes reduce the military's reputation as a chauvinistic or sexually fascist institution, but carry with them new fears about sexual impropriety on bases between members, which may discredit the service. Sexism off-base continues to suggest that it prevails on-base. For example, Marines United was a Facebook page that posted thousands of depictions of nude and partially unclothed female servicemembers and veterans (McLaughlin & Stapleton, 2017). Some of the photos were "revenge porn," and some may have been solicitous (Cusack, 2014, p. 175; Moore, 2017; Rosewarne, 2016, p. 114).

Claims about the photos varied significantly. Some people involved said that images were not posted "maliciously and many women submitted their own photos" (McLaughlin & Stapleton, 2017). Some alleged victims were derided as being manipulative participants disavowing their roles as bisexual prostitutes. Elle Audra, a tattoo model, described the webpage as promoting "slut shaming and rape culture mentality" (McLaughlin & Stapleton, 2017). Some comments on the site supported her characterizations. Commenters blamed the victims, saying, "Women whose images were posted brought this on themselves," and they "should be raped" (McLaughlin & Stapleton, 2017). One comment said, "Admit nothing, deny everything, make counteraccusations" (McLaughlin & Stapleton, 2017). Like inmates, who have bragged about having sex with wardens' wives, one commenter said of an investigation into the website, "It would be hilarious if one of these FBI or (Naval Criminal Investigative Service) f***s found their wife on here" (McLaughlin & Stapleton, 2017). There may have been dozens of similar sites operated by cronies. Marines United alone had 30,000 members. Many members attempted to reject women from the group, which was supposed to be exclusively comprised of male servicemembers and veterans, but included females, civilians, and catfish (Cusack, 2017).

Prostitution is a severe problem in the military. It occurs in offices, locker rooms, bathrooms, barracks, military housing, parks, parking lots, tactical obstacle courses, and other areas. Prostitutes (e.g. veterans and dependents) may visit bases and servicemembers may prostitute themselves; and it occurs at military functions (e.g. escorts). Phillip A. Spight was a pimp, who was enlisted in the military. He ran an escort service that operated on and off the base. Spight prostituted members and non-members to other servicemembers and civilians. He was prosecuted by the military, but explained that during his operation, he was unconcerned about being arrested by the state police. "It has happened in the past that clients have turned in their escorts and owners…to the police because they did not get what they expected" (Spight, 2005, p. 11). He said that his lack of fear was rational because "[i]n this line of work you get all kinds of clients[: b]usinessmen, judges, lawyers, cops, dope dealers, etc." (Spight, 2005, p. 11). He described the protection offered to each party in the form of silence as a "sacrifice" (Spight, 2005, p. 11). "Life is full of fun. Sometimes you have to make those sacrifices to get what you're seeking[; so] do the clients" (Spight, 2005, p. 11). "Those escorts that might be performing illegal acts are told right off the bat, not to talk about their calls, unless it is on a need to know basis" (Spight, 2005, p. 8). Spight defended against allegations that prostitution is a patriarchal infection within the military and society. "I say they're paying for love. Many say they are paying for a quickie. Not just that, many are like me and you. They are lonely, divorced, and shy, single[; horny], low self-esteem or just in love with you or your picture on the website" (Spight, 2005, p. 11). He claimed that prostitutes cannot pay all of their bills and expenses with a military salary; and they turn to prostitution to supplement their income.

> I'm…[speaking] based on an adult business owner's point of view. Even though many people have their own opinions as to what the average escort, dance, stripper, etc., really do[es] in this line of work, you would be surprised. In some cases, it's not what you think. Meaning, you will always have a bad apple in a bunch, even at the grocery stores. But you have to see why you have those so called bad apples. You have to see that many will do what they have to do to make ends meet. Regardless of what it is. That's just life. You would lie; steal, cheat, etc. to get what you want. Why do you think people are out there selling drugs? Life is not easy at all…if you don't have the tools to get where you want to be. That is the reason you make sacrifices….[Y]ou decide to make…life better for you regardless of the outcome, [which] can include breaking the law, which we have all done at some point in our lives (Spight, 2005, p. 8).

Spight blamed society for creating unreasonable moral standards that hinder survival and correlate with duplicity.

> You sometimes have to put your pride to the side to make it happen. I have plenty of times. It's sad to say that the cops charging the escort for prostitution,…whether they committed this crime or not…, are the same ones that use the service. They are sometimes the same cop the escort serviced the other day. Still today, that is one of the main reasons I don't trust the system. They love to come after the business owners, hoping for a scare to get us to shut down, and every day, someone does (Spight, 2005, p. 8).

He complained that his due process rights were violated in order to punish him more severely. "I have still not been to court. They even served me with an outdated warrant, ransacked my home, confiscated and kept my records and computer equipment, hoping that I would get scared and shut down my business" (Spight, 2005, p. 9). He said that the government attempted to shame him. "They went so far as to have local news crews run stories throughout the state…labelling me as the owner of some kind of giant prostitution ring" (Spight, 2005, p. 9). However, he said that their shaming tactics "[d]idn't work" to deter, reform, or punish him (Spight, 2005, p. 9). He explained that because he "love[s] to fight back," their tactics have had no effect, even though he "still" had "not seen a judge" in "[a]lmost two years" after his arrest (Spight, 2005, p. 9).

He was affected by their rogue and passive-aggressive attempts to severely punish him for crimes that are difficult to prove. "I spent over ten thousand dollars to get out of jail on bail" (Spight, 2005, p. 9). While awaiting trial he continued to pay costly legal bills. He explained the fruitlessness of attempting to prosecute prostitution charges; but also identified the motive. "The legal system makes good money off of escort services…finally to go to court to be found not guilty. [T]he bad thing about it is that the system already knows, before they even arrest you, that you will be found not guilty, but you will contribute a sizable amount of money to gain your freedom" (Spight, 2005, p. 9). The system acts as an operation to regulate sexual vice, but not constitutionally punish offenders.

Spight described a cycle of moral decay caused by and resulting in the government experiencing weak power to enforce morality.

> You are going to be a target because the state wants that money, and besides, the officers would love to harass you so that they can see your escorts. I remember a situation where one of my escorts was busted for prostitution,…though no sex was performed....She was told by the arresting officer that he would drop the charges if she would go out with him. She refused, and guess what[,]…she was arrested and hauled off to jail. She got out the following day, and he actually called the service on his off time to meet with her" (Spight, 2005, p. 9).

He explained that morality laws are inapplicable to escort services. Spight compared prostitution to a fundamental right to have consensual sex in private; and suggested that escort services sufficiently attenuate remuneration from sex as not to violate pandering and prostitution laws. Police officers seeking sex will arrest escorts for hooking, thereby proving the state's powerlessness and justice members' willingness to break the law (Cusack, 2017). "The law says that what happens between two consenting adults is their business, but they never say anything about money exchange. To me, that is entrapment, especially if they set it up" (Spight, 2005, p. 9).

Despite having witnessed victimization, the officer's law-breaking sexual deviance, and moral decay within the government and society, Spight maintained that some law enforcement officers are law-abiding and "good" (Spight, 2005, p. 9). "The system is not right at all, but you still have to keep in mind, there are good cops and bad cops; they are human as well" (Spight, 2005, p. 9). However, he felt that many law enforcement officers were motivated by lust even when responding to calls to protect victims, for example domestic violence (Fernandez v. California, 2014).

> I remember I got arrested in my own house for PI (Public Intoxication)...[—i]n my own house! What happened was, I called the cops on my girlfriend, and they took me to jail. I just called them to remove her because we were fighting. The point of what I'm getting at is my girlfriend was a model type and everyone loved her. When the cops arrived[,] this particular officer thought that he had the opportunity to get rid of me, so that he could sweet talk her. Of course, she didn't fall for it[; but,] they do try. Constantly patrolling my house, hoping to see the girl that he is in love with that he saw on the website. They would even see cars in my driveway and run the escorts' plates just to find out where they live. [However,] officers are not the only ones[, who] do that (Spight, 2005, p. 9).

Spight compared officers' behavior to "stalkers" (Spight, 2005, p. 9). He said that because escorts "[g]et plenty of those," they "have to be very careful" and leery of police encounters (Spight, 2005, p. 9). This would impair their ability to call police to assist them to exit sex trafficking and seek protection from abusive pimps, who may threaten to abandon, report, harm, rape, rob, and kill them (Lyter, 2016; McMahon & Francis, 2010; Parker, 2016; Woody, 2016). Avoiding police encounters "is one reason why a lot of escorts rather have someone drop them off, instead of driving their own cars to work" (Spight, 2005, p. 9). Being unable to comply with police officers' demands for favoritism with prostitutes caused Spight to worry that he would "go to jail for just owning a business of referrals" (Spight, 2005, p. 9). Spight bragged about police powerlessness and his knowledge of and ability to defend against criminal charges using contract law because hookers "are not even, by law, employees. They are considered by law as independent contractors who are willing to help" him "make some money" (Cusack, 2017; Spight, 2005, p. 9).

At Spight's court martial hearing the trial counsel described how Spight operated his business from a military base.

> Now, where did the accused find his prostitutes? Well, he was sitting at the largest military instillation in the world, and he recruited his prostitutes

> from active duty soldiers and dependent wives….[N]ot only did Fort Hood, Texas supply him with prostitutes, Fort Hood, Texas also provided him with free office space, the accused was leasing his office space rent free. You see, the accused ran his prostitution business out of his government quarters. Yes, ladies and gentlemen, in post housing (Spight, 2005, p. 34).

Trial counsel depicted Spight as being a remorseless psychopath, a label that has been used to describe typical military members. Like prison inmates, military members may enter the service because they suffer from mental illness (e.g. psychopathy), which worsens as they serve their commitments (Cusack, 2015; Cusack, 2016; Witt & Conroy, 2008).

A deviant person (e.g. psychopath) may justify deviance by extolling a virtue (e.g. charisma) (Gerth & Mills, 1946). For example, a servicemember may justify patronizing a prostitute because it alleviates tension, which minimizes rage and domestic violence (APA, 2013). A callous narcissist may claim that giving gifts in exchange for sex is morally inferior to prostitution (Prasad, 1999). Research on sex buyers ("johns") demonstrated their belief that direct exchange of payment for sex is morally superior to gift exchange because the sex market offers transparent pricing, independence from the traditional family structure, and forthrightness typically absent from interpersonal relationships (Hartford, 2014; McMahon & Francis, 2010; Prasad, 1999).

> [Prostitution creates] moral economies for their participants: they are economies embodying moral beliefs about individual autonomy, democratic equality, and unambiguous, nondiscretionary fulfillment of obligations. Critics of the market do a disservice in ignoring moral appeals of market exchange. Sociological analyses that pit norms against self-interest ignore the ways in which norms can enable and constrain self-interested market behavior (Prasad, 1999, p. 181).

This research supports Spight's assertion that morality laws impair servicemembers' abilities to survive. Spight's argument that the government benefits from prosecuting prostitution by charging court fees and employing judges, attorneys, staff, corrections and law enforcement officers, and other members, illustrates how prostitution is a market economy on which the government capitalizes (Gerth & Mills, 1946). Yet, when properly regulated, sex-buying can be a victimless crime and market industry that protects workers and clients. By legalizing and regulating prostitution the government could extoll its virtuousness even though it may cause significant harms (e.g. budgetary crises and secondary effects) (Cusack, 2014; Gerth & Mills, 1946). It may also relieve some servicemembers of burdensome secrecy and increase taxable revenue.

CHAPTER ELEVEN

AGENTS AND EMPLOYEES

Agents and employees may breach their duties causing public criticism even though they lack direct control over the system, law, and society. Due to culture, training, and pressure, they may begin to think that fear of termination, guilt by implication, and threat of exposure justify deviance and permissiveness (Marx & Engels, 1988). They may believe that to be a team player and a good person, they must ignore deviance (Hobbes, 2013; Kant, 1788; Schaeffler, 1999). They may also feel that the greater good would be to cover indiscretions in order to preserve the government's image to maintain power, which ultimately acts on the people's behalf to protect the majority from immoral and violative conduct.

Employees and agents lack sufficient power to feel in control of the workplace environment (Marx & Engels, 1988). Sexual deviance may give them a feeling of being in control; for example, they may feel as if sexual deviance in their workplaces is a mechanism for not selling their souls to the government or their employers. They may bring their personal attitudes toward sex into the office because they do not believe that they are accountable for filling leadership roles. They may also fear revenge under color of law or use of the system to obfuscate evidence of revenge. For example, they may believe that if they reported a colleague's threats then they would be ignored by the system.

They may only expose their knowledge of institutional deviance when they stand to gain. Low-level employees may expose each other because destructive behavior may feel like empowerment (Siegel, 2010). Although they may be accused of acting resentfully, despite selfish intentions, they fulfill their obligations. Thus, they strengthen the Leviathan because they are empowered as people to intervene when government members fail to use their power evenly to enforce rules (Dressler & Garvey, 2012).

Fig. 11.1, Tallahassee City Hall, Tallahassee, Florida.

An example of employee misconduct was paraded in the press when scandal erupted at Tallahassee City Hall after numerous disciplined and unconfronted misdeeds and crimes were discovered, including immoral sexual conduct that occurred in a public restroom (Alcock, 2014). Disciplinary action was partially implemented after a female custodial worker used a male security guard's phone inside City Hall's restroom to record a lewd exhibition. While inside the City Hall building, the security guard played the video for other men. A city electrician exposed himself to a custodial worker; and she offered to have sex with other employees and simulated sex with some employees. Some of the misconduct was investigated. As a consequence, the female custodial worker was dismissed. The contracted security guard was investigated by his private employer, which found that he had not been involved in sexual misconduct. However, he was barred from working in City Hall and disciplined for not maintaining a safe and professional distance from other employees. The city said that when they learned about the behavior, which embroiled them in public scandal, and occurred along with several other illegal activities, the city "took" "action" to "focus on the importance of" "respecting all people" because such "disheartening" behavior would "not be tolerated in the workplace" (Alcock, 2014).

Fig. 11.2, Tallahassee City Hall bathroom where an explicit video was recorded, Tallahassee, Florida.

Exposure of secretaries, court reporters, interpreters, bailiffs, and other employees' improprieties may demonstrate bloodthirst in public humiliation. Incidents may provide the public with excuses to question the system and all of its employees. Reasoning, such as "where there's smoke, there's fire" and "one bad apple spoils the bunch" may allow the public to buy into the idea of systemic moral decay that excuses their sexual foibles. Sloughing powerless employees articulates the Leviathan's might without disrupting its essential functions or calling on more powerful employees to implement moral authority in their own lives or the lives of their superiors.

Becoming sensitive to institutionalized immorality may symbolize to blue collar workers and white collar staff that they have ascended or will be invited into the oligarchy; however, acquiescence to institutionalized immorality threatens powerless employees, who may be treated as dispensable players (Heine, 2005). It also demonstrates that they have drifted from the protection and authority of external control and social morals. Their participation signifies that immorality is preferred by the people, not just the rulers; and therefore, irrational and unpopular morality laws should be stricken and unenforceable under the state's police power.

Justice employees may have deviant sex not only as a bribe or power exchange, but to avoid courtship at work (Prasad, 1999). Casual sex may limit affairs of the heart, damaging "office spouses," and abuse of authority (e.g. in prisons) (Christiansen v. Everglades College, 2015; White, 2014). Staff and employees may view sexual impropriety differently than other kinds of professionals, such as officers and judges. For example, judges, prosecutors, social service staff, and police officers may hold distinct views about causes of rape; deterrence and prevention; and veracity of the allegations based on their professional judgement and experience, personal attitudes, and role within the justice system (Feldman-Summers & Palmer, 1980).

Staff and employees may ascend through the ranks, for example practice law, work as magistrates, or serve as judges. Their experiences at lower-levels of power may inform their decision-making and influence their conduct (Cernovich, 2010; Marx & Engels, 1988). Impropriety manifesting in small towns may be particularly damaging because illusions are formulated and shattered as employees work in more powerful or prominent positions (Durkheim, 2008). Ascent through the ranks preserves culture and maintains power for those, who institutionalize traditional and sexual deviance. Justice systems in "largely rural" areas are "hardly reflections of" "modern," liberated, or progressive American morals (Hayes, 2014, p. 192). They reflect "efficient law that elite legal professionals [have] wished to implement" (Hayes, 2014, p. 192). A justice system "is both a legal and a social space, and individuals in…surrounding locale[s] [have] gathered as much to convene and gossip with neighbors and friends as to observe legal processes at work" (Hayes, 2014, p. 192). Lawyers may amass former colleagues, associates, acquaintances, friends, and relatives connected to "the task of presenting legal arguments to the court from ordinary litigants" (Hayes, 2014, p. 192). The public may believe that they, "in most cases, still learned the trade in the local law offices of their elder colleagues, not in professional law schools" (Hayes, 2014, p. 192). Magistrates and judges are "often poorly trained by the standards of prominent professionals. Finally, the local [people] acting as jury members [are] sometimes personally acquainted with one or both of the litigants. This familiarity, of course, impede[s] their ability to deliberate as impartial, 'truth' seeking bodies" (Hayes, 2014, p. 192). Members of the system may also serve as jurors. "The fact that the faces representing the legal power of the state [are] often familiar ones influence[s] the ways in which witnesses conduct themselves on the stand" (Hayes, 2014, p. 192). Some top officials have "proceeded in the same conversational and casual tone" from when they worked as staff "merely rehashing intimate tales before old pals" rather than effectuating justice (Hayes, 2014, pp. 192-193).

Fig. 11.3, Chi Omega Sorority House, Tallahassee, Florida.

Ted Bundy is an example of a sexual deviant, who rose to prominence through the justice system. Psychopath Bundy placated to powerful figures, including Republican Washington Governor Daniel J. Evans, who wrote a letter of recommendation for Bundy to attend law school in Utah; and Judge Edward D. Cowart, who was a former police officer. Bundy was sentenced by Judge Cowart to die by electric chair in Dade County, Florida for the murder of two Florida State University Chi Omega sorority sisters. Judge Cowart seemed to be engaged by Bundy when he issued his sentence.

> Take care of yourself, young man. I say that to you sincerely; take care of yourself, please. It is an utter tragedy for this court to see such a total waste of humanity as I've experienced in this courtroom. You're a bright young man. You'd have made a good lawyer, and I would have loved to have you practice in front of me, but you went another way, partner. Take care of yourself. I don't feel any animosity toward you. I want you to know that. Once again, take care of yourself (Wilkins & Peterson, 2009).

Bundy's ability to propitiate powerful people became evident when he attended the Republican Convention in Miami, Florida in 1968 as a supporter of Republican Presidential candidate Nelson Rockefeller. He worked on Rockefeller's campaign, and then worked with Washington Governor Daniel J. Evans, who later served in the U.S. Senate. He assisted Washington Republican Party chairman, Ross Davis. He was appointed by Governor Evans to the Seattle Crime Prevention Advisory Committee, which involved working with police and discussing policies affecting hitchhikers, one of whom Bundy later raped and killed.

During Bundy's trial, the media was "entranced by" Bundy's "celebrity" (Cusack, 2013; Grossman & Friedman, 2011, p. 97). Further fueling morbid sexual interests, the media graphically focused on the victims' injuries while repeatedly describing Bundy's attractiveness and appeal (Cusack, 2014; Cusack, 2015; Cusack, 2015). This is "a prime example of how Euro-American media and the homogenously Euro-American male Republican Party, along with U.S. 'law enforcement,' view harming women as noble, courageous, and admirable" (Wilkins & Peterson, 2009). "If he could have kept his murders and rapes hidden behind 'color of law' as most American police and politicians do, he likely could have been a Senator or Presidential Candidate for the Republican Party" particularly because the "Euro-American male media and the U.S. [j]ustice [s]ystem's seemingly homosexual attraction to Bundy" made him "well-liked and well connected" (Wilkins & Peterson, 2009). This extreme behavior may be one reason that "men's innate role as protector[s] for their children and [wives] seems to be dissipating into oblivion in this current society" (Marx & Engels, 1988; Wilkins & Peterson, 2009). Employees like Bundy "have undoubtedly taken the lead in this disgusting, disturbing phenomenon" (Wilkins & Peterson, 2009). For example, "[p]olice in Seattle, who once-upon-a-time were advised by mass rapist/murderer Ted Bundy, do not punish this" deplorable "behavior at a government level and seemingly, the society at large in that area accepts it as normal" (Wilkins & Peterson, 2009). People, who rise through the ranks, influence the entire system (Chin, 2013; Cusack, 2015). For example, "Republicans (and some Democrats also) have always been cop-apologists and would never remotely chastise one of their 'heroes' for murdering and/or raping yet another American citizen;" but, "the facts remain that King County-Seattle area government officials not only [accepted] beloved mass murderer Ted Bundy as a Republican politician, but also as a police policy maker" (Wilkins & Peterson, 2009).

> 'Black' Americans and all American women have always had to 'fight' for inalienable rights in this country; and the fact the aforementioned are the primary targets for contemporary and otherwise government-sanctioned murders, rapes, and manipulations, should not surprise anyone. The 'mainstream' media in this country make the Ted Bundy's…and thug police out to be heroes, because, coincidentally, they primarily target said aforementioned people. However, after 9/11, European American men ('[W]hitey' is the term Euro-American media and their 'bloggers' use for themselves) have increasingly become just as 'disposable' to the hegemony as women and '[B]lacks' (Wilkins & Peterson, 2009).

Ted Bundy, a manipulative government insider, would "be proud of his Republican and police pupils of the Northwest. The sad truth is, the U.S. government and media are also proud" (The Asian Riff, 1847; Wilkins & Peterson, 2009). When insiders climb and destabilize the appearance of a morality-making government, the sexual oligarchy may feel threatened, but ultimately benefit as expectations are lowered. People's desire to lead moral lives without government supervision remains in crisis due to lack of leadership and uncertainty about the future direction of politics and social climate regarding sexual matters.

CHAPTER TWELVE

CUSTOMS AND BORDER PROTECTION (CBP) AND IMMIGRATION AND CUSTOMS ENFORCEMENT (ICE)

Customs and Border Protection (CBP) and Immigration and Customs Enforcement (ICE) have been accused of serious immorality even though they serve as line of defense against sex crime. For example, they have a responsibility to prevent materials, such as snuff films and child pornography, from being imported or exported (Cusack, 2014; Cusack, 2015; Cusack, 2016; Cusack, 2016). For more than two centuries, federal customs agents have used Congress' commerce power to enforce morality legislation, even though morality is a state police power (18 U.S.C. §§ 1460-1463, 2017). Federal use of customs to enforce morality has survived various challenges, including those made under the First, Fifth, and Fourteenth Amendments (Moran, 2015; U.S. v. One Package of Japanese Pessaries, 1936). Due to the internet, their strategies to uphold morality laws have shifted from focusing on the mail to human trafficking at the border (18 U.S.C. § 2252B-C, 2017). For example, more than 17 indictments resulted recently after ICE investigated a Thai sex trafficking ring using counterfeit visas and passports (ICE, 2016). Hundreds of women, called "flowers," were "owned" and traded for money in American "houses of prostitution where they" were "forced to work long hours—often all day, every day—having sex with strangers" (ICE, 2016). Poor women and children, who do not speak English, promised to repay traffickers between $40,000 and $60,000. Their photographs and services were advertised on websites, such as Backpage and Eros. Their lives and families were threatened to assure compliance until they repaid their debts for pimping services, including surgical enhancements (Cusack, 2016).

Customs officers may take suspected victims and violators into custody. They have repeatedly been accused of flagrantly violating their duties to protect detainees (BFC News, 2015; Cusack, 2014; Cusack, 2015; Cusack, 2016). The climate in customs offices appears to be more sexually charged than other government agencies (Werner & Strickler, 2015). Dozens of officers have been indicted and hundreds of complaints of sexual misconduct have been filed in the past five years. Although approximately 15,000 agents work for CBP, "a string of cases" involving "on or off duty" agents, describe gruesome "sex crimes against women or children," and have tarnished their organization's reputation (Werner & Strickler, 2015). Only recently CBP said it implemented a "zero tolerance policy" against sexual abuse (Werner & Strickler, 2015).

Agents have been alleged to commit rape, sexual abuse, and sexual harassment, including having detainees unnecessarily strip, masturbate, fellate, sodomize, and ingest semen (Cusack, 2015; Cusack, 2015). "Indiscretions like drunken skinny dippy;" "sex-ring[s];" "acquiescent behavior occurring in the office with no attempt to disguise the vulgar language;" "strip 'pornopoly';" "male coworkers" "grop[ing]" each other's "private parts" and "influenc[ing]" each other "to have sex;" "sexual innuendos;" "obscene phone calls and various sexual-aids placed in co-workers mailboxes;" "swinger parties" at supervisors' homes; sexual harassment against men and women; coercion; violation; verbal abuse; and gender, race, and age discrimination are common in U.S. Department of Homeland Security (DHS) and customs (Candiotti, Levitt, & Cratty, 2012; Dvorak, 2009; Klausner, 2015; Moran, 2015).

Sexual misconduct reports commonly have been made against male and female customs agents and inspectors, who get "promoted in record time;" yet, customs has dismissed relatively few people (Dvorak, 2009). One ICE employee said, "When I started with the agency I was told by my superiors that I was nothing more than" my body "and if I played my cards right I'd move up real fast" (Cusack, 2015; Dvorak, 2009). Those employees, who resisted "the sexcapades quickly" have attempted to transfer, but "once word got out [that] they refused to partake in sex games they were ostracized" (Dvorak, 2009). An employee said, "It is a very eerie feeling to have to work among" sexual violators, who "seem to want to always be in your space for no reason" (Dvorak, 2009). The "thing is that they all cover up for each other and lie for each other at every level whenever they are caught in the act" (Dvorak, 2009).

ICE sustained its "organizational culture" with "[t]alk of sexual favors" (Dvorak, 2009). Talk of "orgies was a company staple" that was prevalent at employees' going-away parties (Dvorak, 2009).

> Because this type of culture is perpetuated and fostered from the highest levels of the agency the new employees who unknowingly are targeted by these sexual...[pursuers] do not have a chance of justice when they are reporting these acts of misconduct in the mistaken belief that the agency administrators share the same values of integrity that they do. The rank and file officers who didn't engage in obscene behavior were left to do the job

> of many since much of this behavior took place while on duty, in government buildings and vehicles. Even though these employees were being caught on government cameras, [and] walked in on by fellow officers at their offices with large glass doors or windows, nothing brought an end to the sexcapades.
>
> However, employees who dared to fight the establishment on sexual innuendo were often taught a painful message. Constant berating, promotion denials (though qualified) and crappy, often humiliating details would await those who dared to say 'no' (Dvorak, 2009).

ICE has been described as a "good ole boy" club that cannot "make the harassment stop" (Cusack, 2015; Dvorak, 2009).

Complainant, Julia Davis, reported harassment and adverse actions by Senior Supervisor, Kevin Crusilla. Davis "had no idea that the management was in a habit of attacking victims who dared to complain, instead of disciplining perpetrators. She would later discover that a victim of stalking, battery and harassment was subject to even greater danger by seeking protection from the agency" (Dvorak, 2009). DHS retaliated by frivolously deploying a Black Hawk helicopter to threaten her, and repeatedly invading her home to "get her to stop with the sexual harassment charges" (Dvorak, 2009). She was offended by her colleagues, who had taken the same "oath to protect and defend the Constitution" but had not "take[n] the same oath…seriously" (Dvorak, 2009). Because they make insincere commitments and severely retaliate, supervisors have told employees "to let it go'" and not "worry about it" (Dvorak, 2009). Davis said, "DHS needs to clean house and fire these people from start to finish because they are making a mockery of the U.S. legal system. National security is an illusion" (Dvorak, 2009). Stricter "hiring standards," such as maintaining a moral lifestyle "as a condition of employment" may be possible (Dvorak, 2009). Moral conduct may be demanded by employers as long as standards do not deprive DHS employees of their constitutional rights to privacy, equal protection, and free speech (Cusack, 2014).

Customs employees must be trained to remember their obligations rather than view anti-sexual harassment policies as a "conflict of interest" with institutionalized deviance (Dvorak, 2009). Training should demonstrate how to "create loyalty to America;" "treat their employees with respect;" and "earn the respect of their officers at all pay grades in order to rebuild morale and trust" (Dvorak, 2009). "If these issues are not resolved quickly," then "all the employees" may inevitably experience harassment, coercion, threat, and retaliation (Dvorak, 2009). However, customs agencies do not recognize a systemic "problem," but identify particular offices as needing to "fix the climate" (Dvorak, 2009).

CONCLUSION

"Moral panic is a troupe of American history" dating "to the Salem witch trials. Events like these have colored the country's folklore, literary tradition, and media practices. Perhaps a propensity for widespread fear of the unknown is a necessary excess of American democracy….that is belief in the equality of opinions and the distrust of the opinions of others" (Mignanelli & Siggelakis, 2017, p. 120). Although the press and court has an "uncanny" way of perverting sex crimes, their revelry in sexual deviance reveals how debased the oligarchy has become (Glenn, 2004; Mignanelli & Siggelakis, 2017, p. 120). Exposure allows the public to presume to assess how much depravity may abound within the government. "[C]onfrontation with the uncanny" is "the act of reinterpreting an old and benign cultural institution in such a way that it becomes the very essence of our deepest fears" (Mignanelli & Siggelakis, 2017, p. 120). "[W]hereas the moral panics of old were geographically limited, the advent of technology—especially social media—has allowed information, and thus social-psychological frenzy, to move effortlessly from coast to coast and across borders" (Mignanelli & Siggelakis, 2017, p. 72). Yet, in some contexts, such as on social media and in courtrooms, perpetuation of moral decay is encouraged and viewed by some as being a fundamental part of the American way of life. "[A]ttention" "may also benefit communities. Awareness has dispelled rumors about locals' participation in or ambivalence" toward sexual deviance (Cusack, 2016, p.19). Their inattention would allow the oligarchy to hide; but, their distinction brings issues to the public forum. Without the media, press coverage would be completely run by the oligarchy and become a self-reinforcing method to oppress the people, not liberate them from tyranny as the First Amendment was designed.

Because "there are likely no legal consequences for simply exacerbating moral panic, even when such actions impact society's most vulnerable members," the press is not to blame. "Indeed, any attempt to impose legal consequences" for "exacerbating moral panic" "would likely conflict with the principles of freedom of speech and personal liberty that lie at the heart of the American system of government" (Mignanelli & Siggelakis, 2017, p. 121). "While in the throes of trepidation it can be tempting to utilize the power of the state to halt a disturbing phenomenon, the social consequences of doing so might prove regrettable" (Mignanelli & Siggelakis, 2017, p. 121). People, who exploit cases of sex abuse for titillation "reject" "sensible impulses" (Kant, 1788). They may "check[]" their "inclinations so far as they might be opposed to" the "law," but use "free will" to participate in deviance while appearing to be "moral" (Kant, 1788).

When sexually deviant legislators publicly exploit victims and oppress other deviants by authorizing police power to enforce morality, they exhibit "self-conceit" (Kant, 1788).

> This propensity to make ourselves in the subjective determining principles of our choice serve as the objective determining principle of the will generally may be called self-love; and if this pretends to be legislative as an unconditional practical principle it may be called self-conceit….No special kind of feeling need be assumed for this under the name of a practical or moral feeling as antecedent to the moral law and serving as its foundation (Kant, 1788).

Arguably, when they are not exposed as deviants, their efforts may benefit society to some extent despite resultant stratification. "This effect is on one side merely negative, but on the other side, relatively to the restricting principle of pure practical reason, it is positive" (Kant, 1788). "The negative effect on feeling (unpleasantness) is pathological, like every influence on feeling and like every feeling generally" (Kant, 1788). Sexually deviant members of the justice system may not commit crimes, but deviate from externally imposed traditions that are not mandated by law.

The possibility of disappointing the public and divesting them of false beliefs about the extent of the law and society to standardize morality may be inconsequential to them, even if they realize that exposure may threaten or harm their careers. Moral "law is something positive in itself, namely, the form of an intellectual causality, that is, of freedom," from deviance, ostracization, and lusty enslavement (Kant, 1788).

> [I]t must be an object of respect; for, by opposing the subjective antagonism of the inclinations, it weakens self-conceit; and since it even breaks down, that is, humiliates, this conceit, it is an object of the highest respect and, consequently, is the foundation of a positive feeling which is not of empirical origin, but is known a priori (Kant, 1788).

"Therefore respect for the moral law is a feeling which is produced by an intellectual cause, and this feeling is the only one that we know" (Kant, 1788).

The effect on society of sexual oligarchy and anarchy is institutionalization of deviance, which essentially revises subculture; and eventually may change laws through legislative means or through lack of enforcement. "[E]verything that presents itself as an object of the will prior to the moral law is by that law itself, which is the supreme condition of practical reason, excluded from the determining principles of the will which we have called the unconditionally good" (Kant, 1788). "[T]he mere practical form which consists in the adaptation of the maxims to universal legislation first determines what is good in itself and absolutely, and is the basis of the maxims of a pure will, which alone is good in every respect" (Kant, 1788). Progressive ideologies may emerge and allow alternative sexualities and gender roles openly to flourish and receive equal treatment. Therefore, the spiral causes and results from some "good" and "bad" destruction of moral authority; but, the means are tainting "good" destruction, while stalling it, and facilitating and causing "bad" destruction (Kant, 1788; Schaeffler, 1999).

Despite increasing tolerance toward, if not demand for, protection for minority sexualities and privacy rights that break tradition, the government has not banned moral opinions or guarded against the people's power to reject immorality and immoral actors (e.g. not pass legislation granting special protection for homosexuals). Although police power may not be constitutionally "illegitimate to regulate" certain types of immoral, "private sexual behavior," some members of society, such as public and private employers, may self-impose regulation (Dickinson v. McCarty, 1994; Givens v. Board of Regents, 2007; Samuela Quesada, 2011; Sigman v. John Marshall Law School, 2014). U.S. Supreme Court Justice Antonin Scalia said that an employer "may refuse to offer a job because the applicant is a Republican; because he is an adulterer; because he went to the wrong prep school or belongs to the wrong country club;...because he is a womanizer;...or even because he hates the Chicago Cubs" (Romer v. Evans, 1996, pp. 652-653). Organizations, corporations, municipalities, and sovereigns need not hire and empower officers, judges, clerks, guards, attorneys, and others suspected of legal immorality, for example adultery. However, those people may represent stability to government employees and their associates (e.g. defense attorneys) when they are self-serving, secretive, and unwilling to confront others. Yet, the people's power to investigate immorality in government may be constrained by employers' abilities to hire moral supervisors and investigative agents.

When people desiring moral communities, leaders, and laws stir and reprove their governments, then they may continue to hold onto moral traditions that benefit themselves and their futures (Chopin, 1837; Liptak,

2016; Primus, 1998). Conservative Justice Scalia even suggested that moral critics could pick and choose which nontraditional conduct could merit disapproval. "I had thought that one could consider certain conduct reprehensible—murder, for example, or polygamy, or cruelty to animals—and could exhibit even 'animus' toward such conduct. Surely that is the…sort of 'animus' at issue here" (Romer v. Evans, 1996, p. 644). Laws that ban cruelty, murder, and other harmful crimes, such as child pornography, (i.e. *malum in* se) are distinct from social and criminal consequences for consensual and harmless sexual conduct (e.g. swingers' clubs) (i.e. *malum prohibitum*) (Lawrence v. Texas, 2003). If a government of the people wishes and intends to reclaim moral authority through leadership, careful exemplary practices, and outspoken opposition to immoral acts, then legislative and administrative polices may constitutionally be used to accomplish their goals, directives, and desires.

Vibrato may resonate within the government, but environments toxified with sexual immorality may result in contagion. By interacting with these people, members of the public may experience social contagion, pressure, suggestion, approval, or other decision-making or morality-evaporating forces and influences that reverberate and move in cycles throughout their homes, communities, public areas, and political arenas. People in the justice system (e.g. jurors) may be influenced, weakened, or overpowered by saturation and exposure to sexual details, which chip at their moral compasses and inundate them with negative, morally disempowering, and suggestive courses of action. Inevitably, some citizens witnessing sexual scandals, may be disgusted or offended, and then resolve to keep moral lives or take a "moral high ground" (Durkheim, 2008; Graham, 2009).

REFERENCES

18 U.S.C. §§ 1460-1463 (2017).

—. § 2252B-C (2017).

—. §§ 2241-2245 (2016).

29 U.S.C.S. § 201 (1997).

42 U.S.C. § 1983 (1997).

—. § 1997e (2017).

AA Mechanical v. Superior Court, 190 Ariz. 364 (1997).

Abrams, D., Cahn, N., Ross, C., Meyer, D., & McClain, L. (2015). *Contemporary Family Law.* St. Paul, MN: West Academic Publishing.

Aero Spark Plug Co. v. B. G. Corporation, 130 F.2d 290 (1942).

Aiken, H. D. (1962). *The Age of Ideology.* New York, NY: Memoir Books.

Alcock, A. (2014, September 15). Sex scandal at Tallahassee City Hall. WCTV. Retrieved from http://www.wctv.tv/home/headlines/Sex-Scandal-At-Tallahassee-City-Hall-275196621.html

Alden v. Maine, 527 U.S. 706 (1999).

Allen, B. & Bosta, D. (1981). *Games Criminals Play*. Susanville, CA: Rae John Publishers.

Allen, I. R. (1982, April 28). Dornan attacks Goldwater. United Press International (UPI). Retrieved from http://www.upi.com/Archives/1982/04/28/Dornan-attacks-Goldwater/1495388814400/

Almodovar, N. J. (2011, September 11). List of rapist corrections officers/ jail guards. Police, Prostitution, and Politics. Retrieved from http://www.policeprostitutionandpolitics.com/index.php?option=com_content&view=article&id=63:list-of-rapist-corrections-officer-unverified&catid=1:latest-news&Itemid=41

Alter, C. (2016, November 9). Hillary Clinton collides again with highest glass ceiling. *Time.* Retrieved from http://time.com/4564142/hillary-clinton-gender/

American Civil Liberties Union (ACLU). (n.d.). Words from prison: Sexual abuse in prison. Retrieved from https://www.aclu.org/other/words-prison-sexual-abuse-prison

American Psychological Association (APA). (2013). *Desk Reference to the Diagnostic Criteria from DSM-5.* APA: Arlington, VA.

Americans for Effective Law Enforcement (AELE) (2007). Civil liability for sexual assaults on prisoners. *Americans for Effective Law Enforcement Monthly Law Journal, 8,* 301-312. Retrieved from http://www.aele.org/law/2007JBAUG/2007-08MLJ301.pdf

Anderson, C. I. & Hunsaker, P. L. (1985). Why there's romancing at the office and why it's everyone's problem. *Personnel*, *62*(2), 57-63.

Applewhite v. City of Baton Rouge, 380 So.2d 119 (La.App. 1 Cir. 1979).

Ashcroft v. Free Speech Coalition, 535 U.S. 234 (2002).

Attorney General v. The Book Named "Tropic of Cancer," 184 N. E. 2d 328 (1962).

Ausband, S. C. (2000). *Myth and Meaning: Myth and Order.* Macon, GA: Mercer University Press.

Bacon-Blood, L. (2016, September 21). Here's what the FBI had on Harry Morel, St. Charles' corrupt DA. NOLA.com. Retrieved from http://www.nola.com/crime/index.ssf/2016/09/fbi_evidence_harry_morel_corrupt_da.html

—. (2016, December 9). U.S. senator asks whether ex-DA Harry Morel got sweetheart deal. NOLA.com. Retrieved from http://www.nola.com/crime/index.ssf/2016/12/us_senator_asks_if_ex-da_harry.html

Baehr v. Miike, 910 P. 2d 112 (1996).

Balduzzi, B. (2013). A taxing divorce: A solution to DOMA's tax inequities in same-sex divorce. *Boston University Public Interest Law Journal*, *22*, 201-241.

Barayuga, D. (2006, January 25). Fox's testimony affirms his sexual misconduct. *Star Bulletin, 11,* 25. Retrieved from http://archives.starbulletin.com/2006/01/25/news/story03.html

Barnes v. Glen Theatre, 501 U.S. 560 (1991).

Baumeister v. Plunkett, 673 So.2d 994 (1996).

Baum, G. (2006). *Religion and Alienation.* Maryknoll, NY: Orbis Books.

Beck, A. J., et al. (2014). Sexual victimization reported by adult correctional authorities, 2009–11. U.S. Department of Justice (DOJ). Retrieved from https://www.bjs.gov/content/pub/pdf/svraca0911.pdf

Beerthuizen, M. G. C. J. & Brugman, D. (2010). Sexually abusive youths' moral reasoning on sex. *Journal of Sexual Aggression, 18*, 125-135.

Begley, S. (2015, October 26). Gloria Steinem on Playboy, Amy Schumer and when not to vote for women. *Time.* Retrieved from http://time.com/4085396/gloria-steinem-amy-schumer-playboy-book/

Benoit v. Capitol, 617 So.2d 477 (La. 1993).

Berman v. Parker, 348 U.S. 26 (1954).

BFC News. (2015, July 13). Customs officer in sex for cargo. Retrieved from https://www.youtube.com/watch?v=FhJvhiIZ_FQ

Bilowit v. Dolitsky, 124 N.J.Super 101 (Ch. Div. 1973).

Blackburn, A. G., Fowler, S. K., Mullings, J. L., & Marquart, J. W. (2011). When boundaries are broken: Inmate perceptions of correctional staff boundary violations. *Deviant Behavior, 32*(4), 351.

Blackburn, A. G., Mullings, J. L., & Marquart, J. W. (2008). Sexual assault in prison and beyond: Toward an understanding of lifetime sexual assault among incarcerated women. *The Prison Journal, 88*(3), 351.

Blackhurst, R. & McGinn, B. (2016). *Amanda Knox.* Los Gatos, CA: Netflix.

Bolivar, L. (2005, December 4). Theater group socio-drama tackles domestic violence. *Sun Sentinel.* Retrieved from http://articles.sun-sentinel.com/2005-12-04/community/0512010633_1_domestic-violence-domestic-abuse-social-justice

Bond v. U.S., 564 U.S. 2083 (2011).

Bonner, J. (n.d.). Cop forces woman to have sex in patrol car, threatens to "ruin her life" with arrest if she tells anyone: Lawsuit. Courthouse News Service. Retrieved from http://filmingcops.com/cop-rapes-woman-in-patrol-car-threatens-to-ruin-her-life-with-arrest-if-she-tells-anyone-lawsuit/

Boswell, D. (2016, April 7). Email conversation with Attorney Don Boswell. West Palm Beach, FL.

Bowers v. Hardwick, 478 U.S. 186 (1986).

Brandes, H. (2016, March 8). Ex-Oklahoma cop sentenced for rape had earlier victim—attorney. MSN. Retrieved from http://www.msn.com/en-us/news/crime/ex-oklahoma-cop-sentenced-for-rape-had-earlier-victim-attorney/ar-AAgviDY?li=BBnbfcL

Brandl, S. G. (2014). *Criminal Investigation.* Thousand Oaks, CA: Sage Publications.

Browne, G. (1999). The shadow formula: How to catch a crooked cop. *Women Police, 33*(3), 44.

Brown, W. (2006). *Regulating Aversion: Tolerance in the Age of Identity and Empire.* Princeton, NJ: Princeton University Press.

Bryan, C. (2014, May 15). Former Trenton Mayor Tony Mack sentenced to nearly 5 years. CBS Philly. Retrieved from http://philadelphia.cbslocal.com/2014/05/15/former-trenton-mayor-tony-mack-sentenced-to-nearly-5-years/

California Government Code § 815 *et seq.* (2016).

California v. LaRue, 409 U.S. 109 (1972).

Caminetti v. U.S., 242 U.S. 470 (1916).

Campbell, C., Moore, J., Maier, W., & Gaffney, M. (2015). Unnoticed, untapped, and underappreciated: Clients' perceptions of their public defenders. *Behavioral Sciences & the Law, 33*(6), 751-770.

Candiotti, S., Levitt, R., & Cratty, C. (2012, August 17). ICE chief of staff on leave on heels of DHS job discrimination lawsuit. CNN. Retrieved form http://www.cnn.com/2012/08/16/us/dhs-discrimination-suit/

Carey v. Population Services International, 431 U.S. 678 (1977).

Carline, A. (2011). Criminal justice, extreme pornography and prostitution: Protecting women or promoting morality? *Sexualities, 14*(3), 312-333.

Carroll, H. L. (2015). Social cognitive factors associated with verbal bullying and defending (Order No. AAI3646953). Available from PsycINFO. (1724426408; 2015-99190-212).

Cass, S. A., Levett, L. M., & Kovera, M. B. (2010). The effects of harassment severity and organizational behavior on damage awards in a hostile work environment sexual harassment case. *Behavioral Science Law, 28,* 303–321.

Cernovich, M. (2010, March 22). The dirty truth about public defenders. Crime & Federalism. Retrieved from http://www.crimeandfederalism.com/2010/03/the-dirty-truth-about-public-defenders.html

Cheeseman, K. A., Mullings, J. L., & Marquart, J. W. (2001). Inmate perceptions of security staff across various custody levels. *Corrections Management Quarterly, 5*(2), 41.

Cheeseman, K. A. & Worley, R. M. (2006). A "captive" audience: Legal responses and remedies to the sexual abuse of female inmates. *Criminal Law Bulletin, 42*(4), 439-455.

Chin, W. Y. (2013). Law and order and white power: White supremacist infiltration of law enforcement and the need to eliminate racism in the ranks. *Journal of Law & Social Deviance, 6*, 30-98.

Chopin, F. (1837). *Etude* in E minor, Op. 25 No. 5.

—. *Prelude* in E-Minor (op.28 no. 4).

Christiansen v. Everglades College, No. 15-10711 (11th Cir. 2015).

Chudnow v. Chudnow, 2001 WL 672511 (Mich. April 27, 2001).

Clarke, M. T. (2007, August 15). Six Florida federal prison guards convicted, sentenced on rape and corruption charges. Prison Legal News. Retrieved from https://www.prisonlegalnews.org/news/2007/aug/15/six-florida-federal-prison-guards-convicted-sentenced-on-rape-and-corruption-charges/

Clason, S. S. (2009). Rhetorical strategies in closing arguments: A case study of a southwest U.S. federal public defender office (Order No. AAI3349362). Available from PsycINFO. (622072862; 2009-99170-080).
City of Cleburne, Texas v. Cleburne Living Center, 473 U.S. 432 (1985).
City of New York v. State, 562 N.E.2d 118 (1990).
City of New York v. State, 655 N.E.2d 649 (1995).
Coalition for Economic Equity v. Wilson, 122 F.3d 692 (1997).
Coelho, P. (2006). *The Alchemist.* San Francisco, CA: HarperOne.
Cohen, A. (2015, October). Consultation for Adam Cohen of AIDS Healthcare Foundation. Los Angeles, CA.
Cohen, D. (1995). The development and utilization of a work orientation typology for the study of public defender job satisfaction (Order No. 9613768). Available from ProQuest Dissertations & Theses Global: Business; ProQuest Dissertations & Theses Global: Health & Medicine; ProQuest Dissertations & Theses Global: Social Sciences. (304261731).
Coker v. Georgia, 433 U.S. 584 (1977).
Complex News. (2016, October 8). Trump caught on hot mic saying 'grab them by the p*ssy'. Retrieved from https://www.youtube.com/watch?v=tl5HJBnPitU
Conroy, S., Henle, C. A., Shore, L., & Stelman, S. (2017). Where there is light, there is dark: A review of the detrimental outcomes of high organizational identification. *Journal of Organizational Behavior, 38*(2), 184-203.
Conway v. Deane, 401 Md. 219 (2007).
Copeland, S. (2016). Prison life: My world in the hellish Florida state prison system. *Journal of Law & Social Deviance, 12*, 226-243.
Counting Crows. (1999). Color blind. on *Cruel Intentions*. Hollywood, CA: Virgin Records.
Cox Broadcasting Corp. v. Cohn, 420 US 469 (1975).
Cox, J. W. (2016, April 26). Naval Academy teacher is removed amid widening sexual misconduct scandal. *The Washington Post.* Retrieved from http://www.msn.com/en-us/news/us/naval-academy-teacher-is-removed-amid-widening-sexual-misconduct-scandal/ar-BBsfUU2?li=BBnb7Kz&ocid=mailsignout
Cox, W. (2014). *Miami Panic: Story of Wayne Cox and the Shenandoah Rapist.* Xulon Press: Maitland, FL.
Crace, J. (1999). *Quarantine.* New York, NY: Picador.
Craig v. Boren, 429 U.S. 190 (1976).

Cropanzano, R., Folger, R., & Goldman, B. (2003). Deontic justice: The role of moral principles in workplace fairness. *Journal of Organizational Behavior, 24*(8), 1019-1024.

Cusack, C. M. (2003). Conversations with inmates at Women's Detention Center. Miami, FL.

—. (2010). Conversations with inmates at Turner Guilford Knight (TGK) Correctional Center. Miami, FL.

—. (2011). Busting patriarchal booby traps: Why feminists fear minor distinctions in child porn cases, an analysis of social deviance within gender, family, or the home (*etudes* 4). *Southern University Law Review, 39*, 43-70.

—. (2012). ADR and yama, the first limb of Yoga Sutra. *Australiasian Dispute Resolution Journal, 23*, 131.

—. (2012). Alternative dispute resolution and niyama, the second limb of Yoga Sutra. *In Factis Pax, 6*, 107.

—. (2012). Boob laws: An analysis of social deviance with in gender, family, or the home (*etudes* 2). *Women's Rights Law Reporter, 33*, 197.

—. (2012). Busting patriarchal booby traps: Why feminists fear minor distinctions in child porn cases, an analysis of social deviance within gender, family, or the home (*etudes* 4). *Southern University Law Review, 39*, 43 (2011).

—. (2012). Tit-for-tat about tats on tots: An analysis of social deviance with in gender, family, or the home (*etudes* 3). *Children's Legal Rights Journal, 32*, 50-62.

—. (2012). Two films, one law. *Entertainment & Sports Law Journal, 23*, 3.

—. (2013). A feminist inquiry into intimate partner violence law, policy, policing, and possible prejudices in Alaska. *Journal of Law & Conflict Resolution, 5*(2), 24-32.

—. (2013). Celebrity justice and gossip blogs: Demographic characteristics of victimized and allegedly criminal celebrities featured on top gossip blogs. *Journal of Law & Social Deviance, 5*, 244-295.

—. (2013). Comparative sexology: Nonconsensual insemination in the United States and the European Union. *Sexologies, 23*, e19.

—. (2013). How the content of online pornography depicts expressed consent for insemination. *Online Journal of Communication & Media Technology, 3*, 91.

—. (2013). Kent make-up their minds: Juveniles, mental illness, and the need for continued implementation of therapeutic justice within the juvenile justice and criminal justice systems. *American University Journal Gender, Society, Policy & Law, 22*, 149-165.

—. (2013). Nonconsensual insemination: A pilot study. *Online Journal of Social Science Research, 2*, 61-72.

—. (2013). Nonconsensual seminal transmission, *Criminal Law Bulletin 1*, 49.

—. (2013). Obscene squirting: If the government thinks it's urine, then they've got another thing coming. *Texas Journal of Women & Law*, 22, 45-69.

—. (2013). To-get-her forever: A man hater's right to same-sex marriage. *Journal of Law & Public Policy, 10*, 63-98.

—. (2014). 50 state survey of prosecutors' willingness to prosecute nonconsensual insemination. *Family & Intimate Partner Violence Quarterly, 6*, 7-32.

—. (2014). Differences in skin tone among Hispanic inmates in Florida's prisons. *Ethnicity and Race in a Changing World: A Review Journal, 5*(1), 37-44.

—. (2014). Does size matter in the field?: Female police bodies in online television. *The Qualitative Report, 19*(18), 1-18.

—. (2014). In opposition of cultural institutionalization of speech following U.S. intervention into foreign governments. *Barry Law Review, 19*, 297-311.

—. (2014). No stroking in the pokey: Promulgating penological policies prohibiting masturbation among inmate populations. *Journal of Law & Social Deviance, 7*, 80-124.

—. (2014). *Pornography and the Criminal Justice System.* Boca Raton, FL: CRC Press.

—. (2015). *Animals, Deviance, and Sex.* Cambridge, UK: Cambridge Scholars Publishing.

—. (2015). Best interest fact-or-fiction: Considering deception and danger facing children whose parents work undercover. *Journal of Law & Social Deviance, 9*, 303-353.

—. (2015). *Criminal Justice Handbook on Masculinity, Male Aggression, and Sexuality.* Springfield, IL: Charles C Thomas.

—. (2015). *Hair and Justice: Sociolegal Significance of Hair in Criminal Justice, Constitutional Law, and Public Policy.* Springfield, IL: Charles C Thomas.

—. (2015). *Laws Relating to Sex, Pregnancy, and Infancy: Issues in Criminal Justice*. New York, NY: Palgrave Macmillan.

—. (2016). *Laws, Policies, Attitudes and Processes that Shape the Lives of Puppies in America.* Sussex, UK: Sussex Academic Press.

—. (2016). Save the white tiger. *Journal of Law & Social Deviance, 12,* 1-42.

—. (2016). *Twins and Deviance: Law, Crime, Sex, Society, and Family.* Cambridge, UK: Cambridge Scholars Publishing.

—. (2017). Double glazed: Reflection, narcissism, and Freudian implications in twincest pornography. *Journal of Law & Social Deviance, 13,* 1-69.

—. (2017). *Fish, Justice, and Society* (in press).

Cusack, C. M. & Telesco, G. (2012). Nonconsensual insemination: Intimate partner violence, patriarchy, police education and policy. *Journal of Law & Social Deviance, 4*, 151-171.

Cusack, C. M. & Waranius, M. (2012). Nonconsensual insemination and pornography: The relationship between sex roles, sex crimes, and "STRT," "Gay," and "Shemale" films on Youporn.com. *Journal of Research in Gender Studies*, *2*(2), 15-33.

—. (2015). Visual detection of sex offenders and consequential biases among Christians. *Journal of Law & Social Deviance, 10,* 42-67.

Cusack, J. (2017). The Bad Beginning. *A Series of Unfortunate Events.* Paramount Television: Los Angeles, CA.

Daoud, A. (2008, February 20). Conversation with Alex Daoud at his home. Miami Beach, FL.

David, L. & Mehlman, P. (1993, April 15). The Smelly Car. Seinfeld. USA: Castle Rock and West-Shapiro.

Davis, J. (2013, February 23). Email conversation with Senator Jim Davis about sexually explicit nudity in the public sphere. NC HB 34 § 14-190.9(a2) (2013).

Davis v. U.S., 3:03-CV-0415, 474 F. Supp. 2d 829 (N.D. Tex. 2007).

Denis, L. & Wilson, E. (Edward N. Zalta, ed.). (2016). Kant and Hume on morality. *The Stanford Encyclopedia of Philosophy.* Retrieved from https://plato.stanford.edu/archives/fall2016/entries/kant-hume-morality/

Denmark, F. L., Krauss, H. H., Halpern, E., & Sechzer, J. A. (2006). *Violence & Exploitation Against Women & Girls.* Boston, MA: Blackwell Publishing.

De Vries, M. & Sobis, I. (2016). Increasing transparency is not always the panacea. *The International Journal of Public Sector Management, 29*(3), 255-270.

Dial, K. C. & Worley, R. M. (2008). Crossing the line: A quantitative analysis of inmate boundary violators in a southern prison system. *American Journal of Criminal Justice: AJCJ, 33*(1), 69-84.

Dickson, T. (2016, February 12). Glynn County public defender faces federal drug charges in Macon. *The Florida Times-Union*. Retrieved from http://jacksonville.com/news/crime/2016-02-12/story/glynn-county-public-defender-faces-federal-drug-charges-macon

Dickinson v. McCarty, 1994 U.S. Dist. LEXIS 15838 (1994).

DiFranco, A. (1993). Willing to fight. On *Puddle Dive.* Buffalo, NY: Righteous Babe Records.

—. (2012). ¿Which side are you on?. On *¿Which Side Are You On?*. Buffalo, NY: Righteous Babe Records.

Dilman, M. (2016, June 25). Phone and e-mail conversation James P. Tarquin, P.A. Ocala, FL.

Dodrill v. Dodrill, 2004 WL 938476 (Ohio Ct. App. April 28, 2004).

Doe v. Denning, Case No. 1:08-cv-01265, (ND. Ill. 2007).

Dostoyevsky, F. (2001). *Crime and Punishment.* Mineola, NY: Dover Publications.

Dowd, M. (2016, April 2). Trump does it his way. *The New York Times.* Retrieved from https://www.nytimes.com/2016/04/03/opinion/sunday/trump-does-it-his-way.html?_r=0

Dressler, J. & Garvey, S. P. (2012). *Cases & Materials on Criminal Law.* Eagan, MN: West.

Dugard, J. (2012). *A Stolen Life: A Memoir*. Simon & Schuster: New York, NY.

Dun, J. & Joseph, T. (2015). "Twenty Øne Piløts." The Judge on *Blurryface*. New York, NY: Fueled by Ramen.

Durkheim, D. E. (2008). *The Elementary Forms of Life.* New York, NY: Oxford University Press.

Dvorak, K. (2009, December 8). Acting CBP Commissioner retires—leaves stained legacy. For the Record. Retrieved from http://kimberlydvorak.blogspot.com/2009/12/acting-cbp-commissioner-retires-leaves.html

Easley v. Apollo Detective Agency, 69 Ill. App. 3d 920 (1979).

Eggert, D. (2016, March 14). Michigan prosecutor charged with hiring prostitutes hundreds of times. NOLA.com. Retrieved from http://www.nola.com/crime/index.ssf/2016/03/michigan_prosecutor_charged_wi.html

Eisenstadt v. Baird, 405 U.S. 438 (1972).

Equality Foundation of Greater Cincinnati v. City of Cincinnati, 128 F.3d 289 (1997).

Erlanger, H. S., Epp, C. R., Cahill, M., & Haines, K. M. (1996). Law student idealism and job choice: Some new data on an old question. *Law & Society Review, 30*(4), 851-864.

Eustachewich, L. (2016 August 10). 'Pimp' ex-cop busted again on prostitution charges. *New York Post.* Retrieved from http://nypost.com/2016/08/10/pimp-ex-cop-busted-again-on-prostitution-charges/

Farberov, S. (2015, October 7). Woman screams out 'no! no! why?' after married father-of-two cop she accused of raping her on the hood of his squad car is found not guilty. *Daily Mail.* Retrieved from http://www.dailymail.co.uk/news/article-3263709/No-No-Hysterical-accuser-cries-court-married-father-two-cop-claimed-raped-hood-car-gunpoint-NOT-guilty.html#ixzz3sqoFlHCL

Federal Tort Claims Act (FTCA), 28 U.S.C. Sec. 1346 (2017).

Feldman-Summers, S. & Palmer, G. C. (1980). Rape as viewed by judges, prosecutors, and police officers. *Criminal Justice & Behavior, 7*(1), 19-40.

Ferber, M. A. & Loeb, J. W. (1997). *Academic Couples: Problems and Promises*. Urbana, IL: University of Illinois Press.

Fernandez v. California, 571 U.S. 127 (2014).

Filming Cops. (n.d.). Chief of police charged with aggravated rape of 4-yr-old child. Retrieved from http://filmingcops.com/chief-of-police-charged-with-aggravated-rape-of-4-yr-old-child/

—. Cop indicted for child sexual abuse, instructing 9-yr-old girl to touch his sexual organ. Retrieved from http://filmingcops.com/cop-indicted-for-child-sexual-abuse-instructing-9-yr-old-girl-to-touch-his-sexual-organ/

—. Cop points gun at woman, rapes her at gunpoint after she stops at checkpoint. Retrieved from http://filmingcops.com/cop-points-gun-at-woman-rapes-her-at-gunpoint-after-she-stops-at-checkpoint-lawsuit/

Finnegan, M. (2015, May 14). Loretta Sanchez's public image a factor in Senate race. *LA Times.* Retrieved from http://www.latimes.com/local/political/la-me-pc-loretta-sanchez-image-california-senate-20150514-story.html

Fisher, J. (2012, November 8). Two NYPD cops, acquitted of raping woman in her apartment, going to prison. *New York Daily News.* Retrieved from http://www.nydailynews.com/new-york/prison-nypd-cops-acquitted-rape-court-article-1.1198902

Fitzpatrick, J. L., Sanders, J., & Worthen, B. R. (2011). *Program Evaluation and Alternative Approaches and Practical Guidelines.* Upper Saddle River, NJ: Pearson.

Fla. Stat. §§ 112.311-.326 (2000).
--§ 112.532 (1997).
Fleming, M. (2016, June 29). Why does Hugh Hefner keep contributing to this Senate candidate? CalWatchDog.com. Retrieved from http://calwatchdog.com/2016/06/29/sanchez-hefner/
Florida Department of Law Enforcement. (FDLE, n.d.). *Law Enforcement Officer Ethical Standards of Conduct*. Retrieved from http://www.fdle.state.fl.us/cms/CJSTC/Officer-Requirements/LE-Ethical-Standards-of-Conduct.aspx
Flynt, L. & Eisenbach, D. (2011). *One Nation Under Sex.* New York, NY: Palgrave Macmillan.
Folgero, I. S. & Fjeldstad, I. H. (1995). On duty-off guard: Cultural norms and sexual harassment in service organizations. *Organizational Studies, 16*(2), 299-313.
Foucault, M. (1995). *Discipline & Punish: The Birth of the Prison.* New York, NY: Vintage Books.
Fowler, S. K., Blackburn, A. G., Marquart, J. W., & Mullings, J. L. (2010). Inmates' cultural beliefs about sexual violence and their relationship to definitions of sexual assault. *Journal of Offender Rehabilitation, 49*(3), 180.
—. (2010). Would they officially report an in-prison sexual assault? An examination of inmate perceptions. *The Prison Journal, 90*(2), 220.
Fox News. (2007, July 12). Florida State representative accused of offering to perform oral sex claims innocence. Retrieved from http://www.foxnews.com/story/2007/07/12/florida-state-representative-accused-offering-to-perform-oral-sex-claims.html
—. (2014, November 25). Sentenced: State Rep. Bill Kramer headed to jail on sexual assault charge. Retrieved from http://fox6now.com/2014/11/25/sentenced-state-rep-bill-kramer-headed-to-jail-on-sexual-assault-charge/
—. (2016, March 16). Ex-stripper judge found dead inside Nevada home. Retrieved from http://www.foxnews.com/us/2016/03/16/ex-stripper-judge-found-dead-inside-nevada-home.html
Fradella, H. F. & Vogel, B. (2009). An empirical analysis of the relationship between law, morality, and personal conduct: Implications for theory and policy. *Applied Psychology in Criminal Justice, 5*(2), 203-236.
Franco, J. (2010, February 13). "Howl" interview at Berlinale. Interview of James Franco with Irina JF. Retrieved from https://www.youtube.com/watch?v=gon5EdS6OAE

Frank, J. (1973). *Courts on Trial: Myth and Reality in American Justice*. Princeton, NJ: Princeton University Press.

Franklin, D. (2016, January 8). Oklahoma County public defender facing charges for driving under the influence of drugs. Kfor.com. Retrieved from http://kfor.com/2016/01/08/oklahoma-county-public-defender-facing-charges-for-driving-under-the-influence-of-drugs/

French, P. A. (2005). Inference gaps in moral assessment: Capitalism, corporations and individuals. *International Social Science Journal, 57*(3), 573-584.

Frug, G. E., Ford, R. T., & Barron, D. J. (2006). *Local Government Law*. St. Paul, MN: West.

Ga. Code Ann. § 26-9901 (1972).

Garcia, S. M., Darley, J. M., & Robinson, R. J. (2001). Morally questionable tactics: Negotiations between district attorneys and public defenders. *Personality & Social Psychology Bulletin, 27*(6), 731-743.

Gerth, H. H. & Mills, C. W. (1946). *From Max Weber: Essays in Sociology*. New York, NY: Oxford University Press.

Ginsberg, A. (1956). "Howl." Poetry Foundation. Retrieved from https://www.poetryfoundation.org/poems-and-poets/poems/detail/49303

Ginsberg v. New York, 390 U.S. 629 (1968).

Givens v. Board of Regents of the University System of Georgia, 2007 U.S. Dist. LEXIS 99047 (2007).

Glenn, H. P. (2004). *Legal Traditions of the World*. New York, NY: Oxford University Press.

Gloucester County School Board v. G. G., 572 U.S. 2442; No. 16-273; 137 S. Ct. 369 (2016).

Goldfeder, M. & Sheff, E. (2011). Children of polyamorous families: A first empirical look. *Journal of Law & Social Deviance, 5*, 150–243.

Gonzales v. Martinez, 403 F.3d 1179 (10th Cir. 2005).

Goodnough, A. (2007, September 29). Town is shaken after prosecutor's arrest in a child-sex sting. *The New York Times*. Retrieved from http://www.nytimes.com/2007/09/29/us/29florida.html?_r=0

Gordon Mullane, S. (2014). Conversation with Sharon Gordon Mullane. Office of the State Attorney in Broward County, Florida. Miami, FL.

Gottschalk v. San Francisco, 964 F. Supp. 2d 1147 (2013).

Graham, L. (2009). Senator Graham questions Supreme Court nominee Elena Kagan. Youtube.com. Retrieved from https://www.youtube.com/watch?v=4ac0AcPQLt4

Gramiak, T. (2016, November 30). Conversation with Ware State Prison Warden Tom Gramiak. Waycross, GA.

Greenberg, M. A. (2010). Conversation with Murray A. Greenberg. Florida International University. Miami, FL.

Greeley, A. M. (2004). *Religion in Europe at the End of the Second Millenium: A Sociological Profile*. Piscataway, NJ: Transaction Publishers.

Greenfield, S. H. (2009, December 6). The public defender made me do it. Simple Justice. Retrieved from http://blog.simplejustice.us/2009/12/06/the-public-defender-made-me-do-it/

Gries, S. (2016, April 15). My night at the Playboy mansion with Donald Trump. *Politico.* Retrieved from http://www.politico.com/magazine/story/2016/04/apprentice-contestant-donald-trump-2016-playboy-mansion-213815

Griffin, J. (1961). *Black Like Me*. Boston, MA: Houghton Mifflin Harcourt.

Griswold v. Connecticut, 381 U.S. 479 (1964).

Grossman, J. L. & Friedman, L. M. (2011). *Inside the Castle: Law and the Family in 20th Century America.* Princeton, NJ: Princeton University Press.

Gruber, A. (2008). Conversation with Professor Aya Gruber. Florida International University. Miami, FL.

Gudorf, C. E. (2009). Conversation with Professor Christine E. Gudorf. Florida International University. Miami, FL.

Haberfeld, M. R. & Cerrah, I. (2008). *Comparative Policing: The Struggle for Democratization.* Thousand Oaks, CA: Sage Publishing.

Halberstam, M. (2016, June 20). Conversation with Rabbi Mendy Halberstam, Esq. Jackson Lewis P.C. Miami, FL.

Halderman v. Pennhurst State School & Hospital, 673 F.2d 647 (1982).

Hall, J. (2014, November 18). Stoughton public defender accused of sharing child porn. WHDH. Retrieved from http://www.whdh.com/story/26729641/stoughton-public-defender-accused-of-sharing-child-porn

Hall v. Colorado DOC, No. 1:08-cv-00999-DME-MEH U.S.D.C. (D. Colo. 2008).

Hartford, P. (2014). *Waiter to the Rich and Shameless: Confessions of a Five-Star Beverly Hills Server*. Hillhurst Literary.

Harvey, W. (2015). Wish my FTO had told me. *Law & Order, 63*(6), 54-56.

Harvin, M. (2016, June 21). New York is next state to open professional licensing to undocumented students. Will others follow? Good Call. Retrieved from https://www.goodcall.com/news/new-york-next-state-

open-professional-licensing-undocumented-students-will-others-follow-07649
Hayes, M. A. (2014). Sex in the witness stand: Erotic sensationalism, voyeurism, sexual boasting, and bawdy humor in nineteenth-century Illinois courts. *Law & History Review, 32,* 149-202.
Heggenmiller v. Edna Mahan Correctional Institution for Women, 128 Fed. Appx. 240 (3rd Cir. 2005).
Heilbrum, K. (2009). *Evaluation for Risk of Violence in Adults: Best Practices for Forensic Mental Health Assessments*. New York, NY: Oxford University Press.
Heimbach, D. R. (2004). *True Sexual Morality: Recovering Biblical Standards for a Culture in Crisis.* Wheaton, IL: Crossway.
Heine, S. (1985). *Existential and Ontological Dimensions of Time in Heidegger and Dogen*. Albany, NY: State University of New York Press.
—. (2004). *Opening a Mountain: Kōans of the Zen Masters*. Oxford, UK: Oxford University Press.
—. (2005). *White Collar Zen: Using Zen Principles to Overcome Obstacles and Achieve Your Career Goals.* Oxford, UK: Oxford University Press.
Heyward, G. L. (2015). *Corruption Officer.* New York, NY: Atria.
Hickman, S. E. & Muehlenhard, C. L. (1999). By the semi-mystical appearance of a condom. How young women and men communicate sexual consent in heterosexual situations. *The Journal of Sex Research, 36*(3), 258-272.
Hilton, P. (2008, October 3). Paris for President. Los Angeles, CA: SwagHouse Boys.
Hinton, M. (1998, December 8). Fallin bodyguard resigned before divorce case filed. *The Oklahoman.* Retrieved from http://newsok.com/article/2635804
Hobbes, T. (2013). *Leviathan. The Project Gutenberg EBook.*
Hochschild, A. R. (1996). The emotional geography of work and family life. In *Gender Relations in Public and Private*, ed. L. Morris & E. S. Lyon. New York: St. Martin's Press.
Holley, P. (2016, March 16). Prosecutor known for fighting prostitution charged with paying for sex hundreds of times. *The Washington Post.* Retrieved from http://www.msn.com/en-us/news/crime/prosecutor-known-for-fighting-prostitution-charged-with-paying-for-sex-hundreds-of-times/ar-BBqwM7q?li=BBnbcA1&ocid=mailsignout

Hudson, D. L. (2002, September 13). Secondary-effects doctrine. Newseum Institute. Retrieved from http://www.newseuminstitute.org/first-amendment-center/topics/freedom-of-speech-2/adult-entertainment/secondary-effects-doctrine/

Huffington Post. (2008, October 22). Inside Ashley Dupre's rise to prostitution fame: A book excerpt. Retrieved from http://www.huffingtonpost.com/2008/09/21/inside-ashley-dupres-rise_n_128031.html

Hunter, G. (2009, May 15). Sexual abuse by prison and jail staff proves persistent, pandemic. *Prison Legal News.* Retrieved from https://www.prisonlegalnews.org/news/2009/may/15/sexual-abuse-by-prison-and-jail-staff-proves-persistent-pandemic/

Hunter v. Pittsburgh, 207 U.S. 161 (1907).

Hutchison v. State, 624 P.2d 1116 (1980).

Inquiry Concerning a Judge, 937 So. 2d 643 (2006).

In re Inquiry Concerning a Judge, 76 So. 3d 898 (2011).

In re Marriage of Glatfelter, 2005 WL 950472 (Cal. Ct. App. April 26, 2004).

In re Marriage of Meagher, 31 Cal. Rptr. 3d 663 (Ct. App. 2005).

In re Opinions of the Justices, 232 Ala. 60 (1936).

In the Matter of E.P.L., 26 Misc. 3d 336 (2009).

In the Matter of the Estate of Marshall G. Gardiner, 29 Kan. App. 2d 92 (2001).

Israel, J. (2014, October 8). This is the way the war on pornography ends. ThinkProgress. Retrieved from https://thinkprogress.org/this-is-the-way-the-war-on-pornography-ends-466fc4b53109#.wr88lii97

Jenaé, J. (2016, March 14). Judge accused of sexting while sitting on judicial conduct board. KLTV. Retrieved from http://www.kltv.com/story/31467865/texas-judge-accused-of-sexting-while-sitting-on-judicial-conduct-board

Jones, S. J. (2015). Recommendations for correctional leaders to reduce boundary violations: Female correctional employees and male inmates. *Women & Criminal Justice, 25*(5), 360-378.

Julien, W. M. (2016, April 17). Telephone conversation with William Julien. Law Office of William M. Julien, P.A. Boca Raton, FL.

Kahneman, D. (2011). *Thinking, Fast and Slow.* New York, NY: Farrar, Straus and Giroux.

Kamick, S. T. (2003, February 3). The case of the bestselling author: Why Perry Mason is an American icon. *The Weekly Standard*, *8*, 35-39.

Kant, I. (Kingsmill Abbott, T., trans.). (1788). *The Critique of Practical Reason.* Project Gutenberg: Matthew Stapleton. Retrieved from http://www.gutenberg.org/cache/epub/5683/pg5683-images.html

Katz, J. (1988). *Seductions of Crime: Moral and Sensual Attractions of Doing Evil*. New York: Basic Books.

Keenan, J. (2013, March 17). Email conversation with Professor Jesse Keenan.

Kelo v. City of New London, 545 U.S. 469 (2005).

Kertscher, T. (2010, March 3). Former Racine mayor Becker gets 3 years prison in sex sting. *Journal Sentinel.* Retrieved from http://archive.is/20161209080223/.jsonline.com/narchiveews/wisconsin/86273007.html

Klausner, A. (2015, October 20). ICE boss 'coerced employees into attending sex parties at his home that took place while his children watched TV in the next room'. *Daily Mail.* Retrieved from http://www.dailymail.co.uk/news/article-3281153/ICE-boss-coerced-employees-attending-sex-parties-home-took-place-children-watched-TV-room.html

Knox, A. (2014). *Waiting to Be Heard.* New York, NY: Harper.

Kohn, L. S. (2010). What's so funny about peace, love, and understanding? Restorative justice as a new paradigm for domestic violence intervention. *Seton Hall Law Review, 40*, 517-594.

Kooistra, P. (1989). *Criminals as Heroes: Structure, Power, and Identity.* Bowling Green, OH: Bowling Green University Popular Press.

Koons, J. E. (2009). Engaging the odd couple: Same-sex marriage and evangelicalism in the public square. *Women's Rights Law Reporter, 30,* 255-287.

Koss, M. & Goodman, L. A. (1994). *No Safe Haven: Male Violence Against Women at Home, at Work, and in the Community.* Washington D.C.: American Psychological Association.

Kothmann v. Rosario, No: 5:13-cv-28-Oc-22, 2013, U.S. Dist. LEXIS 193557 (M.D. Fla. 2013).

Krause, K. (2016, November 25). North Texas federal prison guards who had sex with inmates cut deals to avoid sex offender registration. *The Dallas Morning News.* Retrieved from http://www.dallasnews.com/news/crime/2016/11/25/north-texas-federal-prison-guards-sex-inmates-cut-deals-avoid-sex-offender-registration

Lamothe, D. (2016, March 18). 'Sexually suggestive' relationship ends career of Air Force general who ran air war. *The Washington Post.* Retrieved from http://www.msn.com/en-us/news/us/%E2%80%98sexually-suggestive%E2%80%99-relationship-ends-career-of-air-force-general-who-ran-air-war/ar-BBqB5wS?li=BBnbcA1&ocid=mailsignout

Lanoue, C. S. (2011). Just sex: Sexual ethics for twentyfirst century Christian. FIU Electronic Theses and Dissertations. Paper 498. Retrieved from http://digitalcommons.fiu.edu/etd/498

Lanphear, J. B. (2015). Inherent racial biases woven into America's criminal justice institutions: A reexamination of *To Kill a Mockingbird*. *Journal of Law & Social Deviance 10*, 69-136.

Lanterman, J. L., Boyle, D. J., & Ragusa-Salerno, L. (2014). Sex offender risk assessment, sources of variation, and the implications of misuse. *Criminal Justice & Behavior, 41*(7), 822-843.

Lao-Tzu. (1996). *Taoteching.* San Francisco, CA: Mercury House.

Lauer, C. (2016, October 18). Prosecutors: Indicted former judge tried to bribe witnesses.

NewOK. Retrieved from http://newsok.com/article/feed/1094376

Lawrence v. Texas, 539 U.S. 558 (2003).

Lawton v. Steele, 152 U.S. 133 (1894).

Layne, S. R. (2015). What happened to "till death do us part"?: Bringing back fault as the exclusive ground for divorce. *Journal of Law & Social Deviance, 9*, 80-147.

LeBlanc, G. (2017, February 5). My House Men's Group. New Orleans, LA.

Leflore, R. (2016). Arnold Schwarzenegger, Hugh Hefner, and Wilt Chamberlain at the Playboy Mansion 1977. Reddit. Retrieved from https://www.reddit.com/r/OldSchoolCool/comments/3lg2dx/arnold_schwarzenegger_hugh_hefner_and_wilt/

Lerman, A. E. & Page, J. (2016). Does the front line reflect the party line? The politicization of punishment and prison officers' perspectives towards incarceration. *The British Journal of Criminology*, *56*(3), 578-601.

Lerner-Wren, G. (2012). Email conversation with 17th Circuit Judge Ginger Lerner-Wren. Fort Lauderdale, FL.

Lewis v. City of New Orleans, 415 U.S. 130 (1974).

L'Hote v. New Orleans, 177 U.S. 587 (1900).

Lietz, J. J. (1981). Ranking social stigma: Would you want one for a friend. *Perceptual & Motor Skills, 53*(2), 353-354.

Limbaugh, D. (2010). *Crimes Against Liberty: An Indictment of President Barack Obama.* Washington, D.C.: Regnery Publishing.

Lips, H. M. (2006). *A New Psychology of Women: Gender, Culture, and Ethnicity (3rd ed.).* Long Grove, IL: Waveland Press.

Liptak, A. (2016, September 5). Sonia Sotomayor and Elena Kagan muse over a cookie-cutter supreme court. *The New York Times.* Retrieved from https://www.nytimes.com/2016/09/06/us/politics/sotomayor-kagan-supreme-court.html?_r=0

Lobel, S. A., Quinn, R. E., St. Clair, L., & Warfield, A. (1994). Love without sex: The impact of psychological intimacy between men and women at work. *Organizational Dynamics, 23,* 4-17.

Loe, M. (1996). Working for men-at the intersection of power, gender, and sexuality. *Sociological Inquiry, 66*, 399-421.

Los Angeles v. Alameda Books, 535 U.S. 425 (2002).

Lopez v. Lopez, 102 N.J.Super. 253 (Ch. Div. 1968).

Louisville Gas Co. v. Coleman, 277 U.S. 32 (1928).

Lovelace, L. (2006). *Ordeal.* New York, NY: Citadel.

Loving v. Virginia, 388 U.S. 1 (1967).

Lynch, D. R. (1997). The nature of occupational stress among public defenders (Order No. AAM9702125). Available from PsycINFO. (619244511; 1997-95003-142).

—. (1999). Perceived judicial hostility to criminal trials: Effects on public defenders in general and on their relationships with clients and prosecutors in particular. *Criminal Justice & Behavior, 26*(2), 217-234.

Lyter, T. (2016, August 25). Email conversation with Tommi Lyter. Pensacola Police Department. Pensacola, FL.

MacLaine, S. (2012). *I'm Over All That: And Other Confessions.* New York, NY: Atria Books.

Macy v. Dep't of Justice, EEOC Appeal No. 0120120821, 2012 WL 1435995 (April 12, 2012).

Madonna. (2015). All seeing eye. on *Rebel Heart.* Santa Monica, CA: Interscope Records.

—. (2015, March 11). The Madonna interview. Howard Stern. Retrieved from https://www.howardstern.com/news/2015/3/11/the-madonna-interview-ten-things-you-need-to-know/

Malin, H., Tirri, K., & Liauw, I. (2015). Adolescent moral motivations for civic engagement: Clues to the political gender gap? *Journal of Moral Education, 44*(1), 34-50.

Maloy v. Board of County Commissioners of Leon County, Florida, 946 So. 2d 1260 (2007).

Marcellus, M. (2009, October 28). Conversation with Madsen Marcellus, Esq. McGill & Marcellus, P.A. North Miami Beach, FL.

Marie, J. (2014, September 30). I'm a prison guard who married an inmate. *Cosmopolitan.* Retrieved from http://www.cosmopolitan.com/sex-love/news/a31640/secret-life-of-marrieds-prison-guard-married-inmate/

Martinez-Garcia, O. I. & Guerra-Pujol, F. E. (2012). The futility of the libertarian fetish for freedom: Milton Friedman's capitalism and freedom. *Journal of Law & Social Deviance*, *4*, 1-39.

Martinez, L. R., Ruggs, E. N., Sabat, I. E., Hebl, M. R., & Binggeli, S. (2013). The role of organizational leaders in sexual orientation equality at organizational and federal levels. *Journal of Business & Psychology, 28*(4), 455-466.

Martinez v. U.S., 311 F. Supp. 2d 1274 (D.N.M. 2004).

Marx, K. & Engels, F. (1988). *The Economic and Philosophic Manuscripts of 1844 and the Communist Manifesto.* Amherst, NY: Prometheus Books.

Maryland v. Craig, 497 U.S. 836 (1990).

Masson v. *New Yorker Magazine,* 501 U.S. 496 (1991).

Mastropasqua, K. (2015, October 16). Inmate relationships with prison staff. Journalist's Research. Retrieved from http://journalistsresource.org/studies/government/criminal-justice/inmate-relationships-prison-employees-research-roundup

Matlin, C. (2008, March 11). The map of shame: A guided tour of Washington's sex-scandal locales. Slate. Retrieved from http://www.slate.com/articles/news_and_politics/politics/2008/03/the_map_of_shame.html

Matthew Shepard and James Byrd, Jr. Hate Crimes Prevention Act. Pub. L 111-84 § 4701 *et seq.* (2009).

McAfee, M. (2015, October 4). Amber Rose's SlutWalk. CNN. Retrieved from http://www.cnn.com/2015/10/04/living/amber-rose-slutwalk-feat/

McCullen v. Coakley, 573 U.S. 2522 (2014).

McLaughlin, E. C. (2016, February 16). Lawsuit alleges Georgia prison supervisor raped women inmates. CNN. Retrieved from http://edition.cnn.com/2016/02/15/us/georgia-prison-rapes-lawsuit/index.html

McLaughlin, E. C. & Stapleton, A. (2017, March 9). Secret Marines group is still sharing nude photos amid scandal. CNN. Retrieved from http://www.cnn.com/2017/03/08/politics/marines-united-photos-investigation/

McMahon, P. (2016, February 23). Broward lawyer, arrested on child porn charges, accused of abusing minors. *Sun Sentinel.* Retrieved from http://www.sun-sentinel.com/local/broward/fl-child-porn-lawyer-20160222-story.html

McMahon, T. & Francis, C. (2010, February 19). Consultation for Terri McMahon and Curtis Francis. Exclusive Match. North Miami Beach, FL.

McMullan, P. (2010, February 10). The Woman behind Harold Ford. *The Daily Beast.* Retrieved from http://www.thedailybeast.com/articles/2010/02/10/the-woman-behind-harold-ford.html

McWilliams, M. (2012, August). Conversation with Margaret McWilliams about a transgender runaway. Assistant Public Advocate. Juneau, AK.

Megale, E. (2011). The invisible man: How the sex offender registry results in social death. *Journal of Law & Social Deviance, 2*, 92-157.

"Memoirs of a Woman of Pleasure" v. Attorney General of Massachusetts, 383 U.S. 413 (1966).

Merrymen, J. H. (2007). *The Civil Law Tradition*. Palo Alton, CA: Stanford University Press.

Michael, G. (1987). Father figure. On Faith. New York, NY: Columbia.

Mignanelli, N. & Siggelakis, S. (2017). No laughing matter: Phantom clowns, moral panic, and the law. *Journal of Law & Social Deviance, 13*, 70-121.

Mikkelson, D. (2017, January 15). Four things about King. Snopes.com. Retrieved from http://www.snopes.com/history/american/mlking.asp

Miller, H. (1994). *Under the Roofs of Paris*. New York, NY: Grove Press.

Miller v. California, 413 US 15 (1973).

Miller v. Keating, 349 So.2d 265 (La. 1977).

Millwood-Jones v. Holder, CV 214-035, 2016 U.S. Dist. LEXIS 36741 (S.D. Ga. 2016).

Minnick, B. A. (2016, June 20). Telephone and e-mail conversation with Bruce Alexander Minnick, Esq. The Minnick Law Firm. Tallahassee, FL.

Mint News Press. (2015, November 27). Sacramento police officer gets life in prison for raping 75 year-old stroke victim. Reuters. Retrieved from http://www.mintpressnews.com/211605-2/211605/

Minuti, M. (1988). Employer liability under the doctrine of negligent hiring: Suggested methods for avoiding the hiring of dangerous employees. *Delaware Journal of Corporate Law, 13*, 501.

Miranda v. Arizona, 384 U.S. 436 (1966).

Mirow, M. C. (2014). The age of constitutions in the Americas. *Law & History Review*, *32*, 229-235.

Monell v. New York City Dept. of Social Services, 436 U.S. 658 (1978).

Monks, C. P., Smith, P. K., & Swettenham, J. (2005). Psychological correlates of peer victimisation in preschool: Social cognitive skills, executive function and attachment profiles. *Aggressive Behavior, 31*(6), 571-588.

Moore, J. (2017, March 25). Jacob Moore, Nathalia Silva, Elizabeth Gordon, Danielle Teemer, Selamawit Yakob, John Piratsky, Durann Dungee, Samuel Prempeh, Ahmani Dawson, and Kiara Roberto. Law, Gender, and the Digital: From Revenge Porn and Cyberbullying to Cyberstalking and Cyberlove. Southeastern Women's Studies Association (SEWSA). Kennesaw State University. Atlanta, GA.

Moore v. City of East Cleveland, Ohio, 431 U.S. 494 (1977).

Moran, G. (2015, October 19). ICE bosses accused of sex parties. *The San Diego Union Tribune*. Retrieved from http://www.sandiegouniontribune.com/news/watchdog/sdut-complaint-alleges-swingers-parties-for-ice-agents-2015oct19-htmlstory.html

Morning, T. (2016, September 25). Smith County Judge Joel Baker resigns. CBS. Retrieved from http://www.cbs19.tv/news/local/smith-county-judge-joel-baker-resigns/324710845

Morrissey, P. (2013). *Autobiography*. London: Penguin Classics.

Morris v. Eversley, 282 F. Supp. 2d 196 (S.D.N.Y. 2003).

National Center on Sexual Exploitation (NCSE). (n.d.). Retrieved from http://endsexualexploitation.org/dirtydozen-2016/

Neal, B. (2009). *Sex, Murder, and the Unwritten Law.* Lubbock, TX: Texas Tech University Press.

Nielsen, M. O. & Zion, J. W. (2005). *Navajo Nation Peacemaking.* Tucson, AZ: University of Arizona Press.

Neumann-Ribner, M. (1993). When good cops go bad: Can a city be held liable for a rape or murder committed by an on-duty police officer? *San Diego Justice Journal, 1*, 457.

New Orleans Campaign for a Living Wage v. City of New Orleans, 825 So.2d 1098 (2002).

Northup, L. A. (2006). Myth-placed priorities: Religion and the study of myth. *Religious Studies Review, 32*(1), 5–10.

Obergefell v. Hodges, 576 U.S. 2593 (2015).

O'Brien, D. (1996). *Power to Hurt: Inside a Judge's Chambers: Sexual Assault, Corruption, and the Ultimate Reversal of Justice for Women.* New York, NY: Harpercollins.

Okorocha, O. (2013). Field sobriety tests: Criminal injustice. *Journal of Law & Social Deviance, 5*, 298-325.

Orgeron v. McDonald, 639 So.2d 224 (1994).

Orovitz, S. (2012). Free bird: No right to qualified immunity for police who retaliate against the middle finger gesture. *Journal of Law & Social Deviance, 3*, 1-77.

Osborne v. Lyles, 587 N.E.2d 825 (1992).

Paris Adult Theatre v. Slaton, 413 U.S. 49 (1973).

Parker, K. (2016, September 11). Email conversation with Katrina Parker. The WellHouse. Leeds, AL.

Peltier, M. (2012, September 11). Jennifer Carroll sex scandal: Florida Lieutenant Governor accused of misconduct by former aide Carletha Cole. Retrieved from http://www.huffingtonpost.com/2012/07/12/lt-governor-jennifer-carroll-lesbian-sex-scandal-florida_n_1668318.html

People v. Ryan, 82 N.Y.2d 497 (1993).

Pierce v. Society of the Sisters of the Holy Names of Jesus and Mary, 268 U.S. 510 (1925).

Platt, A. & Pollock, R. (1974). Channeling lawyers: The careers of public defenders. *Issues in Criminology, 9*(1), 1-31.

Playboy. (n.d.). Playboy Foundation. Retrieved from http://www.playboyenterprises.com/home/content.cfm?content=t_template&packet=0007B308-45F5-1C7D-9B578304E50A011A&artTypeID=0007B451-BB99-1C76-8FEA8304E50A010D

Poe v. Ullman, 367 U.S. 497 (1961).

Pollock, J. M. (2013). *Ethical Dilemmas and Decisions in Criminal Justice.* Belmont, CA: Cengage Learning.

Powell v. State, 270 Ga. 327 (1998).

Prager, I. G., Moran, G., & Sanchez, J. (1996). Job analysis of felony assistant public defenders: The most important tasks and most useful knowledge, skills, and abilities. *Psychology, Crime & Law, 3*(1), 37-49.

Prasad, M. (1999). The morality of market exchange: Love, money, and contractual justice. *Sociological Perspectives*, *42*(2), 181-214.

Pribble, S. (2008, July 31). Conversation with Scott Thomas Pribble. Office of the Public Defender, 15th Judicial Circuit. West Palm Beach, FL.

Price Foley, E. (2009, February). Conversation with Professor Elizabeth Price Foley about healthcare. Florida International University. Miami, FL.

Primus. (1998). The devil went down to Georgia. On Rhinoplasty. Cotati, CA: Prairie Sun Recording.

Proust, M. (2003). *In Search of Lost Time.* New York, NY: Modern Library.

Public Defender Dude. (2007, December 15). Retrieved from http://publicdefenderdude.blogspot.com/2007/12/why-are-ex-public-defenders-so-often.html

Rattner, A., Turjeman, H., & Fishman, G. (2008). Public versus private defense: Can money buy justice? *Journal of Criminal Justice, 36*(1), 43-49.

Reddington, F. P. & Kreisel, B. W. (2009). *Sexual Assault: The Victims, the Perpetrators, and the Criminal Justice System*. Durham, NC: Carolina Academic Press.

Regents of the University of California v. Bakke 438 U.S. 265 (1978).

Renton v. Playtime Theatres, 475 U.S. 41 (1986).

Riley v. Olk-Long, 282 F.3d 592 (8th Cir. 2002).

Ring, K. A. (2004). *Scalia Dissents.* Washington, D.C.: Regenery Publishing.

Rogers, P. (2014, December 5). Former State Rep. Keith Farnham pleads guilty to child porn charges. NBC Chicago. Retrieved from http://www.nbcchicago.com/news/politics/Former-State-Rep-Keith-Farnham-Pleads-Guilty-to-Child-Porn-Charges-284884331.html

Romer v. Evans, 517 U.S. 620 (1996).

Rosewarne, L. (2016). *Cyberbullies, Cyberactivists, Cyberpredators: Film, TV, and Internet Stereotypes.* Santa Barbara, CA: Prager.

Rosoff, S., Pontell, H., & Tillman, R. (2014). *Profit without Honor.* Upper Saddle River, NJ: Pearson Education.

Ross, R. (2016, July). Telephone conversation with Rob Ross, Esq. about sexual harassment at Keiser University. West Palm Beach, FL.

Roth v. U. S., 354 U.S. 476 (1957).

RS 14:89 (2016).

Samuel Quesada, A. J. (2011). Legislating morality: Montesquieu's case for the regulation of sexual morals (Order No. AAI3441751). Available from PsycINFO. (906333259; 2011-99170-125).

Santo, A. (2015, June 17). Preying on prisoners. The Marshall Project. Retrieved from https://www.themarshallproject.org/2015/06/17/preying-on-prisoners#.LDlq1y9tp

Saunders, E. J. (1988). A comparative study of attitudes toward child sexual abuse among social work and judicial system professionals. *Child Abuse Neglect, 12*(1), 83-90.

Saunders v. Hunter, 980 F. Supp. 1236 (1997).

Schaeffler, R. (1999). *Reason and the Question of God: An Introduction to the Philosophy of Religion*. New York, NY: The Crossroads Publishing Co.

Schiller, F. (2004). *On the Aesthetic Education of Man.* Mineola, NY: Dover Books.

Schmitz, M. (2017). The Juvenile Justice and Delinquency Prevention Act's (JJDPA's) contempt provision: Time to amend. *Journal of Law & Social Deviance 13,* __.

Schwabach, J. M. (1994). Gender differences in ethical judgments. *Retrospective Theses and Dissertations,* paper 11319. Retrieved from http://lib.dr.iastate.edu/rtd/11319

Scott v. Moore, 114 F.3d 51 (5th Cir. 1997).

Segal, R. A. (1999). *Theorizing about Myth.* Amherst, MA: University of Massachusetts Press.

Segrave, K. (1990). *Sex and Politicians: Affairs of State.* Boston, MA: Branden Publishing Company.

Shalvi, S., Dana, J., Handgraaf, M. J. J., & De Dreu, C. K. W. (2011). Justified ethicality: Observing desired counterfactuals modifies ethical perceptions and behavior. *Organizational Behavior and Human Decision Processes, 115*(2), 181-190.

Shamir, J. (2013). The influence of age on the attitudes towards the rule of law: The case of immigrants from the former Soviet Union. *Journal of Law & Social Deviance, 5,* 1-100.

Sheer, R. (2008). *The Pornography of Power.* New York, NY: Hachette Book Group.

Sidanius, J., Liu, J. H., Shaw, J. S., & Pratto, F. (1994). Social dominance orientation, hierarchy attenuators and hierarchy enhancers: Social dominance theory and the criminal justice system authors. *Journal of Applied Social Psychology, 24*(4), 338–366.

Siegel, L. J. (2010). *Criminology.* Belmont, CA: Wadsworth.

Sigman v. John Marshall Law School, 2014 U.S. Dist. LEXIS 44647 (2014).

Singer, P. (2007). Email conversation with Professor Peter Singer. Kendall, FL.

Singhal, R. (2013, September). Conversation with 17th Circuit Judge Raag Singhal. Weston Bar Association. Weston, FL.

Sista Souljah. (2006). *Coldest Winter Ever.* Pocket Star: New York, NY.

Skiba, M., Hoppus, M., & Barker, T. (1999). Blink-182. What's my age again?. on *Enema of the State.* Seal Beach, CA: Kung Fu Records.

—. (2001). Blink-182. Stay together for the kids. on *Take Off Your Pants and Jacket.* Los Angeles, CA: Jerry Finn.

Skolnick, J. H. (1994). *Justice without Trial.* New York, NY: MacMillan College Publishing Company.

Slidell Police Department. (2015). Conversations with officers at Covington Police Department, Louisiana Office of State Parks Enforcement Division, Louisiana State Police, Mandeville Police

Department, New Orleans Police Department, Pearl River Police Department, Slidell Police Department, and St. Tammany Police Department. Southeast Louisiana.
Slifkin, N. (2006). *Man and Beast: Our Relationships with Animals in Jewish Law and Thought.* Brooklyn, NY: Yashar Books.
Slut Leanne. (2011, March). Conversation with Slut Leanne. Around the World with Slut Leanne. A flight between Juneau, AK and Havana, Cuba.
Smith, B. V. & Loomis, M. C. (2013). After Dothard: Female correctional workers and the challenge to employment law. *Florida International University Law Review 8*, 469-500.
Smith, H. (2009). *The World's Religions, Revised and Updated: A Concise Introduction.* New York, NY: Harper Collins.
Smith v. Cochran, 216 F. Supp. 2d 1286 (N.D. Okla. 2002).
Snider, M. (2017, February 13). 'Playboy' brings nudity back to magazine. *USA Today*. Retrieved from http://www.usatoday.com/story/money/business/2017/02/13/playboy-brings-nudity-back-magazine/97868038/
Sollecito, R. & Gumbel, A. (2012). *Honor Bound: My Journey to Hell and Back with Amanda Knox.* New York, NY: Simon & Schuster.
Sooner Politics. (2015, June 24). The governor who planned her wedding at the Playboy mansion. Retrieved from http://soonerpolitics.blogspot.com/2015/06/the-governor-who-planned-her-wedding-at.html#ixzz4WAa7j11o
Spight, P. A. (2005). *Escorts and Prostitutes: A Real Court Martial.* Middletown, DE.
Stein, J. H. & Cropanzano, R. (2011). Death awareness and organizational behavior. *Journal of Organizational Behavior, 32*(8), 1189-1193.
Stepp v. Stepp, 2004 WL 626116 (Ohio Ct. App. March 31, 2004).
Strickman, L. (2008). Conversation with Dean Leonard P. Strickman. Florida International University. Miami, FL.
Sutton, J. (2002). Conversation with Dr. Jamie Sutton. Florida International University. Miami, FL.
Taylor, R. W. & Fritsch, E. J. (2011). *Juvenile Justice Policies, Programs, & Practices.* New York, NY: McGraw-Hill Education.
Telesco, G. (2013). Conversation with Rev. Grace Telesco, Ph.D. Wilton Manors, FL.
Teproff, C. (2014, June 26). Father vs. daughter: Former Miami Beach Mayor Alex Daoud sued for his house. *Miami Herald.* Retrieved from http://www.miamiherald.com/news/local/community/miami-dade/miami-beach/article1972934.html

The Asian Riff. (1847). The Wonderful Lamp.
The New York Times. (1991, February 17). A secret payment stirs up Florida. Retrieved from http://www.nytimes.com/1991/02/17/us/a-secret-payment-stirs-up-florida.html
The Smiths. (1985). That joke isn't funny anymore. on *Meat Is Murder*. Liverpool and Ridge Farm, Surrey, UK: Amazon Studios.
The Washington Times. (2000, August 11). Sanchez pays price for Playboy Mansion party. Retrieved from http://www.washingtontimes.com/news/2000/aug/11/20000811-011820-1548r/
Thibaut, M. (2016, May 20). Matthew Thibaut, Esq. Ciklin, Lubitz, & O'Connell. West Palm Beach, FL.
Thoreau, H. D. (2013). *Walden.* York, UK: Empire Books.
Thornber v. City of Fort Walton Beach, 568 So. 2d at 917 (Fla. 1990).
Timmerman, G. & Bajema, C. (2000). The impact of organizational culture on perceptions and experiences of sexual harassment. *Journal of Vocational Behavior, 57*(2), 188-205.
Toch, H. & Grant, J. D. (2005). Extending the approach to interagency problem solving. *Police as Problem Solvers: How Frontline Workers Can Promote Organizational and Community Change (2nd ed.),* pp. 317-327. American Psychological Association: Washington, D.C.
Turner v. Safely, 482 U.S. 78 (1987).
Turner v. State, 494 So.2d 1292 (La.App. 2 Cir.1986).
Uniform Code of Military Justice (UCMJ). (2017). Article 120.
—. (2017). Article 134.
U.S. Conference of Catholic Bishops. (2006). *Compendium Catechism of the Catholic Church.* Washington, D.C.: Libreria Editrice Vaticana.
U.S. Department of Justice (DOJ). (2009, September). The Department of Justice's efforts to prevent staff sexual abuse of federal inmates. Office of the Inspector General Evaluation and Inspections Division. Retrieved from https://oig.justice.gov/reports/plus/e0904.pdf
U.S. Immigration Customs Enforcement (ICE). (2016, October 5). ICE investigation results in 17 sex trafficking indictments in Minnesota. Retrieved from https://www.ice.gov/news/releases/ice-investigation-results-17-sex-trafficking-indictments-minnesota
U.S. v. Dost, 636 F. Supp. 828 (S.D.Cal. 1986).
U. S. v. One Package of Japanese Pessaries, 86 F.2d 737 (2d Cir. 1936).
U.S. v. Wade, 388 U.S. 218 (1967).
U. S. v. Windsor, 570 U.S. 2679 (2013).
Valenti, J. (2007). *Full Frontal Feminism.* Berkeley, CA: Seal Press.

Van Gieson, J. C. (1990, December 9). Sex scandal shaking up legislature. *Orlando Sentinel.* Retrieved from http://articles.orlandosentinel.com/1990-12-09/news/9012090184_1_lippman-harassment-jennings

van, Der Lee, R., Ellemers, N., & Scheepers, D. (2016). Mastering moral misery: Emotional and coping responses to intragroup morality (vs. competence) evaluations. *Cognition & Emotion, 30*(1), 51-65.

Vankin, J. (2015, July 12). Alberto Randazzo. *Inquisitr.* Retrieved from http://www.inquisitr.com/2246425/alberto-randazzo-nypd/

Village of Arlington Heights v. Metropolitan Housing Development Corp., 429 U.S. 252 (1977).

Village of Belle Terre v. Boraas, 416 U.S. 1 (1974).

Vronsky, P. (2007). *Female Serial Killers.* New York, NY: Berkley Books.

Walker, L. E. A. (2016). *The Battered Woman Syndrome*. New York, NY: Springer Publishing Company.

Walsh, S. M., Eckhardt, K., & Russell, S. (2006). Sex, lies, and law: Moral turpitude as an enforcer of gender and sexuality norms. *Sexuality Research & Social Policy: A Journal of the NSRC, 3*(2), 37-51.

Walter, D. D. (2008). Conversation with Professor David D. Walter. Florida International University. Miami, FL.

Waranius, M. E. (2011). What up with DADT: Addressing confusion from inside the military. *Journal of Law & Social Deviance, 1*, 56-84.

Ward v. Rock Against Racism, 491 U.S. 781 (1989).

WCVB. (2014, October 7). Stoughton lawyer arrested on child porn charges. Retrieved from http://www.wcvb.com/article/stoughton-lawyer-arrested-on-child-porn-charges/8209485

Weiss, M. S. (2003). Toward an understanding of public defender motivations (Order No. 3085122). Available from ProQuest Dissertations & Theses Global: Social Sciences. (305265814).

Werner, A. & Strickler, L. (2015, May 4). “Disturbing” sex abuse within agency that patrols U.S. border, says former top official. CBS News. Retrieved from http://www.cbsnews.com/news/u-s-border-patrol-has-a-sex-abuse-problem-says-whistleblower/

What about Bob? (1997, February 9). *New York Times Magazine,* 17.

White, C. (2014, December). Conversation with Cindy White about Keiser University employment conditions. Keiser University. Miami, FL.

Whitehead, J. T., Blankenship, M. B., & Wright, J. P. (1999). Elite versus citizen attitudes on capital punishment: Incongruity between the public and policymakers. *Journal of Criminal Justice, 27*(3), 249-258.

Whitman, W. (1855). Song of Myself. Retrieved from

http://www.english.illinois.edu/maps/poets/s_z/whitman/song.htm

Wilkins, B. A. & Peterson, H. (2009, August 30). Ted Bundy: The Seattle police advisor, Republican, and serial killer. Operation Nation. Retrieved from http://operation-nation.com/?p=193

Williams, C. L., Giuffre, P. A., & Dellinger, K. (1999). Sexuality in the workplace: Organizational control, sexual harassment, and the pursuit of pleasure. *Annual Review of Sociology, 25,* 73-93.

Wilson, A. M. (2016). Witches and guns: The intersection between Wicca and The Second Amendment. *Journal of Law & Social Deviance, 16,* 43-109.

Wiltermuth, S. S., Bennett, V. M., & Pierce, L. (2013). Doing as they would do: How the perceived ethical preferences of third-party beneficiaries impact ethical decision-making. *Organizational Behavior and Human Decision Processes, 122*(2), 280-290.

Witt, P. & Conroy, M. A. (2008). *Evaluation of Sexually Violent Predators (Best Practices in Forensic Mental Health Assessment).* New York, NY: Oxford University Press.

Woody, B. A. (2016, September 21). Email conversation with Brent A. Woody. West Florida Center for Trafficking Advocacy. Tarpon Springs, FL.

Woolley, M. L. (2007). Marital rape. A unique blend of domestic violence and non-marital rape issues. *Hasting Women's Law Journal, 18,* 269.

Worley, R. M. (2016). Memoirs of a guard-researcher: Deconstructing the games inmates play behind the prison walls. *Deviant Behavior, 37*(11), 1215-1226.

Worley, R. M., Tewksbury, R., & Frantzen, D. (2010). Preventing fatal attractions: Lessons learned from inmate boundary violators in a southern penitentiary system. *Criminal Justice Studies, 23*(4), 347.

Worley, R. M. & Worley, V. B. (2011). Guards gone wild: A self-report study of correctional officer misconduct and the effect of institutional deviance on "care" within the Texas prison system. *Deviant Behavior, 32*(4), 293.

—. (2013). Games guards play: A self-report study of institutional deviance within the Texas department of criminal justice. *Criminal Justice Studies, 26*(1), 115.

Worley, R., Marquart, J. W., & Mullings, J. L. (2003). Prison guard predators: An analysis of inmates who established inappropriate relationships with prison staff, 1995-1998. *Deviant Behavior, 24*(2), 175-194.

WTOL. (2010). Attorney denies John Stamos had fling with 17-year-old. Retrieved from http://www.wtol.com/story/12796507/attorney-denies-john-stamos-had-fling-with-17-year-old

Young v. American Mini Theatres, 427 U.S. 50 (1976).

Youtube.com. (2007, September 18). FL attorney general arrested soliciting 5 yo. Retrieved from https://www.youtube.com/watch?v=AuHOAfVEjGY

Zak, P. J. (2011). The physiology of moral sentiments. *Journal of Economic Behavior & Organization, 77*(1), 53-65.

Zoroya, G. (2013, July 31). Adult magazines dropped from shelves at Army exchanges Military Intelligence. *USA Today*. Retrieved from http://www.usatoday.com/story/nation/2013/07/31/pornography-playboy-army-px-penthouse/2606105/

INDEX